June '93.   Misses

AA

CW00385518

b.

Produced by the Publishing Division of
The Automobile Association

Maps prepared by the Cartographic Department of
The Automobile Association.
© The Automobile Association 1991

Cover Illustration	Blue Chip Illustration
Illustrations	Allan Roe
Crossword	Roger Prebble
Head of Advertisement Sales Tel 0256 20123 Ext 21544	Christopher Heard
Advertisement Production Tel 0256 20123 Ext 21545	Karen Weeks

Typeset by Bookworm Typesetting, Manchester
Printed and bound by BPCC Hazell Books Ltd

A CIP catalogue record for this book is available from the
British Library

Published by The Automobile Association, Fanum House,
Basingstoke, Hampshire RG21 2EA.

ISBN 0 74950 196 0

CONTENTS

Introduction
4

Tea-time Crossword
5

How to use this book
Including an example of an A-Z entry
7

An A-Z of towns in England, Scotland and Wales
9

Readers' Recommendations Forms
227

Index
Teashops and hotels listed by name
231

National Grid
241

Atlas
242

INTRODUCTION

This year's edition of *Let's Stop for Tea* has over 300 new entries – from the simple tea room tucked away in a country village to the luxury hotels recognised in food guides – but all having in common a commitment to producing quality teatime refreshments.

Ten years' ago a customer took pot luck when ordering a cup of tea. Now, in 1991, many establishments are reviving the traditional tea, giving people the chance to slip off their diet régimes and indulge themselves in chocolate fudge cake or scones and cream as well as sampling a good cup of tea.

The revival of interest in tea as a mid-afternoon meal is accompanied by an increase in the variety of teas available. Whilst tea bags are still used by the majority of caterers, there are a growing number of establishments using loose-leaf tea, believing that this is the only way to enjoy its full flavour and quality. Then there are the so-called speciality teas which are now appearing on menus: no longer are Orange and Passion Flower or Oolang Peach Blossom or even Gunpowder rarities to puzzle the tea-drinking public. A spirit of adventure has crept into the tea market which is now preparing for tea to become an acceptable alternative to after-dinner coffee. For the health conscious, herbal teas and de-caffeinated teas are on the supermarket shelves and are being introduced on tea room menus, and for those with a sense of humour, teapots of all shapes, colours and sizes can be found in specialist china shops such as you find in Covent Garden. The tea-lover is indeed extremely well catered for

Many thanks to all our readers who have sent in their recommendations of good tea places they have found. AA inspectors follow up all your letters and also tour the country in search of quality tea rooms to include in this guide. There are no doubt many other places which they have not unearthed and we hope that you, our readers, will continue to contribute to this effort by sending in details of the tea rooms which have impressed you by the quality of their pots of tea and their baking. You will find a form you can complete on page 227 of this book.

Meanwhile, to give you a little entertainment, we offer you a crossword puzzle to test your knowledge of tea and perhaps find the answers to some unusual clues. The contributors of the first five correctly completed crosswords will receive a special AA teapot. Turn to page 6 for entry details.

TEA-TIME CROSSWORD

When you've solved the crossword, rearrange the **8** letters that fall into the **8** circles to form a word related to tea.

Just send this one word with your completed crossword to The Editor, *Let's Stop for Tea* (see page 6).

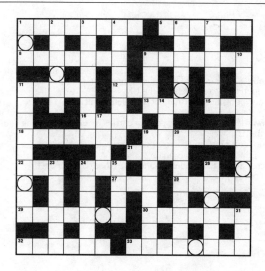

Anagram

ACROSS

1 Cuppa filter that catches every 19 Across (8)

5 1773 tea party venue! (6)

8 Darjeeling cultivator? (7)

9 Makers of tea and a famous dictionary (7)

11 Provide refreshment from tatty crate (5)

12 Obtain some orange tea (3)

13 That woman in the room (3)

15 Number for tea? (3)

16 The last word in Assam enjoyment (4)

18 Transport for tea and Judy Garland (7)

19 Cockney thief plucked from China? (3-4)

21 Butter muffins include special word (4)

22 China collection . . . (3)

24 . . . and part of it (3)

27 Not at home with spout's contents (3)

28 Shouts for Eric's brew (5)

29 Boilers required by 9 Across (7)

30 Relations at the chimps' tea party? (7)

32 Like pleasantly potent tea (6)

33 Japanese tea rite requiring yon crème? (8)

DOWN

1 Daintily drink some Indian potion initially (3)

2 Makes a response to subtle traces (6)

3 Lord's tea-break . . . (8)

4 . . . and a lordly tea (4,4)

6 & 7 A bit more tea for luckless missionary?! (3,3,3,3)

9 Betjeman's tea-shop location (4)

10 Fool's puns about brewing-up units (9)

11 Tea-clipper at Greenwich Pier (5,4)

14 Jug held by 9 Across (4)

17 Tea card? (4)

19 Maybe a late bet that's laid at 4.00pm? (3-5)

20 In a Miami cab, lemon tea is friendly (8)

23 Professional tea-drinker (6)

24 Old Sri Lanka tea (6)

25 Stop lifting tea-containers (4)

26 Gown worn at tea 33 Across? (6)

31 Reserved some delicious hyson (3)

TEA-TIME CROSSWORD

HOW TO ENTER

Competition rules:

- AA staff and their families are excluded from the competition.
- The competition is open only to residents of the UK.
- The close date for receipt by the Publishers of completed entries is 31 August 1991.
- The prizes will be awarded to the first five correct entries received following the close date (see above).
- The Publishers cannot enter into any correspondence regarding the competition and the Editor's decision is final.
- For answers to the crossword, to be released after the close date, send stamped, addressed envelope to:

The Editor
Let's Stop for Tea
The Automobile Association
Editorial Department
Fanum House
Basingstoke
RG21 2EA

Date entry received by Publishers _____

Competitors

Name (BLOCK CAPITALS) _____

Address _____

_____

Tel No _____

HOW TO USE THIS BOOK

The tea places in this book are listed alphabetically by place name throughout England, Scotland and Wales.

Example:

SKYE, ISLE OF   Highland   Map 13 NG52

Pipers Moon
Luib
Tel (04712) 594

For quick reference, if you are visiting an unfamiliar area, every location represented in the guide is shown on the appropriate map in the Atlas section.

The example of a typical entry given on the right should help you to make the most of the information given.

Symbols
A number of symbols may appear in each entry:

Credit Cards:
The following credit cards may be accepted, but check current details when booking:

$\boxed{1}$ = Access
$\boxed{2}$ = American Express
$\boxed{3}$ = Visa

Disabled access:

$\boxed{\&}$ This symbol shows that the establishment has toilets with access for the disabled.

EXAMPLE OF
A TYPICAL ENTRY

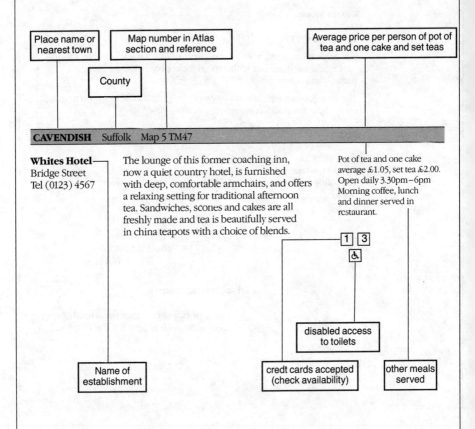

Place name or nearest town

Map number in Atlas section and reference

Average price per person of pot of tea and one cake and set teas

County

CAVENDISH   Suffolk   Map 5 TM47

Whites Hotel
Bridge Street
Tel (0123) 4567

The lounge of this former coaching inn, now a quiet country hotel, is furnished with deep, comfortable armchairs, and offers a relaxing setting for traditional afternoon tea. Sandwiches, scones and cakes are all freshly made and tea is beautifully served in china teapots with a choice of blends.

Pot of tea and one cake average £1.05, set tea £2.00. Open daily 3.30pm–6pm Morning coffee, lunch and dinner served in restaurant.

1 3
&

disabled access to toilets

Name of establishment

credt cards accepted (check availability)

other meals served

ABBERLEY   Hereford & Worcester   Map 07 SO76

The Elms
Tel (0299) 896666

This lovely Queen Anne house has just gone through a major refurbishment, and the three lounges are lovelier than ever with an inviting array of deep seating. Formal teas are available throughout the year, but are particularly pleasant during the summer within sight of the lovely grounds – ten acres of well-kept gardens and lawns. There is a selection of very good teas and a refreshing infusion of fresh peppermint leaves. Scones, cakes and biscuits and The Elms' own rich fruitcake are all made on the premises, and locally grown strawberries and cream are available in season.

Pot of tea £1 full afternoon tea £6.50
Open all year, every day, 3–6pm (for afternoon tea)
Meals available

1 2 3 &

ABBERLEY   Hereford & Worcester   Map 07 SO76

Manor Arms at Abberley
Tel (0299) 896507

This is a charming country inn standing in the centre of old Abberley Village. The pleasant and efficient staff serve good tea, and there is a selection of sandwiches and homemade cakes, biscuits and scones.

Set tea £4.50
Open Apr–Oct, every day, 3–5pm

1 2 3

ABBOTSBURY   Dorset   Map 03 SY58

Ilchester Arms
Tel (0305) 871243

Set in the centre of Abbotsbury village, the Ilchester Arms is an old coaching inn with comfortable lounges, and a conservatory restaurant with garden-style furniture. Homemade cakes and scones are served.

Cream tea £2.00
Open all year, every day, 3.30–5.30pm (for afternoon tea)

1 3

ABERDARE   Mid Glamorgan   Map 03 S000

Servini's Restaurant
2 Cardiff Street
Tel (0685) 873351

Located in the town centre of Aberdare, this restaurant on two levels serves a wide variety of pastries, cakes and pies, and there are cakes and bread on sale at the counter. Speciality ice cream is available. Coach parties are welcome.

Tea 30p
Open all year (except Christmas and Easter and bank holidays), Mon–Sat, 8am–5.30pm
Lunches and snacks available

ABERDARON   Gwynedd   Map 06 SH12

Hen Blas Crafts
Tel (075886) 438

A delightful little teashop/café is set at the back of this interesting craft and gift shop. A range of tea blends is available and a traditional Welsh dresser displays an array of homemade cake – bara brith, chocolate cakes, rum and fruit cakes and Nelson cake. Smoking is not permitted.

Pot of tea 65p
Open Easter–Oct, every day, 9am–6pm
Lunches served

ABERDEEN   Grampian   Map 15 NJ90

Coffee Club
Bruce Miller and Co
363 Union Street
Tel (0224) 592211

This attractive restaurant serves light snacks and teas at the rear of the first floor of this book and music shop. There is a tempting range of home-baked scones, cakes, pancakes and biscuits displayed on the tea trolleys, and a choice of tea blends is available.

Pot of tea 55p
Open all year, Mon–Sat, 9.30am–4.45pm
Lunches and snacks available

ABERDEEN   Grampian   Map 15 NJ90

Music Hall Coffee Shop
Union Street
Tel (0224) 632080

Two rooms of the recently refurbished Music Hall provide spacious and elegant surroundings for afternoon tea. Scones, cakes, gâteaux and biscuits are supplied by local bakers, and there is a choice of Assam, Earl Grey or Darjeeling teas. Tea dances are held in the Music Hall itself every fortnight (except in the summer).

Pot of tea 60p, set afternoon tea £2.50
Open all year, Mon–Sat, 9am–5pm

ABERDOVEY   Gwynedd   Map 06 SN69

Old Coffee Shop
New Street
Tel (065472) 652

In a side street just off the promenade at Aberdovey is this excellent little coffee shop – full of character and offering a friendly welcome. There is a choice of tea blends, and a lovely display of home baking (the scones had just come out of the oven when our inspector arrived). The tempting menu includes light snacks and cold platters.

Pot of tea 50p, speciality teas 75p
Open Feb–Dec (closed 2 weeks in Nov), every day 10am–5pm in summer, 10am–6pm in winter
Hot meals available

ABERFELDY   Tayside   Map 14 NN84

Country Fare
Bridgend
Tel (0887) 20729

This popular little coffee house-cum-restaurant is conveniently located in the main street of Aberfeldy. The emphasis is on home baking – tempting offerings include wholemeal cakes and scones, flapjacks, shortbread and cream cakes. There is a choice of tea blends, and the staff are friendly and helpful. The menu also offers freshly-made quiches, meat and fish dishes and a super salad bowl.

Pot of tea and one cake average £1.05
Open mid Feb–Dec, Mon–Sat, 10am–5pm

ABERGAVENNY   Gwent   Map 03 SO21

Clam's Coffee House
Lion Street
Tel (0873) 4496

Just off the shopping area and near the main car park, this coffee house offers a wide range of food such as barbecued chicken, omelettes, quiche, jacket potatoes and sandwiches, and breakfast is served until noon. Homemade desserts, peach fruit cakes, passion cake, caramel slices and scones can all be enjoyed with a choice of tea blends.

Pot of tea and one cake average £1
Open every day
Light lunches, licensed

ABERLOUR   Grampian   Map 15 NJ24

The Old Pantry
The Square
Tel (03405) 617

This attractive cottage-style restaurant with a beamed ceiling displays an interesting old tin collection. Blue and white checked tablecloths, live fire, tiled floor and everything immaculate and orderly make this an inviting prospect for afternoon tea. There is a range of homemade scones, cakes and biscuits and a choice of tea blends.

Pot of tea 50p
Open all year, Sun–Thu 9am–6pm, Fri–Sat 9am–9pm
Meals available

ABERNETHY   Tayside   Map 11 NO11

Pitblae Cottage Tearoom
Tel (073885) 361

Dating from the 18th century, this old building, with its timbered ceiling and rough stone walls, has been made into a homely little cottage tearoom. There are pretty tablecloths on the tables, and newspapers and magazines for customers to read. Drop scones, shortbread, Vienna shortcake, fruit slice, fairy cakes, sponge cakes and biscuits are among the range of good home-baking available.

Pot of tea 40p
Open Mar–Dec, Mon–Thur and Sat 10am–5pm, Sun 12.30–6pm
Meals and take-away service

ABERYSTWYTH   Dyfed   Map 06 SN58

Pennau Coffee Shop
Rhydypennau
Bow Street
Tel (0970) 820050

A good selection of Welsh and English craftwork is on sale at the Pennau Craft and Coffee Shop. The coffee shop is attractively furnished, with cushioned cane chairs, and there is a selection of homemade scones, pastries, pies and sandwiches; the set Welsh tea includes a Welsh Cake and Bara Brith.

Pot of tea and one cake average 65p, set tea from £1.90
Open Easter–Christmas every day Jun–Sep, otherwise Tue–Sun, 10am–5.30pm

ABERYSTWYTH   Dyfed   Map 06 SN58

Welsh Fudge Shop
Sandmarsh Cottage
Queens Road
Tel (0970) 612721

This small tearoom forms part of the Welsh Fudge Shop and is a must for anyone with a sweet tooth. All sorts of cakes and pancakes are served with a good pot of tea. The atmosphere is friendly.

Pot of tea 55p
Open all year, Mon–Sat 10am–6pm, Sun 12–6pm

ALDEBURGH   Suffolk   Map 05 TM45

White Lion Hotel
Market Cross Place
Tel (0728) 452720

A very attractive comfortably furnished room on the seafront looking out at the fishing boats, with car parking close by. A daily blackboard menu offers a variety of freshly-made dishes and there is a carvery buffet display. Sandwiches, cakes, pastries, scones and gâteaux are all made on the premises and are of very good quality. Earl Grey and Indian tea are available.

Pot of tea and one cake average £1.20, cream tea £1.50
Open every day
Lunches and snacks

$\boxed{1}$ $\boxed{2}$ $\boxed{3}$

ALDWARK   North Yorkshire   Map 08 SE46

Aldwark Manor Hotel
Alne
York
YO6 2WF
Tel (03473) 8146

A splendid 19th-century house looks out onto its own golf course, and guests taking tea outside on warmer days can watch players' progress; in cooler weather the elegant lounge with its live fires provides an alternative setting in which to enjoy freshly-made sandwiches, crumpets, teacakes and a sumptuous selection of homemade cakes. Assam, Darjeeling, Earl Grey, Ceylon and lapsang souchong teas are available.

Pot of tea £1.25–£1.30, set teas £4.25
Open every day, 3–5.30pm for tea

$\boxed{1}$ $\boxed{2}$ $\boxed{3}$

ALFRISTON   East Sussex   Map 05   TQ50

Toucans Family Restaurant
Tel (0323) 870234

Toucans forms part of the Drusillas Park and Zoo which includes the Adventure Playland and other family attractions. As well as home-baked cakes and scones and Sussex cream teas (with a choice of blends), Toucans children's menu offers 'jungle juice'.

Pot of tea 70p, Sussex cream tea £1.85
Open all year, every day (except Christmas), 10.30am–6pm
Meals available

$\boxed{1}$ $\boxed{2}$ $\boxed{3}$ $\boxed{\&}$

ALFRISTON   East Sussex   Map 05 TQ50

The Tudor House Restaurant
High Street
Tel (0323) 870891

This 14th-century building, the gardens at its rear looking over the Cuckmere to the South Downs, houses a restaurant where you can enjoy either a Sussex cream tea or items from an à la carte selection of savouries, sandwiches, scones and a range of cakes from shortbread to gâteau. Everything is made on the premises, and China, Earl Grey or Darjeeling tea are available as alternatives to the standard blend.

Pot of tea and one cake average £1.15, set teas £2.05–£2.50
Open every day (except Christmas Day and Boxing Day) 9.30am–5.30pm

$\boxed{3}$

ALNWICK   Northumberland   Map 12 NU11

Gate Gallery Coffee Shop
12 Bondgate Within
Tel (0665) 6062607

A pretty little coffee/teashop over a craft shop by the walled gateway in the centre of the town. A good range of homemade cakes is served, including delicious carrot cake, date and walnut loaf, fruit quiche, éclairs and gâteau. Full afternoon tea comprises a sandwich, a scone with jam and butter and a fresh cream cake with a choice of tea or coffee type.

Pot of tea and one cake average £1.50, set tea £2.50
Open every day 9.30am–4.30pm (closed Sun & Wed after 2.30pm in winter)

ALRESFORD (NEW), Hampshire Map 04 SU53

Tiffin
50 West Street
Tel (0962) 734394

A two-storey teashop on the busy main street with pine tables, padded upright chairs and no smoking permitted upstairs. Various set teas are served: Tiffin Tea with a salmon and cucumber sandwich, a cream tea and a watercress tea – this being a watercress-growing area. Homemade cakes are displayed in a cool cabinet and Indian, Earl Grey and China tea are available.

Pot of tea and one cake average £1.20, set teas £1.85–£2.25
Open every day (except Sun Jan–Mar)

ALSTON Cumbria Map 12 NY74

Brownside Coach House
Tel (0434) 381263

This old rustic-style coach house dates from 1689, and from the attractive, beamed interior are views of the south Tyne valley and the Pennines. Good home baking is accompanied by a friendly homely welcome from Mrs Graham, the proprietress.

Pot of tea 40p, set afternoon tea £2.70
Open Easter–end Sep, Wed–Mon, 10am–6pm

ALSTONEFIELD Staffordshire Map 07 SK15

Old Post Office Tea Room
Alstonefield, Nr Ashbourne
Tel (033527) 201

A converted post office – part of a 17th-century house, and well-known for its odd collection of cups and saucers – is popular with tourists and local people alike for its hospitable service and homemade scones, biscuits, tarts and cakes. A range of tea blends is available, and the set afternoon teas include a substantial one with boiled eggs.

Pot of tea and one cake average £1.30, set teas £2–£3.75
Open mid Mar–mid Nov, Thu–Tue 10.30am–5pm

ALTON Staffordshire Map 07 SK04

Byatt Coffee and Crafts
High Street
ST10 4AQ
Tel (0538) 703037

A quaint tea shop situated opposite the Bulls Head Hotel – and only a mile from Alton Towers Leisure Park – offers both an array of craft items and a two-roomed café offering savoury snacks, sandwiches and a trolley display of scones, Danish pastries, apple pie, cheesecake and gâteaux; there is a choice of tea blends.

Pot of tea 75–80p
Open Thu–Tue

AMBLESIDE Cumbria Map 07 NY30

High Green Gate Guest House
Near Sawrey
Tel (09666) 296

The cosy dining room of an 18th-century farmhouse, now converted to provide a comfortable guest house, serves afternoon tea with home-baked scones, biscuits and cakes; Earl Grey, lapsang and herbal teas are offered as an alternative to Indian. In fine weather seating is available on the front lawn.

Pot of tea 50p, pot of tea and one cake average £1.10, cream tea £1.60
Open Easter–end Oct (may close Thu or Fri), 3–6pm

AMBLESIDE   Cumbria   Map 07 NY30

Rothay Manor Hotel
Rothay Bridge
Tel (05394) 33605

An elegant Regency house in lawned gardens, standing just outside the town on the Coniston Road, offers a good buffet selection of dainty sandwiches (brown or white), sausage rolls, vol-au-vents, scones, fruitcake and cream cakes – all made on the premises. An equally good range of tea blends is available, customers placing their order with Reception before choosing their food.

Pot of tea and one cake average £2.50, set tea £5.75
Open all week
1 2 3

AMBLESIDE   Cumbria   Map 07 NY30

Sheila's Cottage
The Slack
Tel (05394) 33079

This delightful restaurant, in a charming Lakeland stone cottage, is deservedly popular with visitors to the Lakes and local customers alike. In the afternoon the friendly staff and owners Stewart and Janice Greaves serve a wide range of delicious cakes including lemon bread with lemon cheese, spicy bara brith and fresh muffins made with flour ground locally at Muncaster Mill in Eskdale. Swiss food is another speciality of Shelia's Cottage; why not try a Swiss drinking chocolate served with Jersey cream with a slice of rum-flavoured Sachertorte?

Borrowdale teabread 80p
Open Feb–Dec, Mon–Sat, 10.30am–5.30pm
Lunches (booking advisable)

ANNAN   Dumfries & Galloway   Map 11 NY16

Queensberry Arms
47 High Street
DG12 6AD
Tel (04612) 2024

This recently refurbished High Street hotel offers a choice of inviting venues in which to enjoy morning coffee, hot snacks, lunch or afternoon tea; this last comprises an extensive range of sandwiches (plain or toasted) with teacakes, home-baked scones, biscuits, meringues and rich chocolate gâteaux, served with a choice of tea blends.

Pot of tea and one cake average £1.50
Open Mon–Sat
Lunches and hot snacks

1 2 3

ANSTRUTHER   Fife   Map 12 NO50

Scottish Fisheries Museum Teashop
Harbour Head
KY10 3AB
Tel (0333) 310628

This quaint teashop, together with a museum and gift shop, is run by volunteers who are both friendly and knowledgeable about the area. Honest, old-fashioned home baking provides fresh scones, light sponges, jam tarts, coconut macaroons and butterfly cakes. Sandwiches are always freshly made and during the winter months may be ordered toasted as an accompaniment to homemade soups.

Pot of tea 50p
Open every day

ANSTRUTHER   Fife   Map 12 NO50

The Tea Clipper
15 East Green

This small tearoom is part of a guest house that stands in a quaint, narrow street immediately behind the harbour and fisheries museum. Its menu offers homemade soups, jacket potatoes and salads as well as a good range of sandwiches and a selection of home baking which always includes scones, gâteaux and its speciality – chocolate cake.

Pot of tea and one cake average 75p
Open Easter–mid Oct
Snacks

APPLEBY-IN-WESTMORLAND   Cumbria   Map 12 NY62

The Copper Kettle Restaurant
17 Boroughgate
Tel (07683) 51605

A copper kettle and warming pan, jugs and a grandfather clock lend atmosphere to this friendly town-centre café/restaurant (ample parking space nearby) which also sells sweets and chocolates. Afternoon tea comprises brown bread and butter, teacakes and homemade scones and cakes, but the menu also offers a good choice of sandwiches, salads and popular hot dishes.

Pot of tea 50p, set tea £2.20
Open all year, every day (except Sun Nov–Easter)

APPLEBY-IN-WESTMORLAND   Cumbria   Map 12 NY62

Courtyard Gallery
32 Boroughgate
Tel (07683) 51638

Tucked away down a passageway in Appleby is the Courtyard Gallery, which sells original paintings, pottery, glass, jewellery, turned wood and cards. At one end of the gallery, the teashop, overlooking an attractive garden, offers a selection of cakes and biscuits and a wide choice of tea blends and herb teas. No smoking is permitted.

Pot of tea 40p
Open all year (except 2 weeks in Jan), Tue–Sun 10am–5pm, Sun 10.30am–5pm
1

APPLEBY-IN-WESTMORLAND   Cumbria   Map 12 NY62

Victorian Pantry
9 Bridge Street
Tel (07683) 52593

In this attractive licensed restaurant, pleasant and efficient service by waitresses in long skirts adds to the Victorian atmosphere. There is a selection of cakes and scones, and the choice of tea blends includes an English Breakfast Tea.

Pot of tea and one cake average £1.10
Open all year, every day (except Oct–Easter closed Thu), 9am–9pm summer and 10am–5.30pm winter
Restaurant meals served

ARDERSIER   Highlands   Map 14 NH75

The Old Bakehouse
73 High Street
Tel (0667) 62920

This teashop is an old converted bakehouse – now with a conservatory extension, and an inviting place for tea with prints on the walls, pot plants, and pine tables and chairs. There is a good selection of scones, cakes and pastries, and tea blends available include Earl Grey, jasmine and Scottish breakfast. Smoking is not permitted.

Set tea £2.20
Open May–Oct, every day, 10am–6pm

ASHBOURNE   Derbyshire   Map 07 SK14

Ashbourne Gingerbread Shop
26 St John Street
Tel (0335) 43227

This historic half-timbered building stands in the centre of town and is almost always packed out with customers eager to sample the excellent cakes and pastries freshly made in the bakery adjoining the teashop. Gingerbread men are, naturally, a speciality but all the cakes are popular. There are six different blends of tea, and some herbal fruit teas.

Cream tea £1.80
Open Mon–Sat but not bank holidays 8.30am–5pm

ASHBOURNE   Derbyshire   Map 07 SK14

Mrs Cheadle's Old Fashioned Tearoom
The Derbyshire Brass Rubbing Centre
22 King Street
Tel (0335) 300151

The tearoom is situated inside the brass rubbing centre but visitors are welcome even if not visiting the centre. Part 16th century, part Victorian the building houses three brass rubbing rooms, gift shop and tearoom. The latter specialises in locally home-baked cakes in some unusual and tasty variations, notably paradise cake with its blend of orange and coconut sponge. Set teas and a choice of tea blends are available.

Pot of tea and one cake average £1.65, set teas £1.30–£2.40
Open every day 10am–5pm (check for winter opening)
[1] [3]

ASHBURTON   Devon   Map 03 SX77

The Old Saddlery
24 North Street
Tel (0364) 53127

A homely, relaxed teashop in a former saddlery with exposed ceiling beams and an open fire with an attractive stone surround (lit in winter), and fresh flowers in summer. Friendly service is provided by the proprietors who take pride in their home-baked cakes and scones served with local clotted cream. A range of hot snacks and sandwiches is available and a selection of tea varieties.

Pot of tea and one cake average £1.50, cream tea £1.95
Open Sat–Thu
Hot snacks

ASHFORD   Kent   Map 05 TR04

Eastwell Manor
Eastwell Park
Boughton Lees
Tel (0233) 635751

This charming country house hotel is set in 3,000 acres of private parkland and offers much character and comfort. Afternoon tea may be taken in the delightful lounge, and service is very good and extremely efficient. Traditional full afternoon teas are available, as well as Kentish cream teas, and there is a choice of blends, served in beautiful silver teapots. This is an excellent place for a leisurely tea.

Pot of tea and one cake average £2.00, set teas £4.50–£8.00
Open all year, every day, 3.30pm–5.30pm
Meals available
[1] [2] [3]

ASHOPTON WOODLANDS   Derbyshire   Map 08 SK19

The Snake Pass Inn
Tel (0433) 51480

This small inn, built in 1821 for the refreshment of travellers on the newly constructed turnpike between Sheffield and Manchester, now offers teas in a large lounge with ample seating. Particularly popular with ramblers and walkers in this remote part of the High Peak area, it serves a good range of sandwiches, filled rolls, toasted teacakes, scones and cakes, all of which are prepared on the premises.

Set teas £1.50–£1.95
Open every day

ASTBURY MARSH   Cheshire   Map 07 SJ86

Astbury Tea Shop
Newcastle Road
Tel (0260) 277099

A small teashop on the A34 Congleton–Newcastle road, with garden seating as well as indoors among the display of antiques for sale. Light hot snacks are available along with homemade cakes, pastries and sandwiches.

Pot of tea and one cake average £1.15, set tea £2.20
Open Tue–Sun 11am–5pm (check winter opening)
Hot snacks

AUCHENCAIRN   Dumfries & Galloway   Map 11 NX75

Solwayside House Hotel
25 Main Street
DG7 1QU

The teas served in the comfortable lounge of this family-owned and managed hotel include a good-value range of home-baked scones, cakes and biscuits; such sandwich fillings as beef, ham and cheese are always available, and there is a choice of tea blends.

Pot of tea and one cake average 90p
Open every day

AVIEMORE   Highlands   Map 14 NH81

Chinwags Coffee Shop
Red McGregor Hotel
Main Road
Tel (0479) 810256

This smart, modern coffee shop is conveniently located off the Foyer lounge of the Red McGregor Hotel in the centre of Aviemore. There is a selection of scones, croissants, tarts, cookies, cheesecakes and gâteaux, all made on the premises.

Cakes 20p–£1.30
Open all year, every day, 9.30am–6pm
1 2 3 &

BAGSHOT   Surrey   Map 04 SU96

Pennyhill Park
College Ride
Tel (0276) 71774

This stately English country manor house has been tastefully converted for use as a popular and elegant hotel. Afternoon tea can be taken either in the lounge or the conservatory; the staff are very smart and efficient. A choice of tea blends is offered, as well as home-baked scones, sandwiches, fresh fruit tarts and fruit cakes – an excellent prospect for tea.

Pot of tea and biscuits £2, Latymer full tea £6.95
Open all year, every day, tea during the afternoon
Meals available
1 2 3 &

BAKEWELL   Derbyshire   Map 08 SK26

Byways
Water Lane
Tel (0629) 812807

Quite a steep staircase leads to spacious premises – there are three separate rooms, all with polished wooden tables and chairs, and the occasional sofa. Friendly staff add to a homely atmosphere. A good selection of tea is provided, as well as homemade Bakewell tart, cakes, pastries and scones. Children and hikers are welcome.

Pot of tea 50p–60p
afternoon tea £2.30
Open all year (except Christmas), Mon–Sat 10am–6pm or later, Sun 1.30pm–6pm or later
Full menu of freshly prepared food available all day

BAKEWELL   Derbyshire   Map 08 SK26

Marguerite and Stephanie's Coffee Shop
John Sinclair
The Square
Tel (0629) 814164

Located on the first floor of Sinclair's China Shop, the coffee shop is bright, clean and spacious, with pretty floral tablecloths providing a splash of colour. A wide variety of tea blends is offered, and tea is presented in a china tea service on a silver platter. The Bakewell pudding and various cakes, pastries and biscuits are all baked on the premises. The establishment specialises in vegetarian dishes, and holds the 'Heartbeat Award' for healthy eating.

Pot of tea 60p
Open all year, Mon–Sat
9am–4.45pm (Thur 4pm),
Sun 2–5pm
Light lunches and hot
snacks available

BALA   Gwynedd   Map 06 SH93

Sospan-fach
97 High Street
Tel (0678) 520396

This small restaurant-cum-teashop is situated in the main street of Bala. A low beamed ceiling and open fireplace with hanging copper pans add to the character, and a local lady provides quick and friendly service.

Pot of tea 50p, set tea
£3.00
Open Feb–Dec, summer
9am–6pm (closes at
5.30pm Mon), winter
9.30am–5.30pm
Snacks and meals available

BALA   Gwynedd   Map 06 SH93

White Lion Royal Hotel
66 High Street
LL23 7AE
Tel (0678) 520314

An impressive old inn with a large car park to the rear, set in the town's High Street, serves sandwiches, homemade scones and cakes, cream teas and hot snacks in its sun lounge – or on the terrace when weather permits.

Pot of tea and one cake
average 75p
Open every day, 2–6pm
Hot snacks

BALA   Gwynedd   Map 06 SH93

Y Radell
81 High Street
Tel (0678) 520203

Our inspector found a warm Welsh welcome at this small bow-fronted restaurant. Inside, the walls are adorned with bric-a-brac, there are stick-back chairs and the tables are covered with lace cloths. The homemade cakes are tempting, and the tea has a good flavour. No smoking is permitted.

Pot of tea and one cake
from 90p, set teas from
£1.60
Open all year, every day,
9am–5pm Mon–Sat, 12
noon to 5pm Sun
Breakfast, lunches and
snacks available

BAMBURGH　Northumbria　Map 12 NU13

The Copper Kettle Tea Room
21 Front Street
Tel (06684) 315

This is an interesting little cottage tearoom with some fine carved wood panelling and an attractive display counter adding to the period styling and character. There is a wide choice of speciality teas, herbal infusions and fruit teas, as well as a selection of homemade cakes, pastries and scones. A range of sweets, biscuits and preserves are on sale. Smoking is not permitted.

Pot of tea 50p–60p
Open Mar–Nov, every day, 10.30am–5.30pm or 5.00pm Mar and Oct
Hot and cold meals and snacks available, take away snacks

BAMBURGH　Northumbria　Map 12 NU13

Ramblers
5 Lucker Road
Tel (06684) 229

A homely atmosphere and friendly service are a feature of this small family-run tearoom. There is a choice of tea blends, and a selection of gâteaux, cakes, scones and sandwiches. Two rooms are available for guests taking tea, one catering for non-smokers.

Pot of tea 40p–45p
Open all year, every day, 10am–5.30pm
Meals and snacks available
1　3

BAMFORD　Derbyshire　Map 08 SK28

Rising Sun Hotel
Castleton Road
Tel (0433) 51323

Hot meals, snacks and afternoon teas are served in the pleasant restaurant-bar area of this attractive black and white timbered hotel. A set cream tea of two scones, butter, preserves and cream is available, and there is a refrigerated display of mainly bought-in quality gâteaux, desserts and ices. A choice of tea blends is offered.

Pot of tea and one cake average £2.25, cream tea £1.90
Open every day
Meals and snacks, licensed
1　3

BANCHORY　Grampian　Map 15 NO69

Banchory Lodge
Tel (03302) 2625

Delightfully situated in 12 acres of grounds along the River Dee, Banchory Lodge has a wonderful atmosphere that makes guests feel completely at ease. The owners, Dugald and Maggie Jaffrey, who have run the hotel for over 20 years, are enthusiastic about antiques, and Edwardian and Victorian pieces grace the beautiful house, along with the lovely furnishings and fresh flowers. The elegant lounges provide the perfect setting for a relaxing tea, with good-natured staff ensuring an informal and warm hospitality. Homemade cakes, shortbread, scones and freshly-cut finger sandwiches are some of the offerings for afternoon tea.

Pot of tea and one cake average £1.75, set teas from £5
Open Feb–12 Dec, every day, 3–5pm for afternoon tea
Meals available
1　2　3

BANCHORY   Grampian   Map 15 NO69

Country Kitchen Restaurant
Raemoir Road
Tel (03302) 2025

A smaller timber-clad roadside restaurant in a rural setting just north of the village. Popular with locals and visitors alike, there is ample parking, picnic tables and a children's play area. The pine-furnished interior is bright and cheery with a display of crafts and gifts. The menu offers soup, salads, hot dishes and snacks as well as a variety of filled rolls, sandwiches, homemade cakes and gâteaux served by friendly staff.

Pot of tea and one cake from 70p
Open Feb–Dec every day
Light meals and snacks

BANCHORY   Grampian   Map 15 NO69

Raemoir
Tel (03302) 4884

The panelled morning room, dating from 1817, is the setting for afternoon tea here. The beautiful furnishings are complemented by lovely views over the 3,500-acre estate, and the informal and relaxing atmosphere makes a visit here an experience to remember. Homemade cakes and chef's pancakes are among the offerings for tea, as well as a choice of tea blends and herbal infusions.

Teas £3.00–£5.00
Open all year, every day, 3.30–5pm (for afternoon tea)
Meals available

BANFF   Grampian   Map 15 NJ66

George Ellis Coffee Shop
69 High Street
Tel (02612) 2404

The small coffee shop here is located at the back of the first floor of the chemist's shop. The service is pleasant, and there is a good range of homemade cakes, scones and biscuits on the trolley.

Tea 40p
Open all year, Mon–Sat (but closed Wed afternoon), 9am–4.30pm
Light snacks available at lunchtime

BARDEN BRIDGE   North Yorkshire   Map 07 SE05

Barden Tower Tea Room
Near Bolton Abbey

A ruined hunting lodge in the heart of the Yorkshire Dales overlooking the River Wharfe, Barden Tower has old mullioned windows, beams, uneven floors and antique sideboards decorated with blue china – resonant with historical atmosphere. There are six tables and service is friendly. Warm scones with good jam and thick cream and a small selection of good cakes are served with a choice of tea blends.

Pot of tea and one cake average £1.40

BARMOUTH   Gwynedd   Map 06 SH61

Kith 'n Kin
King Edward Street
Tel (0341) 281071

This teashop is part of a well-established family bakery located on the main street near the railway station. There is a bright, fresh, friendly atmosphere here. The bakery supplies a good range of cakes, and a very good locally-made bara brith is served.

Pot of tea 52p
Open all year except 24 Dec–11 Jan, every day (except Sun till 1 Jul), 9am–4.30pm

---

BARMOUTH   Gwynedd   Map 06 SH61

The Old Tea Rooms
Church Street
Tel (0341) 280194

In the main street of Barmouth, this double-fronted teashop has plenty of character. There are padded stick-back chairs, lace cloths on the tables, and a large model of a tea clipper boat is on display. A selection of tea blends is offered, and there is a cake display and a good homemade bara brith. Smoking in not permitted.

Pot of tea 50p–55p, set teas £1.95–£2.25
Open seasonally (limited opening in winter), every day (except Wed early season), 10.30am–5.30pm
Light lunches available

BARMOUTH   Gwynedd   Map 06 SH61

Tyn y Coed
Caerdeon
Tel (0341) 49228

Everything, including the jam, is homemade at this 200-year-old stone-built farmhouse which stands in 16 acres of grounds and gardens beside the A496 three miles east of Barmouth. Sandwiches, teacakes, scones, sponges and fruitcakes are supplemented by such daily 'specials' as honey and ginger cake or pineapple gâteau, and there is a choice of tea blends. Teas are served on the lawn when the weather permits.

Pot of tea and one cake average 90p
Open all year, every day 11am–6pm

BARNARD CASTLE   Co Durham   Map 12 NZ01

The Market Place Teashop
29 The Market Place
Tel (8033) 690110

Oak tables, low beams, stone walls, flagstone floors and an open fire when it is chilly all add to the charm and character of this wonderful little town-centre tearoom. Offerings include Jap cakes, a variety of fresh cream cakes, gâteaux and pastries: teacakes, biscuits, scones and fruit pies. There is a good variety of tea blends, served in silver teapots (and silver hot-water jugs) with Wedgwood china tea service. Staff are always friendly and attentive. This is a really excellent teashop that gives great value for money.

Pot of tea and one cake average £1.60
Open all year, every day (except Jan–Mar closed Sun), 10am (Sun 3pm)–5.30pm
Varied menu available all day

BARTON   Lancashire   Map 07 SD53

The Thirsty Gardener
Barton Grange Hotel & Conference Centre
PR3 5AA
Tel (0772) 862551

Conveniently set beside the A6 between Preston and Lancaster, adjoining Barton Grange Hotel and next to a garden centre, this pleasant little coffee shop serves light meals and afternoon tea, seating being available on the terrace in warmer weather. Salads, quiche, sandwiches with a variety of fillings, scones, shortbread, flapjacks and Danish pastries are on offer throughout the day.

Pot of tea and one cake average £1.25
Open every day
Light meals

BARWICK-IN-ELMET   West Yorkshire   Map 08 SE43

The Copper Kettle
22 Main Street
Tel (0532) 812684

Rails of plates, cups and bric-à-brac decorate the plain walls of a cosy little teashop at the rear of this charming village's drug store. Tables are prettily laid out, service is friendly, and a good range of tea blends accompanies a wide selection of snacks, sandwiches and homemade scones, sponges, gâteaux and fruit pies.

Pot of tea 45–60p, set tea
£2.45
Open Wed–Sat 9.30am–
5.30pm (closes 3.30pm
Tue)
Sunday lunch

BASILDON   Essex   Map 05 TQ78

Café Metro
Allders
East Gate Shopping
Centre
Tel (0268) 527858

There is a feeling of France about the Café Metro, with all the atmosphere of a pavement café, pot plants and trees and soft lighting. Scones, rolls, croissants and various pastries are available, as well as a very good choice of tea blends and herbal teas.

Pot of tea 55p–60p
Open all year (except
Christmas), Mon–Sat,
10am–7.30pm
$\boxed{1}$ $\boxed{2}$ $\boxed{3}$ $\boxed{\xi}$

BASILDON   Essex   Map 05 TQ78

Oliver's
54 Town Square
Tel (0268) 280886

Oliver's is a modern hot bread and coffee shop, with counter service on the ground floor and additional seating upstairs. Home-baked items include cream cakes, jam doughnuts, scones, hot buns and pastries.

Pot of tea 50p, cakes 35p–
75p
Open all year, Mon–Sat,
8.45am–5.45pm

BASLOW   Derbyshire   Map 08 SK27

Cavendish Hotel
Tel (0246) 582311

The Cavendish is set in this Peak District village on the edge of the Chatsworth estate. Afternoon tea is a new venture here: teas are taken in the 'Garden Room', which commands superb views across part of the estate. A choice of tea blends is served in silver teapots, with Wedgwood china and linen napkins. There is a range of cakes, crumpets and scones, and many items include homemade bread.

Set afternoon tea from £2
Open all year, every day,
11am–11pm
$\boxed{1}$ $\boxed{2}$ $\boxed{3}$

BASLOW   Derbyshire   Map 08 SK27

**Crofters Restaurant
and Tea Room**
Goose Green
Eaton Hill
Tel (0246) 883164

Morning coffees and afternoon teas are an event in this little cottage-style restaurant in the heart of Baslow village. Stone walls and coal-effect fires are a feature of the interior. A local baker supplies fruit pies, scones and various pastries.

Pot of tea 55p
Open all year, Tues–Sun,
11am–5pm
$\boxed{1}$

The Canary
3 Queens Street
Tel (0225) 424846

Tucked away on a cobbled back street in Bath, the Canary is a charming place – the décor is simple, with prints on the walls and circular bare-topped tables and wheel-back chairs. It was given the Tea Council Award for Excellence in 1988 and 89, and also judged Top Tea Place of the Year in 1989. There is a wonderful display of home-baked cakes – teacakes and tea breads, wholemeal scones, meringues, fruit tartlets, cakes and pastries. The menu offers a choice of over 40 teas and 10 coffees, and provides informative and entertaining reading. There are ranges of Ceylon, China, India, Assam, Darjeeling and Formosa teas; a selection of blends (including 'Canary Blend' and 'Tea of the Week') as well as many herbal, exotic and fruit teas and infusions. Packets of speciality teas are on sale.

Pot of tea and one cake average £2.25, set teas £1.50–£3.00, clotted cream tea £2.70
Open all year (except Christmas Day and Boxing Day), every day, 8.30am–8pm
Lunches served

Charlotte's Patisserie
Collonade Shopping Centre
Bath Street
Tel (0225) 445895

On the lower ground floor of the new Colonnade shopping centre, Charlotte's has a bright, modern décor, and a mouthwatering display of cakes and pastries. The young staff are quick and friendly and serve a wide range of teas and snacks. Specialist items are baked by the company's own local bakery.

Pot of tea from 80p, set cream tea from £2.25
Open all year, Mon–Sat, 9am–5.30pm

David's
17 Pulteney Bridge
Tel (0225) 464636

In a unique location, this tiny building is built on Pulteney Bridge and has views of the river and the weir beneath. Its charm is helped by very friendly and hard-working staff. A good range of interesting cakes are available – all baked by the staff, and there is a good range of tea served in china pots.

Pot of tea 85p, cream tea £2.25
Open all year, Tue–Sat, 9am–5pm
Breakfast, lunch and dinner available

The Francis Hotel
Queen Square
Tel (0225) 24257

The Francis Hotel faces an attractive little park, and is only a stone's throw from the little narrow shopping streets that are a feature of Bath. Formal teas are taken in the lounge, and are an attraction for residents and visitors alike. There is a choice of tea blends, and sandwiches, scones, gâteaux and fruit tarts are all home-baked.

Pot of tea and one cake average £2.25, set tea £5.25
Open all year, every day, 3.30–6pm (for afternoon tea)

BATH   Avon   Map 03 ST76

No 5 Argyle Street Restaurant
5 Argyle Street
Tel (0225) 444499

Indoor plants, ceiling fans and cane furniture help to create a stylish atmosphere – a fun place to eat any time of day. There is a choice of tea blends. The selection of cakes includes scones, chocolate cake, cookies and brownies.

Pot of tea 50p, scones and clotted cream £1.65
Open all year, every day, 10am–10pm (12 noon–5pm Sun)
Breakfast and lunch available
1 2 3

BATH   Avon   Map 03 ST76

The Priory Hotel
Weston Road
Tel (0225) 331922

Surprisingly, although little more than half a mile from the bustle of Bath, the Priory is everything one expects from a country house hotel. Afternoon tea can be taken in one of the sitting rooms, or, weather permitting, on the terrace overlooking the lovely mature garden. There is a choice of tea blends, and a good range of cakes – all baked on the premises.

Pot of tea and one cake average £2.45, set afternoon tea from £6.50
Open all year, every day, 3.30pm–5.30pm (for afternoon tea)
Meals available
1 2 3

BATH   Avon   Map 03 ST76

The Pump Room
Tel (0225) 444477

In 1786 the present Pump Room replaced a smaller house, and ever since then this has been a favourite Bath meeting place. Elegant portraits of early dignitaries adorn the walls, chandeliers hang from the ceiling, and sedan and Bath chairs are on display. Teatime favourites here are Cobb's original Bath buns, plain and cheese scones, dark chocolate cake, fancy cakes and pastries, and toast and 'gentlemen's relish'. A selection of tea blends is available. The Pump Room Trio play every morning and in the afternoon during summer. A pianist plays in the afternoon at all other times.

Pot of tea and one cake average £3.00, 'Club Tea' £3.75, set teas £5.50–£20
Open all year, every day, 9am–5pm (10am–4.30pm Nov–Feb)

BATH   Avon   Map 03 ST76

Royal Crescent Hotel
16 Royal Crescent
Tel (0225) 319090

Superbly set in the middle of Bath's most famous street, the Royal Crescent offers a splendid afternoon tea in luxurious surroundings. The interior has been modernised, but there is still plenty of period charm and atmosphere – with beautiful antiques, fine paintings, delicate porcelain and lovely soft furnishings. Afternoon tea is served in three of the hotel's pleasant lounges and in the splendid gardens during the summer months. There is a wide choice of different tea blends, served with china service. Traditional teas include assorted finger sandwiches, scones with Jersey cream, hot buttered teacakes and – of course – Bath buns.

Afternoon tea from £4.50
Open all year, every day,
3-5pm (for afternoon tea)
Meals available

1   2   3

BATH   Avon   Map 03 ST76

Sally Lunn's House
4 North Parade Passage
Tel (0225) 461634

Sally Lunn's house must have a claim to being the original tearoom from which all others followed. It is reputedly the oldest house in Bath (excavations have revealed Roman occupation) where, in 1680, Sally Lunn created her much-copied bun – a renowned delicacy. The present owners, Mike and Angela Overton, have done much to make a visit here interesting by opening the original cellars and excavations. However, this is a serious place to come and eat a piece of history. The rich, generous Sally Lunn bun can be served in countless ways – toasted and buttered, filled with sweet jam, cream or butters; with a savoury filling and accompanied by salad it can make a meal. All items here are home-baked, mostly based on the brioche-like bun. A choice of tea blends is available. Smoking is not permitted.

Pot of tea from 80p, Sally
Lunn bun from £1.58, set
teas from £3.08
Open all year (except
Christmas and New Year),
every day, 10am (12 noon
Sun)–6pm
Light meals based on Sally
Lunn bun

BATH   Avon   Map 03 ST76

La Silhouette
7 Green Street
Tel (0225) 460463

Plain woodchip décor, round bare-topped tables, wicker chairs and fresh flowers on the table greet guests to La Silhouette. Cakes – made on the premises – include tea cakes, scones, gâteaux, various slices and Danish pastries. There is a good selection of different tea blends.

Pot of tea and one cake
average £1.75, set teas
from £2.95
Open all year, every day
(but closed Sun Dec–Feb),
9am–5.30pm (Sat 6pm),
12 noon–5.30pm Sun

1   3

BATTLE   East Sussex   Map 05 TQ71

Gateway Restaurant
78 High Street
Tel (04246) 2856

Polished floorboards, wooden tables and wheelback chairs enhance the beamed interior of a very popular licensed restaurant which is open for morning coffee, lunch and dinner as well as afternoon tea. Hot fruit scones with jam and clotted cream, homemade patisserie, snacks and light bites are all recommended, and there is a choice of tea blends.

Pot of tea 55–65p, pot of tea and one cake average £1.10, set tea from £2.25
Open every day

BATTLE   East Sussex   Map 05 TQ71

Netherfield Place
Tel (04246) 4455

This elegant Georgian-style country house hotel stands in 30 acres of beautiful parkland, and is a real haven for those seeking a relaxed and tranquil afternoon tea in luxurious rural surroundings. Tea can be taken in the elegantly furnished lounge in front of a log fire when the weather is chilly, or in the garden, if it is fine. Netherfield offers a choice of tea blends, all served with individuality and traditional style. The professional patisserie includes Madeira cake, homemade shortbread and freshly-baked scones. The hotel has its own walled kitchen garden, and in season guests can enjoy fresh berries with cream. The afternoon tea menu provides excellent value for money.

Set afternoon tea £4.50
Open all year except last week Dec and first week Jan, every day, 3–5.30pm (for afternoon tea)
Meals available
[1] [2] [3]

BATTLE   East Sussex   Map 05 TQ71

The Pilgrims Rest
Tel (04246) 2314

Located next to the abbey in Battle, this early 14th-century building is full of old-world charm. The original beams are exposed, and there are leaded-light windows and wood-burning open fires when the weather is cold. Sussex cream teas are served throughout the afternoon, and tempting offerings include pastries and cakes, fruit scones, hot toast and ice cream surprises.

Set afternoon tea £2.50
Open Apr–Mar, every day, 10am–5.30pm (limited opening during winter)
Morning coffee and lunches available

BEACONSFIELD   Buckinghamshire   Map 04 SU99

Georgian Coffee House
Wycombe End
Beaconsfield
Bucks
Tel (0494) 67855

The Georgian Coffee House is set in an old two-storey building in the centre of the old town. The rooms are well-decorated and inviting, with carpeted floors. A good pot of tea is served by pleasant and attentive staff, and there are homemade cakes, scones and shortbread.

Pot of tea and one cake average £1.70
Open all year except Christmas, Mon–Sat, 9.30am–5.30pm

BEAUMARIS   Gwynedd   Map 06 SH67

Spinning Wheel Tea Rooms
1 Bulkeley Place
Castle Street
Tel (0248) 810338

Situated next to the castle in the main street, this is a bright and inviting tea room. There is an attractive glass case with a wonderful display of homemade cakes, pies and shortbreads, including nutty flapjacks, apple and banana slice and currant slice (our inspector particularly enjoyed the apricot-nut slice). The service is quick and friendly. Boxes of fudge are on sale.

Pot of tea 50p–75p, set tea £2.50–£2.95
Open all year (but may close occasionally in winter), every day, 10am–6pm
Range of meals and snacks served all day

BEAUMARIS   Gwynedd   Map 06 SH67

The Welsh Dresser Tea Shop
30 Castle Street
Tel (0248) 810851

This small shop, with its low ceiling and exposed beams, dates back to the 15th century. Blue carpets are complemented by pretty blue and white tablecloths, and there is a nice cosy, friendly atmosphere. There is a tempting range of homemade cakes, scones and slices, and a choice of tea blends is available. A very good prospect for an enjoyable afternoon tea. Smoking is not permitted.

Pot of tea and one cake average £1.10
Open all year, every day, 10am–7pm
Light meals and snacks available

BEDALE   North Yorkshire   Map 08 SE28

Plummers
North End
Tel (0677) 23432

This old stone-built building is full of character. There are low ceilings and exposed beams; a fire burning in the old-fashioned grate, dark polished tables and matching wheel-back chairs complete the picture of the traditional tearoom. Assorted sandwiches, homemade pastries, scones and cakes are available, accompanied by a good, strong pot of tea (and jug of hot water).

Cream tea £2.50
Open all year, Mon–Sat, 10am–5pm
Morning coffee and lunches available

BEDDGELERT   Gwynedd   Map 06 SH54

Beddgelert Tea Rooms
Waterloo House
Tel (076686) 543

Situated by the river bridge in the centre of the village, these tearooms are part of an antique shop. This is a delightful little place, with antique tables and a lovely old stone-built fireplace. A tempting array of cakes and bara brith is available – all homemade. A choice of good flavour tea comes in brown crockery pots, with bone china cups and saucers.

Pot of tea 50p–55p, cakes from 50p
Open all year, every day (closed midweek, Jan–Mar), 10am–6pm
Light lunches and snacks available

BEDFORD   Bedfordshire   Map 04 TL04

Bedford Swan
The Embankment
Tel (0234) 46565

Set on the riverside at Bedford, this 18th-century hotel has upgraded its public rooms to provide comfortable lounge accommodation where afternoon teas are served. Scones, cakes, gâteaux and sandwiches are available, and the service is efficient and friendly. A choice of tea blends is offered.

Pot of tea and one cake average £1.75, set afternoon tea £3.50
Open all year, every day, 3–5.30pm (for afternoon tea)
Meals available

BERWICK-UPON-TWEED   Northumberland   Map 12 NT95

King's Arms Hotel
(Garden Terrace
Restaurant)
Hide Hill
Tel (0289) 307454

This is a spacious, tastefully decorated self-service restaurant, part of an impressive, stone-built hotel. In fine weather tea can be taken on the patio of the sheltered walled garden. The choice for tea includes shortbread, scones, gâteaux, cheesecakes, malt loaf, pastries and sandwiches. A choice of tea blends is available.

Pot of tea 40p
Open all year, every day,
9.30am – 5.30pm
(occasionally closed Sat
afternoons)
1 2 3

BETWS-Y-COED   Gwynedd   Map 06 SH75

Alpine Coffee Shop
The Railway Station
Tel (06902) 747

This small, bright and fresh coffee shop – decorated in yellow and green – is situated overlooking the railway platform. A good range of snacks is available from the self-service counter, and there is a veranda on the platform if the weather is fine. Fresh cream cakes, fruit cakes, scones and welshcakes are on offer, and the tea has a good flavour and the welcome is friendly.

Pot of tea and one cake
average 87p, set tea £1.20
Open all year (except for
Jan), every day, 10am –
6pm (9am – 7pm in
summer)

BETWS-Y-COED   Gwynedd   Map 06 SH75

**The Buffet Coach
Café**
The Old Goods Yard
Betws-y-Coed Railway
Museum
Tel (06902) 568

An authentic 50-year-old railway carriage seating forty-eight (with additional patio seating) forms part of a complex beside the railway station which also includes a museum, souvenir shop and a miniature railway. A wide range of homemade snack meals, scones and cakes – including Annwen's Parkin, Grandmother's Bara Brith and Lottie's Fruit Cake, for example – is served in a friendly, relaxed atmosphere.

Pot of tea 40p
Open every day 9am –
5.30pm

BETWS-Y-COED   Gwynedd   Map 06 SH75

**Craig-y-Dderwen
Hotel**
Tel (06902) 293

A late-Victorian country house hotel set on the edge of the village in five acres of gardens, grounds and woodland that stretch to the banks of the River Conwy. A choice of set teas is offered and sandwiches followed by scones or homemade puddings are accompanied by a choice of tea blends served in the pleasantly decorated public rooms or out-of-doors when weather permits.

Set teas £1.75 – £3.95
Open every day
1 2 3

BEVERLEY   Humberside   Map 08 TA03

Beverley Arms
North Bar Within
Tel (0482) 869241

This modernised country inn is set in the centre of this attractive market town. Tea is served in the rambling lounge areas. The patio lounge and the old kitchen lounge both have original flagged floors; one overlooks the garden area, the other features the old range recesses. Gâteaux, scones, cheesecakes and pastries are available, and there is a choice of tea blends.

Set afternoon tea £3.75
Open all year, every day,
9.30am – 7pm
Meals available

BEVERLEY   Humberside   Map 08 TA03

Blue Berrys Brasserie
3 North Bar Within
Tel (0482) 881919

A bright modern brasserie at the back of the Face and Body Shop, furnished with comfortable garden furniture and colour-coordinated in cool blue and white. Counter service is quick and friendly and the menu offers a good range of sandwiches, filled croissants, cakes, pastries and gâteaux – the local favourite apparently being banana and walnut cake. A choice of tea blends is available.

Pot of tea and one cake average £1.30
Open Mon–Sat 9am–5pm
Hot & Cold snacks

BEVERLEY   Humberside   Map 08 TA03

The Butler's Parlour
33 Highgate
Tel (0482) 870032

Part of '… and Albert', a unique Victorian arcade of 26 small craft shops, close to the Minster, this is an ideal place to round off a visit to Beverley. Over 30 teas and tisanes are available, and a good choice of coffees freshly ground to order. There is always a range of homemade cakes, gâteau, scones and freshly-made sandwiches.

Pot of tea and one cake average £1.50
Open every day 9.30am–5pm (4.30pm in winter), 10.30am opening Sun

BEVERLEY   Humberside   Map 08 TA03

Tickton Grange Hotel
Tickton
Tel (0964) 543666

About a mile from Beverley, this Georgian country house hotel is set in three and a half acres of gardens. Tea is served in the library, and is ideal for an informal, comfortable and peaceful afternoon tea. There are homemade scones, shortbread, meringues and preserves, and good-quality strong tea is served by the courteous and efficient staff.

Cream tea £2.50
Open all year, every day, 10am–5.30pm
Meals are served

BEWDLEY   Hereford & Worcester   Map 07 SO87

George Hotel
Load Street
Tel (0299) 402117

Afternoon tea at the George Hotel makes a pleasant conclusion to a day out in this charming little town. Served in the comfortable buttery near the foyer, there are fresh scones and an array of pastries from which to choose. Different types of tea include Rwanda, Darjeeling, Earl Grey and Lapsang Souchong.

Pot of tea and one cake average £1.55
Open every day, 2.30–6pm for afternoon tea
Light refreshments also served in the morning, and lunches

BEWDLEY   Hereford & Worcester   Map 07 SO87

Merchants Tea Room
78–80 Load Street
DY12 2AW
Tel (0299) 402436

A friendly teashop beside the River Severn in Bewdley's main street, its fresh, bright interior decked with pictures of the town in bygone days, offers light snacks as well as sandwiches, scones, cakes and pastries; service is pleasant and the atmosphere informal.

Pot of tea and one cake average £1, cream tea £1.95
Open every day

BIBURY   Gloucestershire   Map 04 SP10

Jenny Wren
11 The Street
Tel (028574) 555

In a 250-year-old building with an attractive garden, this small old-fashioned teashop is just outside the charming village on the A433. In a heavily beamed room with a Cotswold stone fireplace, a pine dresser has a tempting array of homemade cakes, biscuits and gâteaux, with additional items available from the menu. Hot lardy cakes and Cornish clotted cream always prove popular. There is a choice of tea blends.

Pot of tea and one cake average £1.30, set tea £2.50
Open all year except probably Christmas, every day, 10am–6pm
Lunches available
Bed and breakfast

BIBURY   Gloucestershire   Map 04 SP10

The Swan Hotel
Tel (028574) 204

Lying deep in the Cotswolds on the banks of the River Coln, this former coaching inn is full of character. Tea can be taken in one of the two charming and comfortable lounges, or in the lovely garden in fine weather. The usual cakes and scones are available, as well as a choice of tea blends served in attractive good-quality china.

Cream tea £2.75
Open all year, every day, 2.30–5.30pm (for afternoon tea)
Meals are available
1 3

BILLESLEY   Warwickshire   Map 04 SP15

Billesley Manor
Alcester
Tel (0789) 400888

This lovely Elizabethan manor house has been converted into an impressive top-class hotel. Teas are served in the comfortable lounge, the attractive panelled bar, or – weather permitting – outside looking onto the extensive lawns and magnificent topiary garden. Scones, biscuits and cakes are all baked on the premises, and a choice of tea blends is available.

Pot of tea and one cake average £3.25, 'Manor House Tea' £5.75
Open all year, every day, 3–6pm (for afternoon tea)
Meals served
1 2 3 &

BINGLEY   West Yorkshire   Map 07 SE13

Camelias
Bingley Station
Wellington Street
BD16 2NG
Tel (0274) 562938

This delightful split-level tea room with Victorian-style art gallery and shop stands beside the railway station, its delicate décor enhanced by lace-clothed tables, an abundance of pot plants and piped classical music. Several substantial homemade snacks and an extensive selection of vegetarian dishes are offered, as well as a good range of cakes and a choice of tea blends.

Pot of tea 60p
Open Tue–Sat 10.15am–4pm, Sun 11.30am–4pm, Mon 11am–4pm
Snacks
1 3

BIRDHAM   West Sussex   Map 04 SU80

The Birdham Tea Parlour and Restaurant
Main Road
PO20 8HQ
Tel (0243) 511341

A charming little cottage, with car parking space in front, serves teas in a small, beamed room at four lace-clothed tables. Brass, houseplants, pictures and a dresser with blue and white china all contribute to the cottage atmosphere. Here you can enjoy a cream tea, fruit flan, apple pie, bread pudding or one of a range of cakes – all home-baked – as well as sandwiches (plain or toasted) and teacakes.

Pot of tea and one cake average £1.50, cream tea £2
Open Tue–Sun, teas from 2.30pm
Lunches, evening meals

BIRMINGHAM   West Midlands   Map 07 SP08

Jonathan's
16–24 Wolverhampton
Road
Oldbury
Warley
B68 0LH
Tel 021–4293757

Visitors to an unusual hotel, which stands beside the A456 near Birmingham, are transported back to the Victorian era and its sitting rooms provide a tranquil setting in which to enjoy a tempting range of sandwiches, homemade cakes and scones (sweet or savoury) with a choice of tea blends. You are welcome to browse among the interesting bric-à-brac – or perhaps play a game of solitaire or chess.

Set teas £5.90
Open every day
[1] [2] [3]

BISHOP'S CLEEVE   Gloucestershire   Map 03 SO92

**North's Village
Bakery**
Church Road
Tel (0242) 672658

The teashop here is on one side of the bakery – quite a pretty little area, bright and pink with white china. The temptation will be to eat too much; the smell from the bakery – bread, sugars, cakes – is irresistible. There is a small selection of good-flavour teas, and a wide choice of cakes and pastries.

Pot of tea and one cake average 90p, set tea £1.20
Open all year, Mon–Sat, 9am–5pm
Hot snacks and light meals available

BISHOP'S CLEEVE   Gloucestershire   Map 03 SO92

**Tarlings Coffee
Shop**
Tarlings Yard
Church Road
Tel (0242) 676500

This bow-fronted shop in a courtyard off Church Street provides a popular meeting place, the cafe being carpeted, well-appointed and attractively adorned with paintings by the proprietor. Most of the cakes are homemade, and guests can choose between Indian, Earl Grey and Darjeeling tea.

Pot of tea and one cake 90p, set tea £1.50–£2.50
Open all year, Mon–Sat, 9am–5pm
Light lunches (homemade quiches etc)

BISHOPS TACHBROOK (ROYAL LEAMINGTON SPA)   Warwickshire Map 04 SP36

Mallory Court Hotel
Harbury Lane
CV33 9QB
Tel (0926) 330214

Tea time visitors to the restaurant of this hotel – a nineteenth-century hall set in the most beautiful Warwickshire countryside – will be offered a generous spread of assorted finger sandwiches, home-baked scones and fruit or sponge cake, with a good choice of Indian, China and herbal tea blends. During the summer months seating is available on a sun-trap terrace overlooking extensive and sumptuous gardens.

Pot of tea and one cake average £4.50, set teas £4.50–£9.75
Open all year (except Christmas Day–New Year), every day, 3.30–5pm for tea
[1] [3]

BLACKPOOL   Lancashire   Map 07 SD33

Pembroke Hotel
North Promenade
Tel (0253) 23434

This hotel's newly refurbished lounge provides the ideal setting for an enjoyable afternoon tea of the highest quality; sandwiches are freshly cut, scones and pastries baked on the premises, and staff are both friendly and efficient.

Set tea £2.10–£3.85
Open all year, every day, 2.30–5pm (for afternoon tea)
Meals available
 [1] [2] [3] [&]

BLACKTOFT   Humberside   Map 08 SE82

**Courtyard
Restaurant**
South Farm Craft
Gallery
Staddlethorpe Lane
Tel (0430) 441082

Part of the South Farm Craft Gallery complex, a collection of craftspeople who work at and demonstrate their crafts. Morning coffee, lunch, afternoon tea and snacks are served as well as a full evening à la carte service. There is a selection of homemade cakes or two set teas – full afternoon tea: sandwiches, scone and preserve, cream cake and tea or high tea: a salad, choice of dessert and tea.

Pot of tea and one cake average £1.70, set teas £2.65–£4.50
Open Wed–Sun 10am–5pm 7–11pm
Snacks & evening meals

BLAIRGOWRIE   Tayside   Map 15 NO14

Riverside Granary
Lower Mill Street
PH10 6AQ
Tel (0250) 3032

A former grain store tucked away in a side street near the river has been carefully converted to create an upstairs gallery selling a range of craft goods and gifts, and a bright, airy ground floor coffee house offering snacks (including its special open sandwiches, served hot or cold), filled rolls, a wide variety of homemade cutting cakes and traybakes and a selection of tea blends.

Pot of tea for two 80p–£1.10
Open every day
Light lunches
1 3

BLAKENEY   Gloucestershire   Map 03 SO60

Brook House
Bridge Street
Tel (0594) 517101

This beautifully-restored seventeenth-century stone house at the head of the village, flanked by a gentle stream and willow tree, was taken over by new owners late in 1989. Its delightful sunny patio offers the ideal setting in which to enjoy a lazy afternoon tea with home-baked scones and cakes. Bed and breakfast is also available all year.

Set cream tea £2.25
Open all year, Tue–Sat 10.30am–5pm, Sun 3.30pm–5.30pm, for afternoon tea
Lunch every day except Mon, Dinner 7pm–10pm Wed, Fri, Sat
1 3

BLAKENEY   Norfolk   Map 09 TG04

The Blakeney
Near Holt
Tel (0263) 740797

A traditional flintstone building, overlooking Blakeney Point from its setting on the quay, serves set teas in a tranquil lounge with fine views and comfortable seating arranged in informal clusters; a choice of Earl Grey, Assam, Darjeeling or Indian tea accompanies an assortment of sandwiches and home-baked scones with jam and cream.

Set tea £2.75
Open every day
1 3

BLAKENEY   Norfolk   Map 09 TG04

The Moorings
3 High Street
Tel (0263) 740054

This small but extremely busy café/bistro is just up the street from the quayside. There are steps up to the entrance leading inside to a mouthwatering array of homemade cakes and pastries, and early in the morning a lovely smell of baked bread. Tasty, yet refreshing tea is served by friendly local waitresses all the day. There is a wide choice of tea blends.

Pot of tea 60p, Norfolk cream tea £2.95
Open all year, every day 10am–5.30pm

BLEASBY   Nottinghamshire   Map 08 SK74

Manor Farm Tea Shoppe
Tel (0636) 830241

A working farm in the heart of the countryside with parking in a field. Homemade fare is served in the garden or in the converted cowshed which has an array of gifts for sale. Sandwiches, teacakes and a selection of cakes including carrot cake and parsnip cake are available.

Pot of tea and one cake average £1, set tea £1.60
Open Easter–Oct Tue–Sun

BOLTON   Greater Manchester   Map 07 SD70

The Village Tea Shop
Last Drop Village
Bromley Cross

This old world teashop with beams, inglenook and copper pans – part of the Last Drop Village Complex – offers a wide variety of home-baked items such as Bakewell tart with cream and syrup or hot gingerbread in addition to its set afternoon or cream teas. There is also a range of fine speciality teas, and pleasant waitresses in Victorian costume add to the atmosphere.

Pot of tea 70–85p, set teas £2.10–£2.50
Open every day 10am–5pm
[1] [2] [3]

BOLTON ABBEY   North Yorkshire   Map 07 SE05

Devonshire Arms Country House Hotel
Near Skipton
Tel (075671) 441

A country house hotel with a wide range of comfortable, well-appointed lounges serves afternoon tea from a trolley in the relaxed atmosphere of its elegant surroundings. Biscuits, scones, pastries, cream cakes and gâteaux are all made on the premises, and there is a choice of tea blends.

Set tea £2.75
Open every day
[1] [2] [3]

BONTDDU   Gwynedd   Map 06 SH61

Bontddu Hall
Tel (034149) 661

Bontddu Hall is a lovely stone-built Victorian country mansion offering unrivalled views over the Mawddach estuary and the mountains beyond. Tea is served in the elegant Green Room, or on the delightful terraces on fine summer days. Freshly made sandwiches accompany a variety of gâteaux, cheesecakes and scones made on the premises, and a choice of tea blends is available. Staff are friendly and very efficient.

Pot of tea and a cake average £1.25, set tea £3.55–£3.95
Open Mar–Nov every day, 2–5pm (for afternoon tea)
Meals available
[1] [2] [3]

BONTDDU   Gwynedd   Map 06 SH61

Farchynys Cottage Garden
Tel (0341) 49245

Visitors exploring the attractive four-acre gardens (admission 50p) of this stone-built mid-Victorian cottage – set beside the A496 between Dolgellau and Barmouth – can afterwards indulge in an afternoon tea where even the preserves are homemade, sandwiches, scones, pastries and cakes being accompanied by a choice of Indian or Earl Grey tea.

Pot of tea and one cake average £1.30
Open Apr–Oct, Sun–Tue, Thu & Fri 11am–6pm, Wed 2.30–6pm

BOOT   Cumbria   Map 07 NY10

Brook House
Tel (09403) 288

Set in a tiny village in Eskdale, this small family-run hotel offers a good cup of tea and tasty home baking to tourists and fell walkers. Items available include Bakewell tart, shortbread, fruitcake, gingerbread, crunch slice and mincemeat tart.

Pot of tea and one cake average £1.15, set teas £1.75–£4.50
Open all year, every day (except 24–26 Dec) 8.30am–8.30pm

1 3

BOSHAM   West Sussex   Map 04 SU80

Drifters
Berkley Cottage
Tel (0243) 573517
(evenings)

Drifters is a small contemporary tearoom featuring homemade cakes and a choice of good, fresh-flavoured tea blends. The plain panelled decor is complemented by pretty lace tablecloths and fresh flowers, and the charming picturesque village setting – well known for its antiques and local crafts. Friendly, personal service is offered by the proprietor, Jane Taverner.

Pot of tea 50p, cakes from 35p
Open Easter–Sep, Tue–Sun and bank holiday Mon, 10.30am–6pm
Morning coffee and light lunches

BOURNEMOUTH   Dorset   Map 04 SZ09

Cumberland Hotel
East Overcliff Drive
Tel (0202) 290722

This large seafront hotel has a particularly well-appointed and spacious lounge, where winged armchairs and deep settees offer comfortable surroundings for a range of tea blends including 12 herbal varieties. A resident pastry chef ensures that there is never any shortage of cakes including carrot cake, date and walnut cake, chocolate brownies and banana bread, and offers a 'gâteaux of the day'. If the weather is fine, tea can be taken on the terrace around the pool.

Pot of tea 90p, set tea £3.95
Open all year, every day, 3–5pm (for afternoon tea)
Meals available

1 3 &

BOURNEMOUTH   Dorset   Map 04 SZ09

Flossie's Restaurant and Take-away
73 Seamoor Road
Westbourne
Tel (0202) 764459

Located among the busy shops of Westbourne, Flossie's is a simply-furnished, cosy place, with red-plush benches and newspapers to read. A long counter displays a wonderful array of homemade cakes (lunchtime vegetarian dishes are also very good). Selections from the counter are taken to tables by the friendly and helpful staff.

Pot of tea and one cake average £1.15
Open all year, Mon–Sat (closed bank holidays), 9am–5pm (later in summer)
Light lunches

BOURNEMOUTH　　Dorset　　Map 04 SZ09

Hotel Miramar
East Over Cliff

Friendly porters in braided uniforms serve tea from a trolley in smart, comfortable lounges in the English country house style, or on the terrace and flower-filled garden – all with panoramic sea views. Cream teas, chocolate chip muffins and hearty fruitcake can be enjoyed with Earl Grey or Assam tea.

Pot of tea and one cake average £1.75, set tea £2.75
Open every day
[1] [2] [3]

BOURTON-ON-THE-WATER　　Gloucesteshire　　Map 04 SP12

Bo Peep Tea Rooms
Riverside
GL54 2DP
Tel (0451) 22005

This riverside establishment on the edge of the village serves not only a selection of sandwiches, scones, fruit flans, slices and gâteaux with a choice of tea blends but also a wide range of hot and cold dishes (including a substantial lunch menu). Its spacious interior, with fitted carpet, panelling and exposed stone walls, is furnished with well spaced and appointed reproduction oak tables and chairs.

Pot of tea and one cake average £1.90, set teas £1.95–£3.35
Open every day
Lunches, hot and cold snacks

BOURTON-ON-THE-WATER　　Gloucestershire　　Map 04 SP12

Small Talk
High Street
Tel (0451) 21596

A bow-windowed Cotswold stone teashop and pâtisserie in the centre of the village with lace tablecloths and cottage-style décor. A wide range of hot and cold lunches are available, and homemade cakes, scones and fruit pies served with a choice of tea blends.

Pot of tea and one cake average £1.35, cream tea £2.35
Open every day 9am–5.30pm
Lunches

BOVEY TRACEY　　Devon　　Map　03 SX87

Moorhouse Farm
Tel (06477) 203

A pretty, personally-run farmhouse teashop, set in a pleasant rural location near Hennock Reservoir, serves Devon cream teas with home-baked bread, scones, teacakes and cakes.

Pot of tea and one cake average £1.60
Open May–Sep, Thu–Sun

BRADFORD　　West Yorkshire　　Map 07 SE13

H. R. Jackson Coffee Lounge
46 Darley Street
Tel (0274) 726621

This pleasant coffee and tearoom, situated in a city-centre china shop and furnished with lounge seating and low tables, is the ideal place to relax after a hard day's shopping. A good range of sandwiches is accompanied by tea (Earl Grey or Indian) served in a white porcelain pot with matching cups.

Pot of tea 50–70p
Open Mon–Sat 10am–4.30pm

BRADFORD-ON-AVON　Wiltshire　Map 03 ST86

Bridge Tea Rooms
24a Bridge Street
Tel (02216) 5537

Though dating from 1675, the interior of this building has been restored in Victorian style with open fires, a range and Victorian furniture and photographs. Even the staff are in period dress. The food is outstanding, a pastry chef cooks all day and cakes are served fresh from the oven. Beginning with freshly-baked croissants; at lunch soups, terrines and a casserole, and always the excellent tea goods which are displayed on a Victorian dresser. There may be summer cake with raspberries and almonds, apple cake, chocolate roulade or strawberry pavlova. The selection changes every day and through the day. A cream tea is available, and a full tea with sandwiches, scones and cake, along with 18 varieties of tea or freshly ground coffee. No smoking is permitted.

Pot of tea and one cake £2, set teas from £2.95–£5.95
Open Mon–Sat 9.30am–6pm, 10.30am–6pm Sun
Lunches

BRAMHOPE　West Yorkshire　Map 08 SE24

The Bakery Coffee House
Golden Acre Park
Tel (0532) 613064

An attractive building – set in gardens just inside the lovely Golden Acre Park, and offering a good self-service range of snacks, scones and cakes which are all made on the premises – provides a welcome refreshment break for those exploring the park. Filled Yorkshire puddings (a local speciality) are highly recommended if the exercise has sharpened your appetite!

Pot of tea 45p
Open Tue–Sat 10am–5pm

BRAMPTON　Cumbria　Map 12 NY56

Oakwood Park Hotel
Longtown Road
Tel (06977) 2436

An impressive Victorian house of red sandstone, set in pleasant gardens just outside Brampton on the Longtown Road, serves an afternoon tea of freshly-prepared sandwiches and home-baked biscuits, scones and cakes in the relaxed atmosphere of its traditional dining room.

Pot of tea 60p, set tea £2.50
Open every day
[1] [3]

BRANDON　Suffolk　Map 05 TL78

Bridge House Tea Rooms
Bridge House
Tel (0842) 813137

At the back of an antique pine shop, this tearoom is an attractive conservatory area overlooking the Little Ouse. Fresh flowers, a greetings card and a menu are on each antique pine table – a most hospitable and informal prospect for tea. The cakes and scones are homemade, and a good strong pot of tea is served (Earl Grey available).

Pot of tea 50p, scone with jam and cream 75p
Open all year, Thu–Tue, 10am–6pm
Light lunches
[1] [3]

BRANDON   Suffolk   Map 05 TL78

Copper Kettle
31 High Street
Tel (0842) 814185

Fresh flowers, lace tableclothes, and a warm welcome await prospective visitors to this small high street teashop. A choice of tea blends is available, and cakes include scones, fruit cakes, chocolate fudge cake, tea cakes, apple pies and gâteaux – all home-baked; sandwiches made with local home-cooked gammon or prawns with lettuce and cucumber are deservedly popular. Smoking is not permitted.

Pot of tea and one cake average £1.55
Open all year, Tue–Fri, 10am–5pm, Sat and Sun, 10am–6pm

BRECHFA   Dyfed   Map 02 SN53

Ty Mawr Hotel
Near Carmarthen
Tel (0267) 202332

The good, wholesome snacks, bread, scones and cakes served at this small, whitewashed hotel at the heart of the village are prepared in its own bakery, using organic flour. Tea is served in the cosy lounge and bar – or outside, if weather permits – customers making their choice from an à la carte snack menu; various tea blends are available.

Pot of tea 55p
Open every day, 10.30am–4.30pm
⬜1 ⬜2 ⬜3

BRECON   Powys   Map 03 SO02

Brown Sugar Restaurant
12 The Bulwark
Tel (0874) 5501

A beamed ceiling and pine tables and farmhouse chairs contribute to the atmosphere of this small restaurant. The tea has a good flavour (choice of blends) and a display of cake offers scones, pastries and tarts. A board of local information brochures is a useful bonus for visitors to the area.

Set teas £1.50–£2.50
Open all year, every day (except Christmas Day, Boxing Day and New Years Day) 10am–9.30pm (winter 5.30pm)
Lunches available

BRECON   Powys   Map 03 SO02

Crusty's Coffee Shop
Country Life and Welsh Flair
High Street
Tel (0874) 2664

Part of a town-centre craft shop, Crusty's is a pine-furnished restaurant – clean and well maintained – with a friendly welcome. There is a very wide selection of pastries, cakes and pies, and bread and cakes are also for sale at the counter. A good pot of tea is served.

Pot of tea and one cake average 90p
Open all year, Mon–Sat 8.30am–5.30pm (Jul–Aug until 6pm), Sun (May–Aug) 10am–5.30pm

BRECON   Powys   Map 03 SO02

Duke's Coffee Shop at the Wellington Hotel
The Bulwark
Tel (0874) 5225

This coffee shop and bistro – open throughout the day – form part of a comfortably appointed town-centre hotel. The à la carte tea-time menu offers hot toast, cream scones, cheesecake, homemade pastries and gâteaux, with speciality teas at the same price as the standard blend.

Pot of tea 50p
Open every day
⬜1 ⬜3

BRIDGEMERE   Cheshire   Map 07 SJ74

Bridgemere Garden World
Near Nantwich
Tel (09365) 381

Signposted from several miles away, and providing ample car parking with level access for the disabled, this huge garden shop includes a self-service coffee house offering an extensive selection of farmhouse-style cakes, pies, scones and cheesecake, all made on the premises and served with coffee or a range of tea blends. More sustantial salad meals and hot snacks are also available.

Pot of tea and one cake average £1.25, set teas (pre-booked parties only) £2.75
Open every day

BRIDGE OF ALLAN   Central   Map 11 NS79

Nibbles Coffee House
33 Henderson Street
Tel (07886) 834290

Tourist information, magazines and newspapers are offered by this small popular coffee shop. As well as an interesting selection of patisserie, desserts – including homemade ice cream – are available, while the set tea comprises two scones (try an apple and cinnamon one) with cream and jam and a pot of tea chosen from a good range of blends. Salads, vegetarian and wholefood snacks are also available.

Pot of tea 45–50p, set tea £1.60
Open every day, 9.30am–5.30pm

BRIDGNORTH   Shropshire   Map 07 SO79

George and Bertie's Coffee House
42 High Street
Tel (0746) 761816

This coffee shop (entered through a bread and cake shop) is in Bridgnorth's busy high street, within walking distance of the Severn Valley Railway. Toast, toasted tea cakes, toasted sandwiches and filled baps are offered, and the cakes are all baked at the proprietor's own bakery in Cannock and delivered fresh every day.

Pot of tea 50p
Open all year, Mon–Sat 9am–5.30pm (Mon–Fri), 8.45am–5.15pm (Sat)
Hot snack meals

BRIDLINGTON   Humberside   Map 08 TA16

Park Rose Pottery & Leisure Park
Carnaby Covert Lane
Carnaby
Tel (0262) 602823

This modern pottery allows visitors free access to see all stages of pottery manufacturing. There is a gift shop, seconds shop and an adventure playground. Tea can be taken in the modern cafeteria where a simple range of fresh gâteaux, scones, snacks and bar meals is available.

Pot of tea and one cake average £1.20
Open every day 10am–5pm
Bar meals

BRIDPORT   Dorset   Map 03 SY49

Toby Jug
41 South Street
Tel (0308) 25774

This small cosy cottage-style tearoom has much character – bay window, exposed beams, wooden tables and chairs. The friendly proprietress serves a good Earl Grey (tea leaves – strainer provided), and a nice selection of scones, cakes and pastries.

Cream tea £1.55
Open all year, Tue–Sat (closed Thu afternoons), 10am–5pm

BRIGHTON   East Sussex   Map 04 TQ30

The Mock Turtle Restaurant
Pool Valley
Tel (0273) 27380

This popular and well-run teashop near the Cannon Cinema displays a varied selection of cakes and gâteaux – all freshly baked on the premises – in its window; homemade scones, biscuits, teabreads and meringues are also available, together with such specialities as cinnamon toast, homemade marmalade and a range of fine teas.

Pot of tea 60–70p, set teas £2.25
Open Tue–Sat

BRIGHTON   East Sussex   Map 04 TQ30

The Royal Pavilion
Tel (0273) 603005

The tour of the royal appartments at Brighton Pavilion (£2.30 admission charge) leads to a first-floor self-service cafeteria. Cakes and scones supplied by local bakeries, and a selection of tea blends is offered. Staff are polite and helpful.

Set tea £1.10
Open all year, every day, Oct–May 11am–4.30pm, Jun–Sep 10.30am–5pm
Lunches and snacks available

BRIMSTAGE   Merseyside   Map 07 SJ38

The Country Mouse
Brimstage Hall
Tel 051–342 5382
Midway between junction four of the M53 and the A540

The barns and stables of an old farmyard have been converted to create a craft centre – one of its units being this quaint tearoom. The array of delicious cakes displayed on a pine dresser includes a selection of sponges and the meringues for which the establishment is well known, and there is a lunch-time menu of hot and cold snacks with an extensive salad bar. Earl Grey tea is available as an alternative to Indian.

Pot of tea and one cake average £1.25, cream tea £1.70
Open all year (except Christmas period), every day, 10am–4.30pm (closed Sun am)

1 3

BRISTOL   Avon   Map 03 ST57

Carwardine's
14–16 The Horsefair
Tel (0272) 268053

In the heart of Broadmead Shopping Centre, this is a branch of the famous Bath tea blenders, and a large retail display of 20 coffees and 40 tea blends is featured here. There is modern booth seating with smoking and non-smoking sections, and a good range of hot and cold dishes plus teabreads, pastries, cakes, gâteaux and ices. Six fine, large leaf teas are on the menu, and six freshly roasted filter coffees.

Pot of tea and one cake average £1.60
Open Mon–Sat
Lunches and snacks

1 3

BROAD CHALKE   Wiltshire   Map 04 SU02

The Cottage House
South Street
Tel (0722) 780266

Attached to the shop and post office, a neat little cottage offers excellent cream teas and such treats as home-baked carrot cake, almond slices, eclairs and shortbread, served with a choice of tea blends; the large inglenook is filled with flowers in summer and a pine dresser displays chutney, jams and marmalade for sale, while on fine days the quiet patio or the garden may be used.

Pot of tea and one cake average £1.50, set teas £1.90–£2.40
Open all year (except Christmas) 8.45am–12.45pm and 1.45–5.30pm (Wed closed 1-3pm), Sat and Sun 1.45–5.30pm. Closed Sat pm New Year–Easter

---

The Coffee Pot
76 High Street
Tel (0386) 858323

This bright, fresh, welcoming restaurant in the High Street offers a range of delicious homemade cakes and sponges as an alternative to its set afternoon tea; tea blends include Old England, Earl Grey and Darjeeling. A friendly husband and wife team provides relaxed, hospitable service.

Pot of tea 75–80p, set teas
£2.30–£2.95
Open Mar–Nov, Tue–Sat

The Coach House
The Green
WR12 7AA
Tel (0386) 853555

A building adjacent to the green – originally built as a barn in 1450, and once the studio of the American artist John Singer Sargent – has recently been restored to provide pleasant surroundings in which to enjoy afternoon tea. Boasting 'Home cooking that's just like Mother's', it offers three set teas, sandwiches (toasted and plain), teacakes, muffins, crumpets and croissants, as well as a wide range of snacks and meals. A choice of tea blends is served with milk or lemon, weak or strong as preferred.

Pot of tea 50p, set teas
£2.30–£4.25
Open Wed–Mon, summer
10am–9pm, winter 10am–
5pm
Meals and snacks
⬜1 ⬜2 ⬜3

Tisanes
Cotswold House
The Green
Tel (0386) 852112

A delightful teashop at the rear of an intriguing shop selling speciality teas and novelty teapots, Tisanes serves a range of teas too numerous to list, including a 'tea of the week'. Gâteaux and tarts are tempting, as are carrot cake, Dutch apple flan and baked cheesecake. A mouthwatering range of sandwiches and rolls are available including salt beef, pastrami and ementhal, and bacon, lettuce and tomato.

Pot of tea and one cake
average £1.55
Open Mon–Wed & Sat
10.30am–5pm & Sun am

Cloud Hotel
Meerut Road
Tel (0590) 22165/22254

A whitewashed three-storey hotel overlooking New Forest healthland serving tea in four interconnecting lounge areas furnished with floral-covered easy chairs. A clotted cream tea, chocolate cake and fruitcake are available and a choice of Earl Grey or Nairobi tea.

Pot of tea and one cake
average £1.40, cream tea
£2.20
Open every day

BROCKENHURST Hampshire Map 04 SU20

The Cottage Hotel
Sway Road
Tel (0590) 22296

True to its name, this is a 16th-century cottage with low doors and ceilings and exposed oak beams – at the rear is a well-kept rockery and lawn with a tea garden terrace. Homemade scones highlight the set cream tea, and China and herb teas are available on request. This is a really attractive setting for a leisurely afternoon tea.

Set teas £2.25–£5
Open all year, every day, 3–5.30pm (for afternoon tea)

BROCKENHURST Hampshire Map 04 SU20

Rhinefield House Hotel
Rhinefield Road
Tel (0590) 22922

Built on the site of an old hunting lodge, this Victorian folly is set in 40 acres of grounds, where fallow deer can occasionally be seen grazing. Scones and a selection of gâteaux are available, and a choice of tea blends is served.

Set tea £3.45
Open all year, every day, 3.30–5.30pm (for afternoon tea)

BROCKENHURST Hampshire Map 04 SU20

Thatched Cottage Restaurant
16 Brookley Road
Tel (0590) 23090

This restaurant is an absolute winner for afternoon tea. Inside this gem of a thatched cottage there are four interconnecting rooms in which to have tea – two with open fires. The menu is mouthwatering, with offerings of scones and clotted cream, finger sandwiches and a selection of cheesecakes – homemade and served warm – including lemon, apple, chocolate, and strawberry. There are also cakes, scones (plain, fruited, wholemeal with walnuts), and a selection of tea blends (Indian, China and English breakfast) and herbal infusions. Several flavours of New Forest ice cream are also available. But one thing really did excite our inspector: '...joy of joys: tea cosies!! A real find.'

Pot of tea 60–75p, 'Complete Cream Tea' £3.60
Open all year (except Jan), Wed–Mon, 2.30–6.30pm (for afternoon tea)

BROOKLAND Kent Map 04 TQ92

The Laughing Frog
High Street
TN29 9QR
Tel (06794) 373

Named after the marsh frog *Rana Ridibunda*, which was introduced into the area in 1955, a quaint, cosy restaurant/guest house with exposed beams and polished oak floors offers set cream teas or an à la carte selection which includes hot and cold sandwiches, scones, teacakes, excellent home-baked pâtisserie and a choice of tea blends.

Pot of tea 65p, set teas £2.25–£3.25
Open every day

BROUGHTON Borders Map 11 NT13

Laurel Bank
Tel (08994) 462

Situated on the A701 on the northern approach to the village, this attractive little gift shop and tearoom was once the village school. Scones, cakes and toasted teacakes are available – all homemade, and there is a choice of Ceylon, Earl Grey, Darjeeling, rosehip, mint or lemon tea. The service is pleasant and efficient. Smoking is not permitted.

Pot of tea from 40p, cakes from 45p
Open Easter–Oct, Sun 12 noon–5pm, Mon–Sat 10.30am–5pm, often weekends only Oct–Easter
Set lunch available (including homemade soup)

BUDE Cornwall & Isles of Scilly Map 02 SS20

Coffee Shop
32 Lansdown Road
Tel (0288) 355973

A small, cottage-style coffee shop on two floors (smoking only permitted upstairs) also offers seating outside for fine days. Fresh décor and bright tablecloths create a pleasant setting in which to enjoy a selection of mainly homemade cakes with Earl Grey or Indian tea. Hot snacks and light lunches are also available.

Pot of tea 45p, set tea £1.75
Open Mon–Sat, 10am–5pm

BUILTH WELLS Powys Map 03 SO05

Cosy Corner Tea Shop
55 High Street
LD2 3AB
Tel (0982) 553585

This pretty restaurant and teashop with black and white timbered walls and beamed ceilings offers a good range of hot snacks as well as sandwiches, scones, teacakes, cheesecake and gâteaux (all homemade). Earl Grey and lemon tea are available as an alternative to Indian.

Pot of tea and one cake average 75p
Hot snacks

BURFORD Oxfordshire Map 04 SP21

Andrews Hotel and Coffee House
High Street
Tel (099382) 3151

This stylish character Cotswold hotel in Burford's attractive high street offers excellent standards of home baking in very comfortable surroundings. Good service is provided by the pleasant staff. A choice of tea blends is offered. A no-smoking room is available.

Pot of tea £1.30, set tea £3.75
Open all year, every day, 10.30am–5pm
1 2 3

BURFORD Oxfordshire Map 04 SP21

Huffkins
High Street
Tel (099382) 2126

This teashop/restaurant is on the first floor – above a bakery shop – and panelled floors, whitewashed walls and wheel-back chairs give an intimate cottage atmosphere. Homemade scones, pastries, croissants and rich tea cakes are available, and a choice of tea blends is served in nice china. No smoking is permitted.

Pot of tea 55p, cream tea £1.95
Open Apr–Nov, every day, 10am–5pm

BURGATE   Hamshire   Map 04 SU11

Ivy Cottage
Salisbury Road
Tel (0425) 654515

The three interconnecting rooms of this 16th-century beamed cottage, beside the A338 just north of Fordingbridge, are furnished with polished tables and Windsor or spindle-backed, cushioned chairs. Attractive china in an ivy design complements a selection of homemade scones and cakes and there is a choice of tea blends.

Pot of tea and one cake average £1.30, set teas £1.60–£2.20
Open every day
Light lunches

BURLEY   Hampshire   Map 04 SU20

Manor Farm Tea Rooms
Ringwood Road
Tel (04253) 2218

This long-established and popular establishment, divided into several dining rooms and a shop, features a very good choice of set teas – including High Tea, Cottage Tea, Huntsman's Tea, Children's Tea and Mother's Tea – all based on fresh, home-baked produce, including homemade jam.

Cottage tea £2.10, high tea £3.95
Open all year, every day (except Mon morning), 10am–5.30pm (5pm in winter)

BURLEY   Hampshire   Map 04 SU20

Old Station Tearooms
Holmsley
Tel (04253) 2468

Just off the A35 Lyndhurst-Bournemouth road, this old railway station has been nicely converted into an extensive tearoom with a large tea garden. The gardens are particularly neat and well-maintained. Scones, shortbread, chocolate gâteaux are available, and efficient aproned ladies serve tea (China or lemon available). There are now complete facilities for the disabled.

Pot of tea and one cake average 79p, set teas £1.51–£2.30
Open all year, Tue–Sun Mar–Dec, Sat–Sun only Jan–Feb, 10am–5.30pm (5pm, Oct–Feb)
Lunches served

BURY ST EDMUNDS   Suffolk   Map 05 TL86

Angel Hotel
Angel Hill
Tel (0284) 753926

Afternoon tea at the Angel is served by efficient uniformed staff in the very comfortable and tastefully decorated hotel lounge. A choice of good-flavoured teas is available, served in bone china. The set tea includes scones with fresh cream and jam, home-baked cakes and scones and hot buttered toast.

Pot of tea £1.50, full afternoon tea £4.50
Open 3.30–5.30pm (for tea)
Meals available
1 2 3

BURY ST EDMUNDS   Suffolk   Map 05 TL86

Porters
Whiting Street
Tel (0284) 706198

This light and airy teashop is nicely furnished – original pictures on the walls, pot plants, wicker chairs and pretty floral tablecloths. Uniformed staff serve scones, croissants, tea bread, gâteaux, homemade cakes, cinnamon toast and sandwiches; a speciality is Lemon Madeira cake with hot lemon sauce. There is a choice of good flavoured tea blends, specially bagged by a local importer.

Pot of tea and one cake average £1.35, tea sets £2.25–£3.50
Open all year, every day, 9.30am–5pm (except Sun, 12 noon–3pm in winter, 11am–5pm in summer)

Bute, Isle of   Strathclyde   Map 10 NS06

Craigmore Pier Tearoom
Craigmore Road
Rothesay
PA20 0AP
Tel (0700) 2867

This seafront tearoom and gift shop, commanding panoramic views of the Cowall Peninsula and Firth of Clyde from its position on the south bay, carries newspapers and confectionery as well as selling snacks throughout the day. Everything is home-baked and enjoyable, but its speciality is the apple, cherry and rhubarb pies which are served with either ice cream or fresh cream.

Pot of tea 35p
Open every day 8am–5pm
Snacks

Bute, Isle of   Strathclyde   Map 10 NS06

Promenade Bistro
The Winter Garden
Rothesay
PA20 0AH
Tel (0700) 2487

Built in the 1920s as a concert and music hall, this fine old building now houses the Heritage Centre, a cinema, souvenir shop and a smart, crescent-shaped bistro and tearoom. Here visitors can enjoy a range of home-baked cakes, huge scones, sandwiches and light meals. In fine weather refreshments are served on the open tea-terrace that encircles the domed roof.

Pot of tea 40p, cream teas £1.45–£1.95
Open every day 10.30am–5pm (also 5.30–9pm for snacks)
1 2 3

BUTTERMERE   Cumbria   Map 11 NY11

Bridge Hotel
CA13 9UZ
Tel (059685) 252/266

An old established Lakeland hotel in a delightful setting on the edge of Buttermere serves both afternoon tea and a more substantial high tea either in its lounge-bar or on the patio in warmer weather. Sandwiches are freshly made, scones, cakes and gâteaux baked on the premises, and both salads and a vegetarian option are available as an alternative to the standard high tea.

Set teas £3–£3.50
Open Jun–Oct every day, 3–5.30pm for tea

BUXTON   Derbyshire   Map 07 SK07

Palace Hotel
Palace Road
Tel (0298) 22001

A magnificent Victorian building overlooking the Roman spa town blends period elegance with comfort. Snacks are served in the bar and lounge area from 10am to 10pm and afternoon tea with cream gâteaux, scones, fruitcake, muffins and teacakes is available between 3 and 5pm. Grosvenor, lemon or decaffeinated teas are available.

Pot of tea and one cake average £2
Open every day
Snacks
1 2 3

CAERNARFON   Gwynedd   Map 06 SH46

Rochelle's
25 Bridge Street
Tel (0286) 5110

A well furnished coffee shop and restaurant situated in the town centre. There is an interesting display of pot plants, mirrors and old pictures, and a 1950s juke box plays old rock and roll records. A range of gâteaux, cheesecakes and scones is served from attractive pink and white crockery. There is a choice of three loose tea blends.

Open Jan–Dec, Mon–Sat, 9am–6pm (9am–9pm Fri–Sat)
Meals served all day

CALDBECK   Cumbria   Map 11 NY33

Monoleys Hotel
Tel (06998) 234

A pleasant stone barn at the centre of the village has been converted to provide a delightful hotel serving a very good afternoon tea in its attractive beamed dining room, the extensive choice of food being matched by a range of tea blends. Cakes, pastries, cheesecakes and gâteaux are all produced on the premises, and residential owners offer friendly service.

Pot of tea 85p, full afternoon tea £4.50 Open every day, 3–5pm for tea
1 2 3

CALDBECK   Cumbria   Map 11 NY33

Watermill Coffee Shop
Priests Mill
Tel (06998) 369

This delightful riverside setting is an ideal spot for a tranquil afternoon tea. The mill was restored in 1985, and now houses craft shops, workshops and a small mining museum as well as this attractive, well-ordered cafe. The friendly helpful staff serve excellent home-baked cakes, wholemeal scones, gingerbread, carrot cake, chocolate rum truffle, sticky walnut flan and tea breads, and choice of tea blends.

Pot of tea and one cake average £1.50 Open mid Mar–Dec Tue–Sun 10.30am–5pm Full meals and light refreshments served all day

---

CALLANDER   Central   Map 11 NN60

Pips Coffee House and Gallery
21–23 Ancaster Square
Tel (0877) 30470

A smart little coffee shop tucked in a corner of the square just off the main street. White furniture creates a bright, airy atmosphere. While walls are heavily adorned with framed pictures. A tasty range of salads and freshly cut sandwiches is offered, with a choice of tea blends. Sweet temptations include cheesecakes and fruit pies served with cream, scones and delicious homemade shortbread.

Pot of tea and one cake average £1.00 Open all year (except winter hol), Thu–Tue, 10am-8pm (5pm Nov-Easter) Lunch, dinner in summer
1 3

CALLANDER   Central   Map 11 NN60

Roman Camp Hotel
FK17 8BG
Tel (0877) 30003

In the peaceful surroundings of this fine country house hotel, set in its own formal gardens on the banks of the River Teith, guests can enjoy a very civilised set afternoon tea offered in either the drawing room, sun lounge or library. Various leaf teas (presented in a silver pot, the first cup being poured by the waitress) accompany a range of nicely-garnished, freshly-made sandwiches and a selection of home-baking that might include scones or pancakes with cream and preserves, shortbread, ginger cake, meringues and gâteaux. Each table is served individually, except on Sunday afternoons when a buffet is provided.

Set tea £8.50 Open every day, 2.30–5.30pm for tea
1 2 3

CALVERTON   Nottinghamshire   Map 08 SK64

Patchings Farm Art Centre
Oxton Road
Tel (0602) 653479

This restaurant – an integral part of the Art Centre, which holds exhibitions, lectures and demonstrations (the latter by prior arrangement) – serves traditional English food throughout the day in a pleasant, smoke-free atmosphere. Here you can enjoy one of two set teas or choose from a selection of biscuits, scones and traybakes, with Earl Grey and fruit teas providing an alternative to Indian.

Pot of tea 60–65p, set teas £2.15–£2.50
Open every day (except Christmas Day and Boxing Day), 9am–10pm
1 3

CAMBRIDGE   Cambridgeshire   Map 05 TL45

Auntie's Tea Shop
1 St Mary's Passage
Tel (0223) 315641

A simply but attractively furnished teashop with lace-clothed tables and fresh flowers stands in a pedestrianised passage opposite Great St Mary's Church, overlooking King's College and the Senate House. Here, efficient and smartly uniformed young waitresses serve an extensive selection of freshly-baked cakes and savouries, with sandwiches made to order, and a good range of speciality teas.

Pot of tea and one cake average £1.25, set tea £3.75
Open every day
1 3

CAMBRIDGE   Cambridgeshire   MAP 05 TL45

Fitzbillies
52 Trumpington Street
Tel (0223) 352500

A small tearoom over a cake shop, the décor is simple: a pine fireplace, prints, clothed tables and fresh flowers. The menu is hand written, offering sandwiches, home-baked scones, cakes, pastries and a choice of Indian, China and fruit teas.

Tea from 65p, set afternoon tea from £1.95
Open all year, Mon–Sat, 10am–5.15pm
1 3

CAMBRIDGE   Cambridgeshire   Map 05 TL45

Henry's Teashop
5A Pembroke Street
Tel (0223) 61206

Part of a shop selling teas, coffees and unusual tea-pots, this is a small tearoom with wood panels, some stained glass, prints and plants. There are wheelback chairs and round tables clothed in white crochet lace, set with vases of dried flowers. Homemade cakes, pastries and a choice of tea blends are served from floral crockery. Smoking is not permitted.

Pot of tea and one cake average £1.50, set teas from £1.50
Open all year, Mon–Sat, 9am–5.15pm

CAMBRIDGE   Cambridgeshire   Map 05 TL45

The Little Tearoom
All Saints Passage
CB2 3LT
Tel (0223) 354188

Situated in the basement of 'Perfect Setting', opposite St John's College, this aptly-named tearoom is furnished in pine and made attractive by pretty crockery and framed watercolours. Its à la carte menu offers a range of snacks throughout the day, all freshly made, well presented and promptly served by friendly staff. As well as the cream tea, there is a more substantial 'Post Tutorial Tea', which includes sandwiches and homemade cake and a scone with cream and jam. A good choice of tea blends is available.

Pot of tea 60–75p, set teas £1.85–£2.95
Open every day
Snacks

CANASTON BRIDGE   Dyfed   Map 02 SN01

Black Pool Mill & Caverns
Near Narberth
Tel (09914) 233

Black Pool Mill, on the bank of the Eastern Cleddau River just off the A40, is a fine example of a water-driven power house. Visitors can enjoy forest and river walks, the caverns, a craft shop and café with a patio for fine weather. The café serves morning coffee, light lunches and teas with mostly homemade cakes.

Pot of tea and one cake average 60p
Open Easter–Oct every day 11am–6pm
Light lunches
1 3

CANTERBURY   Kent   Map 05 TR15

Freebody's Coffee House
Sun Street

Formerly the Sun Inn, dating from 1503, and now part of Debenhams department store, the interior is comfortably modern, furnished in pine with upholstered seating. The menu offers hot dishes, salads, sandwiches, and good quality pâtisserie. The Cream Tea Special is available after 3pm.

Pot of tea and one cake average £1.95, cream tea £1.20
Open Mon–Sat 8.30am–5.15pm
Light lunches

CAPEL CURIG   Gwynedd   Map 06 SH75

Pinnacle Café
Tel (06904) 201

Simple, well-maintained tearooms displaying a variety of bric-à-brac, set beside the A5, offer hot and cold snacks, cream teas and a good selection of homemade scones, cakes and pastries; tea blends include Darjeeling, Ceylon, Assam and Earl Grey.

Pot of tea 45p
Open every day
Snacks

Celtic Cauldron
47–49 Castle Arcade
Tel (0222) 387185

Directly opposite the castle, this tearoom is furnished with farmhouse-style chairs and tables set on bare floorboards. Mostly wholefood baking, snacks and vegetarian meals are offered, with a choice of tea blends, including herbal, served from earthenware pottery.

Pot of tea and one cake average £1.50
Open all year, Mon–Sat, 8am–7pm
Snacks and vegetarian meals available

1 2 3

Chattery Coffee Shop
Excalibur Drive
Thornhill
Tel (0222) 766667

Modern self-service coffee shop in mini shopping centre with waitress assistance for hot meals. Sandwiches, snacks, scones and pastries are offered with a choice of Indian and China teas.

Tea £1
Open Jan–Dec, Mon–Sat,
9am–6pm Mon–Wed,
9am–7pm Thu–Sat
Snacks and hot meals available

New House Country Hotel
Caerphilly Mountain Road
Thornhill
Tel (0222) 520280

A very high quality hotel on the northern outskirts of the city (off the A469) serves afternoon tea both in its elegant lounge and bar areas and on the lawn in fine weather. Set menus include a Welsh Tea with bara brith and Welsh cakes as well as sandwiches and warm scones with cream and preserves; Earl Grey and Darjeeling tea are available as an alternative to the standard blend.

Set teas £2–£5
Open every day

1 2 3

Niki's Coffee Shop and Bakeries
37 Town Wall
St David's Centre
Tel (0222) 396311

This modern, self-service coffee shop in the busy St David's Centre provides a convenient stopping-off place for shoppers. As well as filled rolls, sandwiches, scones, buns and Danish pastries it offers salads, jacket potatoes, cottage pie and pasta dishes.

Pot of tea and one cake average 95p
Open Mon–Sat

Truffles Tea Room
3 Church Street
Tel (0222) 344958

This large, modern, city-centre establishment serves a range of snacks from breakfast time onwards. As well as the set cream tea, visitors can enjoy a range of toasted sandwiches, pastries and gâteaux, with Earl Grey, Darjeeling, Assam or Russian tea if preferred.

Pot of tea and one cake average £1, cream tea £2.25
Open Mon–Sat

Bullough's
Castle Street
Tel (0228) 24202

This stylish, well-run cafeteria is part of Bullough's department store, opposite the Cathedral. There is a salad bar and hot and cold meals are available on a self-service basis. Tea is served in stainless steel pots and a choice of blends is offered. There is a good range of homemade scones, cakes and pastries.

Pot of tea 50–52p
Open Jan–Dec, Mon–Sat,
9am–5.30pm
Lunches available

Cumbrian Kitchen
Court Square
CA1 1QY
Tel (0228) 31951

Part of the Cumbrian Hotel, said to be the oldest in Carlisle, this coffee shop features exposed beams and alcoved seating. Set afternoon teas comprise sandwiches, teacakes, cream cakes and a pot of tea (standard, Earl Grey, Darjeeling or Assam) but meals are available throughout the day – including the fish fingers or bangers with beans and chips so loved by children.

Pot of tea 55p, set tea
£2.25
Open every day, 3–5pm
for teas
Meals and snacks
⬜1⬜ ⬜2⬜ ⬜3⬜

**The Grapevine
Restaurant**
22 Fisher Street
Tel (0228) 46617

Housed in part of the YMCA building, this spacious, bistro-style restaurant is lively, friendly and full of character, and specialities include wholefoods and a wide range of salads as well as teas. The Grapevine offers a choice of teas and herbal infusions, with a wide selection of homemade scones, tea breads, cakes and puddings.

Pot of speciality tea 50p
Open all year, Mon–Sat,
9.30am–4.30pm

**Hudsons Coffee
Shop**
17 Fisher Street
Tel (0228) 47733

Set near the covered market in a pleasant courtyard, this busy, family-run coffee shop offers breakfasts, light snacks and cakes home-baked on the premises; vegetarian meals are always available, and a variety of loose-leaf teas and coffee is served. Smoking is not permitted indoors, but seating is provided in the courtyard when weather permits.

Pot of tea 55p
Open all year, everyday
9.30am–5pm
Snacks available

**Watt's Victorian
Coffee Shop**
11 Bank Street
Tel (0228) 21545

A busy coffee shop with a friendly atmosphere and the delicious aroma of roasting beans. A good range of tea blends is available and well-flavoured leaf tea is served in a traditional pot with strainer, on converted sewing machine tables. There is a wide selection of homemade cakes, scones and biscuits. High class groceries are also stocked.

Pot of tea and one cake
average £1.25, afternoon
tea £2.20
Open Jan–Dec, Mon–Sat,
9.30am–5pm
Light lunches available

CARMARTHEN   Dyfed   Map 02 SN42

Old Curiosity Restaurant
20A King Street
Tel (0267) 232384

Situated in the centre of Carmarthen, close to the castle, this restaurant offers a good selection of cream cakes, gâteaux and scones, as well as full meals and light snacks. One may choose from a variety of tea blends.

Open Jan–Dec, Mon–Sat, 9.30pm–6pm
Cooked meals served throughout the day
1 3

CARMARTHEN   Dyfed   Map 02 SN42

Tuck In
54 King Street
Tel (0267) 233157

Long narrow cafe with plastic furniture. Cheerful staff serve a range of scones, Welsh cakes, cream cakes and fruit pies, as well as a large selection of hot meals. Tea is available by the mug only in the busy period from noon to three o'clock. At other times it can be served by the pot.

Tea and cake 70p
Open Jan–Dec, Mon–Sat, 7.30am–5pm
Snacks and hot meals

CARRBRIDGE   Highland   Map 14 NH92

The Ecclefechan
Tel (047984) 374

A bright modern bistro, patisserie and coffee house set back from the main road in the centre of the village. A choice of teas is offered, and a selection of homemade scones, cakes, pastries (including meringue pies, banana cream pie, Ecclefechan tart and butterscotch tart) and pancakes.

Pot of tea 60p, pot of tea and gâteau £1.50
Open Dec–Oct, Wed–Mon, 10am–10pm
Lunch and dinner

CARRBRIDGE   Highland   Map 14 NH92

Landmark Highland Heritage & Adventure Park
Tel (047984) 614

Large self-service restaurant within the Highland Heritage and Adventure Park (to which an admission fee is payable). There is free admission to the restaurant which offers a wide range of homemade scones, cakes and fruit tarts. Tea is served in stainless steel teapots with sachets of sugar and individual UHT milk cartons (fresh milk is available on request). There is a salad bar and hot meals are also available.

Pot of tea and one cake average £1.00
Open Jan–Dec (except Christmas Day), Mon–Sat, 9.30am–5.30pm (9.30am–4pm Nov–Mar)
Lunch

CARTMEL   Cumbria   Map 07 SD37

The Priory Hotel
The Square
Tel (05395) 36267

The Prior's Refectory adjoins the main hotel, where bow windows and lace-covered tables adorn this attractive tearoom. Tea is freshly made and there is a wide choice of teas. Homemade scones, cakes and gâteaux are available, and the staff are friendly and efficient.

Pot of tea 65p–£1.45, set teas £2.40–£5.75
Open all year, every day, 10.30am onwards

CARTMEL   Cumbria   Map 07 SD37

St Mary's Lodge
Tel (05395) 36379

The front room of this inviting period guest house provides a homely setting for afternoon tea. Genuinely homemade and good cakes and scones accompany China or Earl Grey teas.

Pot of tea and one cake average £1.10, set afternoon tea £3.00
Open Apr–Oct, every day, 2.30–5.30pm

CASTLE ACRE   Norfolk   Map 09 TF81

Castlegate Restaurant
Stocks Green
Tel (0760) 755340

This restaurant, built in Norfolk brick and located at the heart of the picturesque, historic village, was originally a bakehouse; now it offers both a set afternoon tea and an à la carte selection of sandwiches (plain or toasted), home-baked scones, cakes, pastries and gâteaux with a choice of tea blends.

Pot of tea and one cake average £1, set tea £1.95
Open every day
1 3

CASTLE DOUGLAS   Dumfries & Galloway Map 11 NX76

Douglas Arms
King Street
Tel (0556) 2231

This attractive white-painted high street hotel offers afternoon tea in its inviting, comfortably furnished coffee lounge. Scones, fruit pies, sponges, individual cakes and gâteaux are all made on the premises, and the wide range of sandwich fillings includes smoked salmon.

Pot of tea and one cake average £1
Open every day
1 3

CASTLE DOUGLAS   Dumfries & Galloway   Map 11 NX76

184 King Street
Tel (0556) 3878

This bright and cheerfully informal high street restaurant, open for all meals, makes children very welcome and represents excellent value for money. Its cream teas are particularly popular, with home-baked scones and fruit pies and a delectable range of cakes, meringues and gâteaux purchased from a local bakery; both traditional and open sandwiches are available, the range of fillings including vegetarian options.

Pot of tea and one cake average 80p
Open every day
All meals
1 2 3

CASTLE DOUGLAS   Dumfries & Galloway   Map 11 NX76

Threave Garden's Restaurant
Tel (0556) 3586/63276

This spacious, pine-furnished carvery restaurant in magnificent historical gardens serves teas both indoors and on an open terrace. Visitors can choose between the special afternoon cream tea and lighter 'cream snacks', or take their pick from a range of sandwiches, homemade quiche or savoury flan, scones, fruit pies, cakes and gâteaux, with Earl Grey, lemon or Indian tea.

Pot of tea and one cake average £1, set teas £1.45–£2.95
Open Easter–mid Oct, every day
Snacks

CASTLE HEDINGHAM   Essex   Map 05 TL73

Colne Valley Railway Restaurant
Yeldham Road
Tel (0787) 61174

Part of the privately-run Colne Valley Railway, this unusual teashop is a converted 1950s restaurant car, retaining its original seats and tables. There is a good choice of tea, with tempting delicacies such as cinnamon toast, flapjack, scones, sponge cakes and gâteaux, to go with it. The staff are very friendly and welcoming.

Cream tea £2.65
Open Feb–Dec, Tue–Sun, 10am–5pm

CERNE ABBAS   Dorset   Map 03 ST60

Old Market House
25 Long Street
Tel (03003) 680

A Georgian building with large double window front. The décor is simple but pleasant, tables are clothed and well spaced and the crockery is bone china. Tea is served in stainless steel pots. Homemade scones, cakes, sponges and sandwiches are available and lunch is also served. Smoking is not permitted.

Cream tea £1.75
Open Mar–Oct, every day, 10am–5pm
Lunch

CERNE ABBAS   Dorset   Map 03 ST60

The Singing Kettle
7 Long Street
Tel (03003) 3349

This is a small ground floor room in a large, double fronted Georgian house in the village centre, pleasantly decorated with a number of pictures and ornaments and an assortment of wooden tables. A choice of teas is available, and a selection of scones, cakes and shortbread. Tea is served from a stainless steel pot with china crockery. Smoking is not permitted.

Cream tea £1.80
Open Easter–Sep, Tue–Sun, 10.30am–5.30pm
Lunch

CHAGFORD   Devon   Map 03 SX78

Bowlers Tea Shop & Restaurant
22 Mill Street
Tel (0647) 3565

A pretty little shop frontage with a cosy, comfortable interior in pastel shades. Cream teas are available, homemade cakes, scones, gâteaux and a popular speciality 'thunder and lightning' – hot toasted crumpets with golden syrup and clotted cream.

Pot of tea and one cake average £1.60, set tea £1.95
Open Wed–Sat 2–9pm, Sun 12 noon–9pm

CHAGFORD   Devon   Map 03 SX78

Coffee Pot
Tel (0647) 433406

An old white cottage opposite the church is partly crammed with antiques and bric-à-brac. The tearooms are pleasant and well laid out and the walls are hung with paintings for sale. A wide range of fresh cakes is displayed and the cream teas are popular, with a good portion of jam and clotted cream. There are two set teas and a choice of Assam or Earl Grey tea.

Pot of tea and one cake average £1.75, set teas £1.95–£2.95
Open Mon–Sat 9am–6pm, Sun 3–6pm

CHAGFORD   Devon   Map 03 SX78

**The Old Forge
Restaurant & Tea
Rooms**
Tel (0647) 43326

A pretty cottage teashop in the former forge at the centre of the village, personally run by Anne and John Hyslop, providing delicious, wholesome, homemade fare including soup, open and club sandwiches, freshly-baked croissants, brioche, cinnamon rolls, teacakes, pain au chocolate, gâteaux, pastries and farmhouse ice cream (made in the village), plus Devon cream teas with homemade preserves.

Pot of tea and one cake average £1.50, set tea £1.90
Open Thu–Tue
Snacks

CHANNEL ISLANDS   Jersey   Map 16

The Terrace Tea Pot
The Panorama
St Aubin
Tel (0534) 42429

You can choose from more than 80 varieties of tea – infused in silver teapots and drunk from china cups – at this tearoom high above the town, its garden commanding extensive views across the bay. A traditional afternoon tea menu offers hot buttered crumpets and teacakes as well as homemade tipsy tart, apple pie, scones and cakes; anchovy or marmite toast and a range of toasted sandwiches are also available.

Pot of tea and one cake average £1.35
Open May–Sep 11am–1pm (except Sat) and 3.30–5.30pm Mar, Apr, Oct and Nov 11am–1pm (except Sat) and 3–5pm

---

CHANNEL ISLANDS   Jersey   Map 16

Hotel L'Horizon
St Brelade's Bay
Tel (0534) 43101

The unique location of this hotel, commanding spectacular views over St Brelade's Bay, makes the attractive sun terrace a popular summer venue for afternoon tea; during the colder months guests relax to a background of piano music in its comfortably spacious lounges. The tea-time menu offers sandwiches and a sumptuous range of home baking served with a choice of tea blends.

Pot of tea and one cake average £1.75, set teas £1.95–£4
Open every day, 3.30–5.30pm for tea
1 3

CHARMOUTH   Dorset   Map 03 SY39

Stow House
The Street
Tel (0297) 60603

Homemade delights such as Dorset apple cake, Scottish whisky cake, carrot or chocolate fudge cake may be enjoyed in an attractive pink dining room with lace cloths and a display of china plates; though the charming walled garden may be preferred on fine days. Salads, pizza and open sandwiches are served at lunch times, and there is a choice of tea blends.

Pot of tea and one cake average £1.30, cream tea £1.85
Open Easter–Sep Thu–Tue, weekends only in winter
Lunches

CHARMOUTH   Dorset   Map 03 SY39

White House Hotel
2 Hillside, The Street
Tel (0297) 60411

A small hotel in the centre of the town with a well appointed lounge, attractive garden and patio. A choice of tea blends and a selection of scones and cakes are served.

Pot of tea £1.45–£2.00, set teas £1.85–£2.85
Open Jan–Dec, every day, 3pm–5pm

CHARNOCK RICHARD   Lancashire   Map 07 SD51

Emily's
Park Hall Hotel
Tel (0257) 452090

According to the poem inside the menu, this delightful tearoom is named after the lady who recognised that 'Afternoon Tea is better than lunch!', and set about making the Chorley Bun her speciality. Situated in the attractive square at the heart of the hotel, there is an old world charm reflecting a more genteel era which makes this an inviting place to sample other traditional delicacies such as Goosnagh cakes, Dinkie pikelets and Eccles cakes. All the cakes and pastries are baked locally to the recipes used by Emily's grandmother, and are complemented by a range of speciality teas which includes Emily's Special Tea Room Blend.

Pot of tea £1.15, tea and cream cake £2.75
Open all year, every day, 10–5pm (10–6pm weekends)

CHAWTON   Hampshire   Map 04 SU73

Cassandra's Cup
Tel (0420) 83144

Opposite Jane Austen's house in the pretty village of Chawton, Cassandra's Cup is a pleasant place to take tea. A selection of speciality teas is available, and delicious homemade cakes which might include chocolate, orange, coffee, lemon or fruitcake. Service is prompt and courteous.

Pot of tea and one cake average £1.50, set teas £2.20–£2.50
Open Apr–Oct, every day (also Nov, Dec, Wed–Sun and Feb, Mar, weekends), 10.30am–5pm

CHELMSFORD   Essex   Map 05 TL70

Pontlands Park Hotel
West Hanningfield Road
Great Baddow
Tel (0245) 76444

A tastefully modernised country house hotel where tea is served in the comfortably appointed lounge. Salmon and cucumber sandwiches, scones with butter, jam and cream, and continental-style pastries are available. A choice of teas is offered, served in the traditional way by friendly staff.

Pot of tea and one cake average £3.50, set tea £3.50–£5.50
Open every day (except 27–29 Dec and first week Jan) 3pm–6pm

CHELTENHAM   Gloucestershire   Map 03 SO92

Bay Tree
Collenade
Regent Arcade
Tel (0242) 576229

Lifts and level access make this open-plan restaurant – part of an award-winning shopping complex – suitable for wheelchair users. A self-service counter offers jacket potatoes and vegetarian dishes as well as a wide selection of sandwiches and the fresh pastries, scones, sponges and fruitcake are produced by a local bakery. Earl Grey, Darjeeling, lemon, camomile and decaffeinated teas are available.

Pot of tea and one cake average £1.15
Open Mon–Sat, 8.30am–5.30pm

CHELTENHAM   Gloucestershire   Map 03 SO92

Charlotte's
16 Montpellier Walk
Tel (0242) 583947

This wicker-furnished first-floor tearoom above a pastry shop retains many original Regency features. Hot and cold snacks, sandwiches and pastries are prepared on the premises, while cakes are baked in a Bristol bakery. Darjeeling, Assam, Earl Grey and lemon teas provide an alternative to the standard blend.

Pot of tea and one cake average £1.20, set teas £1.60–£3.50
Open Mon–Sat

CHELTENHAM   Gloucestershire   Map 03 SO92

Langtry Pâtisserie & Tearooms
56 High Street
Tel (0242) 575679

A former Regency townhouse, by Sandford Park, which has been shop-fronted and extended. Furnished with pine and pretty lace-covered tables, a wide selection of homemade cakes is displayed. Various tea blends are available and a range of pies, savouries, hot and cold meals and ice cream specialities.

Pot of tea and one cake average £1.20, set teas £2
Open Mon–Sat 9.15am–5pm
Hot and cold snacks

CHESTER   Cheshire   Map 07 SJ46

The Chester Grosvenor
Eastgate Street
Tel (0244) 324024

Whether in the magnificent La Brasserie or the elegant Library lounge, with its quiet sophistication, afternoon tea will be a civilised and memorable occasion at this excellent city centre hotel. The leaf tea is served in delightful silverware and there is a wide range of tempting cakes and pastries.

Pot of tea and one cake average £3.50, set tea £5.45–£7.95
Open all year except 25 & 26 Dec, every day, 3–5.30pm, for set tea
Light lunches and morning coffee

CHESTER   Cheshire   Map 07 SJ46

Chester Visitor Centre
Vicars Lane
Tel (0244) 351609

Styled in the manner of a Tudor courtyard, this cafeteria and restaurant is part of an impressive visitor and tourist centre. There is a limited selection of scones, cakes and pastries with a choice of tea blends. Tea is currently served in plastic pots, but these are to be replaced with stainless steel. Sandwiches and hot meals are also available.

Tea 45p–£1.10, set tea £1.85
Open Jan–Dec, every day, 9am–9pm
1 3

CHESTER   Cheshire   Map 07 SJ46

Next Coffee Shop
37 Eastgate Street
Tel (0244) 329591

A smart in-store coffee shop in Chester's fashionable Eastgate Street. Self-service, with helpful counter staff, various blends of tea are available with some homemade cakes, cream cakes and scones. Light hot dishes, soups, pizza, chilli and excellent salads are also offered.

Pot of tea 50p, cakes 65p–£1.05
Open Jan–Dec, Mon–Sat, 9.30am–5pm
Light lunches

CHESTER   Cheshire   Map 07 SJ46

The Witches Kitchen
19 Frodsham Street
Tel (0244) 311836

An Elizabethan-style building, allegedly haunted, close to the Cathedral. Friendly staff serve scones, gâteaux and various cakes with a choice of tea blends. Hot dishes are served at lunch and dinner and pizzas are available all day.

Set tea £1.95
Open Jan–Dec, Mon–Sun, 9am–6pm (Sun noon–9.30) tea served 2.30pm–6pm
Lunch, dinner

| 1 | 2 | 3 |

CHEWTON MENDIP   Somerset   Map 03 ST65

Chewton Cheese Dairy
Priory Farm
Tel (076 121) 666

Interesting teashop over the Chewton Cheese Dairy. Cheese-making can be viewed from a gallery and the cheddar is on sale, along with other local produce, in the shop next door (closed Sundays). The tearoom is pretty, in pine with bare floorboards. The food display is tempting, and the cakes, scones, soups and pies are all freshly home-baked.

Pot of tea and one cake average £1.10, set tea £1.80
Open mid Feb–mid Jan, every day, 10am–4.30pm
Lunch

CHICHESTER   West Sussex   Map 04 SU80

St Martin's Tea Rooms
3 St Martin's Street
Tel (0243) 786715

The aim of St Martin's is to provide healthy, natural wholefoods, all made on the premises with an emphasis on vegetarian dishes. One orders at the counter from a blackboard menu and food is brought to the table. In addition to hot dishes, soup and Welsh rarebit, a range of scones, flapjacks and cakes is served with a choice of tea blends including herbal varieties.

Pot of tea and one cake £1.80
Open Tue–Sat 9am–6pm (closed Christmas & Bank Hols)
Light lunches and snacks

CHICHESTER   West Sussex   Map 04 SU80

Shepherd's Tea Rooms
35 Little London
Tel (0243) 774761

This excellent teashop produces homemade dishes· using the very best ingredients, beautifully served from pretty crockery, teapots with strainer provided, on lace-clothed tables. A tempting range of cakes is displayed in a cabinet, each individually priced, and toast, teabreads, fruit and plain scones, biscuits, sandwiches and muffins are available. A fine English Breakfast tea is served among a choice of blends, and the Viennese Coffee is not to be missed. A blackboard menu offers lunch-time specials and there is a dining area to the rear.

Pot of tea and one cake from 90p, cream tea £2.50
Open Mon–Sat
Lunches

CHIDEOCK   Dorset   Map 03 SY49

**Betchworth House
Hotel**
Tel (0297) 89478

Small cottage guesthouse on the main road. Tea, scones and cakes are served in the low ceilinged dining room or at tables in the garden. Earl Grey and Jasmine teas are also available.

Pot of tea and one cake average £1.75, set tea £2.25–£2.75
Open Mar–Oct, every day, 2–6pm

CHIPPERFIELD   Hertfordshire   Map 04 TL00

The Two Brewers
The Common
Tel (0923) 265266

Dating from the late 17th century this charming hotel, located on the village common, offers a relaxed and pleasant atmosphere. Tea is served in the comfortable lounge with sugar bowl, milk jug and well flavoured tea. A selection of blends is available.

Pot of tea 90p, full afternoon tea £5.25
Open Jan–Dec, every day, 4–5.30pm (limited on Saturdays)
1️⃣ 2️⃣ 3️⃣

CHIPPING CAMPDEN   Gloucestershire   Map 04 SP13

Bantam Tea Room
High Street
Tel (0386) 78423

Part of a stone-built terrace in the town centre, opposite the medieval market place, a tearoom whose beamed interior is appropriately furnished with oak tables and Windsor chairs offers a wide range of homemade cakes and pastries with a selection of tea blends, three set teas being available. Additional hot and cold dishes are served at lunch time.

Pot of tea 60–75p, set teas £1.80–£2.45
Open every day in summer, Tue–Sat in winter
Set teas served 3–5.15pm
Light lunches
3️⃣

CHIPPING CAMPDEN   Gloucestershire   Map 04 SP13

Greenstocks
The Cotswold House
Tel (0386) 840330

Greenstocks is a café-bar attached to this lovely Cotswold town hotel. Food is served all day from breakfast to supper. For afternoon tea, apart from a wide choice of tea blends, there is the traditional cream tea with homemade scones and Jersey cream, buttered pikelets or cinnamon toast and a variety of cakes and pastries.

Pot of tea 75p, cream tea £2.50
Open Jan–Dec (except Christmas), every day, 9.30am–10.30pm (tea served 2–6.30pm)
Breakfast, substantial lunch and supper
1️⃣ 2️⃣ 3️⃣

CHIPPING NORTON   Oxfordshire   Map 04 SP32

**The Old Bakehouse
Restaurant and
Tearoom**
50 West Street
Tel (0608) 3441

Tiny cottage teashop with flagstone floor, rough cast walls and beamed ceiling. There is a fascinating display of pictures, antiques, object d'art and a fine collection of old teddy bears. Tea is served in traditional style with a selection of blends, Bakehouse pâté, scones, fruitcake and jams. Tables are set with old-fashioned linen and danity bone china. Smoking is not permitted.

Pot of tea 50p, cream tea £2.50
Open Jan–Dec, every day, 10am–6pm
1️⃣ 3️⃣

CHORLEY   Lancashire   Map 07 SD51

Muffins
12 High Street
Tel (02572) 62566

A quaint town centre teashop personally managed by the proprietors. Cakes, pastries and biscuits are baked on the premises and are also sold to take home. Bread and muffins are baked locally. Light lunches and snacks are served fresh from the kitchens and a choice of tea blends is available. Smoking is not permitted.

Pot of tea and one cake average £1, cream tea £1.25
Open Jan–Dec, every day, 9am–4.30pm
Choice of several traditional home-made hot meals

CHRISTCHURCH   Dorset   Map 04 SZ19

Priory Restaurant & Tea Rooms
24 Bridge Street
Tel (0202) 486120

Close to the town centre and Priory, this is a welcoming teashop with additional seating in the small garden. The menu offers morning coffee, light lunches, hot snacks and afternoon teas. The cakes and scones are home-baked and usually include Victoria sandwich, chocolate and coffee sponges and fruitcake served with a good choice of tea blends including herbal varieties.

Pot of tea and one cake average £1.40, set tea £2.20–£2.75
Open Wed–Mon
Hot and cold snacks

CHURCH STRETTON   Shropshire   Map 07 SO49

Acorns Restaurant & Coffee House
26 Sandford Avenue
Tel (0694) 722495

Access to this small, family-run restaurant and coffee shop in the main street is via a narrow staircase, though there are tables available in the garden in summer. All its cakes and pastries – which include parkin and Swiss cake – are made with 100% stoneground flour, and a wide choice of tea blends is served. Light lunches feature unusual hearty soups.

Pot of tea and one cake average £1.10
Open all year (except 1 week Mar and 2 weeks Nov), Wed–Mon
Light lunches

CHURCH STRETTON   Shropshire   Map 07 SO49

Mynd House
Little Stretton
Tel (0694) 722212

A small two star hotel in a peaceful location. Tea is generally served in the comfortable lounge. A large choice of tea blends, crumpets, Danish pastries, meringues and scones are offered.

Pot of tea and one cake average £1.75, set teas £1.75–£3
Open Mar–Dec, every day, 2pm–4.45pm

CHURT   Surrey   Map 04 SU83

The Pride of the Valley Hotel
Jumps Road
Tel Hindhead (0428) 605799

In the friendly, relaxed bar or foyer-lounge areas of this charming country hotel in a popular National Trust area, or at garden or patio tables during the summer months, you can enjoy an afternoon tea of homemade scones, cream and jam served with a choice of Indian or Earl Grey tea; teacakes are sometimes offered as an alternative, and sandwiches will be made on request.

Cream tea £3
Open every day, 3–6.30pm for afternoon tea

CIRENCESTER   Gloucestershire   Map 04 SP00

Rosamond De Marco
Shop 7
Swan Yard
West Market Street
Tel (0285) 659683

Among an old courtyard of interesting shops, this tearoom also sells handmade Belgian chocolates. Continental pâtisserie is the main feature of the menu in this clean, cosy establishment. Tea is served from pretty porcelain crockery, and a selection of blends is available. Smoking is not permitted.

Pot of tea 50p–55p, pâtisserie 45p–£1
Open Jan–Dec, every day, 9.30am–6pm in summer, 10am–5.30pm in winter
Lunches available

CLARE   Suffolk   Map 05 TL74

Ship Stores
22–23 Callis Street
Tel (0787) 277834

This small character tearoom is part of a village shop, though the entrance is separate. There is a cottage atmosphere with wooden tables, upright chairs, bone china crockery and an assortment of pots. Outside seating is also available. There is a blackboard menu offering sandwiches and snacks, and a selection of homemade cakes is displayed.

Tea 30p, set tea 90p
Open Jan–Dec, every day, 10am–6pm
Snacks

CLAWTON   Devon   Map 02 SX39

Court Barn Country House Hotel
Tel (040927) 219

Attractive manor house with five acres of gardens amidst rolling countryside. A lovely setting in which to enjoy traditional afternoon tea. Choose from around twenty-eight speciality tea blends served with scones and Devon cream, homemade jams, marmalades, cakes and pastries. Finalist in Tea Council's 'Best Teas in Britain' award, 1987/89.

Pot of tea and one cake average £1.10, set tea £1.80–£3.75
Open Feb–Dec, every day, 10am–5pm

CLEETHORPES   Humberside   Map 08 TA30

Marples Tea Rooms
6 Seaview Street
Tel (0472) 697188

A well appointed 40s-style tearoom with uniformed staff providing a friendly, efficient service to the strains of old-time music hall piped music. Newly opened and already popular with the locals, with its successful combination of good service and reasonable prices, Marples serves a range of homemade cakes, scones and pastries with a choice of tea blends. Sandwiches and hot snacks are also available.

Pot of tea and one cake average £1.90, set teas £1.65–£1.90
Open Mon–Sat 9.30am–4.15pm, Sun 11am–5pm
Hot and cold snacks

CLEOBURY MORTIMER   Shropshire   Map 07 SO67

The Tea Room
41 High Street
Tel (0299) 270464

A brick-built cottage, with attractive floral displays and wooden garden benches outside, houses a vast collection of teapots both in the gift shop and in a tearoom where the homemade cakes and pastries displayed on a dresser include apple cakes, fruit loaf and bread pudding. A Shropshire cream tea is also available, and various speciality and fruit tea blends are offered as an alternative to Indian.

Pot of tea 40–45p, set tea £1.95
Open Tue–Sat and Bank Holiday Mons
Light lunches

COCKERMOUTH   Cumbria   Map 11 NY13

Headfords Country Restaurant & Tea Rooms
6–7 Lowther West
Tel (0900) 827099

The inviting window display, the attractive décor and the range and quality of the produce make it clear that much thought and care has been taken over this delightful little tearoom. There is a choice of 15 tea blends and seven coffees; freshly baked scones and speciality cakes such as chocolate, rum and walnut cake, chocolate fudge cake and hazelnut and raspberry roulade.

Pot of tea and one cake average £1.35, set teas £1.30–£3.25
Open Mon–Sat, & Sun am
Light lunches
1 2 3

COCKFIELD   Suffolk   Map 05 TL95

Thatchers
Tel (0284) 828246

This delightfully traditional timbered inn has recently been modernised to provide an attractive lounge and restaurant where guests can enjoy either a set cream tea or their choice from a range of sandwiches, teacakes, fruit cake or gâteaux with Indian or Earl Grey tea. Additional tables are provided in a garden which slopes down to a stream where friendly, inquisitive ducks swim.

Pot of tea and one cake average £1.95, set teas £1.95–£3
Open Tue–Sun (restricted in winter)
1 3

COLEFORD   Gloucestershire   Map 03 SO51

Muffins Restaurant
12 St John Street
Tel (0594) 34841

A friendly restaurant in the heart of the lovely Forest of Dean, Muffins is open for various meals from breakfast to high tea. Toasted muffins are the speciality of the house, scones and cakes are all homemade. A variety of blends and herbal teas are available, served in stainless steel pots. The lunch and high tea menus include items suitable for vegetarians.

Pot of tea 45p–50p
Open Jan–Dec, every day, 8am–5.30pm (7pm in school summer holiday), Sun after May noon–7pm

CONISTON   Cumbria   Map 07 SD39

Blue Bird Café
Lake Road
Tel (05394) 41649

Set in a beautiful location on the shore of the lake, near the departure point of the steam yacht Gondola, this café commemorates, in the photographs which adorn it walls, the late Sir Donald Campbell's attempts to gain the water speed record on Coniston Water. The wide range of snacks available includes freshly-prepared sandwiches and homemade scones and cakes.

Pot of tea and one cake average £1.15
Open Mar–end Oct, every day, 9.30am–5.30pm

CONWY   Gwynned   Map 06 SH77

The Quayway
5 High Street
Tel (0492) 592937

Situated above a row of shops, close to the Castle and Quay, with a friendly, simple style, giving good value for money. A blackboard menu offers light meals, toasted sandwiches, homemade cakes and puddings. Well-flavoured tea is served in stainless steel pots at prettily clothed tables.

Pot of tea 65p
Open Jan–Dec, Mon–Sat, 9am–8pm summer, 11am–5pm winter

CONWY   Gwynedd   Map 06 SH77

Victorian Teashop
Hallmark Antiques
7 Berry Street
Tel (0492) 592567

A teashop with a truly Welsh flavour in the heart of the town. Here the tables are set among the antique items for sale which makes for a pleasant and conversational environment. Lace clothed tables, Indian Tree crockery and taped male voice choir music all contribute to the atmosphere. Various snacks and a range of homemade cakes are available with a choice of tea blends.

Pot of tea and one cake average £1.10, set teas £1.40–£4.50
Open every day (except Christmas Day), 8am – 10pm
Snacks

CORRIS   Powys   Map 06 SH71

Teddy Bears' Picnic
Lower Corris
Tel (065 473) 412

The identifying characteristic of this establishment is the collection of teddy bears on display and for sale. For the 'picnic' choose from a range of sweet fare including cookies, hot bread pudding, welshcakes and scones.

Tea 35p
Open from 9th May for season, Sun 2pm–6pm, Tue, Thu and Fri 11am– 6pm

CORSHAM   Wiltshire   Map 03 ST87

Audrey's Tea Room
55 High Street
Tel (0249) 714931

A light, airy tearoom in the main street not far from Corsham Court. A simple menu of scones and homemade cakes is supplemented by a range of sandwiches and light lunches. A choice of tea blends is offered and the set tea comprises as many scones as you can eat, or bread, butter, jam and cake.

Pot of tea and one cake average £1.40, set teas £2
Open every day (except Sun in winter) 9am–2pm 3–5pm
Light lunches

COTEBROOK   Cheshire   Map 07 SJ56

Blue Trees
Jardinerie Garden Centre
Forest Road
Tel (0829) 760433

A teashop within the Jardinerie Garden Centre with a large blackboard menu offering a range of freshly prepared hot snacks, sandwiches and salads at reasonable prices served by friendly, smiling staff. There is a counter display of locally homemade cakes, pastries and fruit pies and a choice of tea blends.

Pot of tea and one cake average £1
Open every day
Hot and cold snacks

COTEHELE   Cornwall & Isles of Scilly   Map 02 SX46

Edgcumbe Arms (National Trust)
Cotehele Quay
Tel (0579) 50434

A pub until 1880 and a tearoom since 1980, this old granite building with its flagstone floor, black-leaded range and pine dresser is an excellent place to relax – perhaps after a visit to Cotehele House. A uniformed waitress service is provided to prettily-clothed tables with fresh flowers. Top-class home-baked cakes include Cornish splits, Tamor Valley cherry cake and Edgcumbe Arms ale and fruit cake.

Pot of tea and one cake average £1.40, Cornish cream tea £2.25
Open Apr–Oct 11am–5pm
Light lunches

COVENTRY   West Midlands   Map 04 SP37

Druckers
66 Hertford Street
Tel (0203) 224941

Conveniently situated in Coventry's busy shopping precinct with nearby car parking, though rather ordinary in appearance, Druckers offers a tempting range of cakes, gâteaux, sandwiches, quiches and croissants made by the company's central pâtisserie. Counter staff are cheerful and friendly.

Pot of tea and one cake average £1.50
Open Mon–Sat 9.30am–5pm
Light lunches

COWBRIDGE   South Glamorgan   Map 03 SS97

Latymers
69 High Street
Tel (0446) 774305

This very modern, good quality restaurant offers a daytime menu of meals and snacks, a range of sandwiches, a cream tea and a refrigerated continental display of cakes and pastries; Earl Grey, Assam, Ceylon and herbal tea blends are available.

Pot of tea and one cake average £1.60, cream tea £4.25
Open Mon–Fri 10.30am–5pm, Sat 10am–5pm, Sun 2.30–5.30pm
Lunches and snacks

CRACKINGTON HAVEN   Cornwall & Isles of Scilly   Map 02 SX19

Trevigue
Tel (08403) 304

Surrounded by National Trust land with wonderful cliff-top views, this 16th-century farmhouse is built around a cobbled courtyard. The interior has whitewashed walls, a Cornish stone floor and solid pine furniture. A short menu offers excellent homemade chocolate or marmalade cake, orange tart, shortbread and ginger biscuits. Light lunches are also available.

Pot of tea and one cake average £1.50
Open Easter–Mid Sep, every day 11am–5.30pm
Light lunches

CRAIL   Fife   Map 12 NO60

Bankhead Farm Tearoom
KY10 3XB
Tel (0333) 50877

On the A917 between Crail and Anstruther stands an unpretentious tearoom – converted from farm outbuildings – which offers ample car parking space and open views across the Firth of Forth. In its friendly atmosphere you can enjoy freshly made sandwiches (plain and toasted) and a delightful selection of home-baked scones and cakes which includes fresh cream sponges and chocolate caramel shortbread.

Pot of tea and one cake average 80p
Open Easter–Mid Mar, every day

CRAIL   Fife   Map 12 NO60

The Beehive
28 High Street
Tel (0333) 50330

A cosy teashop behind a gift shop in the centre of the town. The white roughcast walls are hung with teatowels printed with anecdotes in verse. The selection of home-baked scones and cakes includes chocolate truffles, chocolate, coffee and pineapple and mandarin gâteaux, drop scones and delicious homemade strawberry jam. Sandwich fillings include fresh crab, roast beef and ham and cheese.

Pot of tea and one cake average £1
Open Easter–Aug, half day Wed Mar–Jun

CRAIL   Fife   Map 12 NO60

Honeypot Tea Room
6 High Street
Tel (0333) 50935

Two light, bright open-plan rooms – one non-smoking – and delightful service from the proprietors and their staff. An appetising array of home-baking is displayed including a superb selection of scones: savoury with cheese, chives or mushroom, and sweet treacle, cherry and walnut or ginger and fruit. Drop scones are very popular, as well as the selection of cream cakes and sliceables: date and walnut, fresh blackcurrant, and carrot topped with honey and cream. Home-baked croissants, toasties and freshly-made sandwiches are also available.

Pot of tea and one cake average £1
Open Easter–Oct Tue–Sun

CRATHORNE   North Yorkshire   Map 08 NZ40

Crathorne Hall Hotel
Tel (0642) 700398

Afternoon tea can be taken in the elegant drawing room of this grand Edwardian country house hotel which retains much of the charm and dignity of the period. Freshly-made sandwiches, scones and cakes are available as well as a choice of tea blends.

Pot of tea and one cake average £2.20
Open every day
1 2 3

CRAWLEY   West Sussex   Map 04 TQ23

Tudor Coffee Shop
The George
High Street
Tel (0293) 24215

The George is easily recognised by its gallows sign which spans the High Street. The Tudor Coffee Shop offers a good selection of food, 'Anytimers', 'Just Sweets' and 'Main Dishes', and children are made particularly welcome. Tea is served throughout the afternoon by uniformed staff from china teapots, milk jugs and sugar bowls, with hot fruit scones and pâtisseries.

Set tea £2.15
Open Jan–Dec, every day, 9am–9.45pm
Light meals, lunch and dinner
1 2 3

CREETOWN   Dumfries & Galloway   Map 11 NX45

Moneypool Gallery
1 Harbour Street
Tel (067182) 525

As well as a cosy coffee shop, this attractive 18th-century building houses a studio and gallery; visitors can enjoy hot snacks (homemade soup, toasties and chicken pâté, for example) in addition to sandwiches and a wealth of such temptations as scones, devil's pie, chocolate sherry truffles and caramel shortbread, all made on the premises. Earl Grey and decaffeinated teas are available.

Pot of tea and one cake average 80p
Open Feb–Dec, Mon–Sat
Hot snacks

CREETOWN   Dumfries & Galloway   Map 11 NX45

Moneypool Gallery
1 Harbour Street
Tel (067182) 525

As well as a cosy coffee shop, this attractive 18th-century building houses a studio and gallery; visitors can enjoy hot snacks (homemade soup, toasties and chicken pâté, for example) in addition to sandwiches and a wealth of such temptations as scones, devil's pie, chocolate sherry truffles and caramel shortbread, all made on the premises. Earl Grey and decaffeinated teas are available.

Pot of tea and one cake average 80p
Open Feb–Dec, Mon–Sat
Hot snacks

CRICCIETH   Gwynedd   Map 06 SH43

Granvilles Coffee Shop
High Street
Tel (076671) 522506

A bright fresh coffee shop and restaurant on the main road. Black and gold frontage, cream and black décor with a tiled floor, Victorian fireplace, mock marble topped tables and piped music. A good range of meals is served all day, and there is a display of homemade cakes including bara brith and excellent doughnuts and scones.

Pot of tea and one cake average 90p
Open Apr–Oct, every day 9am–9pm
Meals all day
[1] [3]

CRICKHOWELL   Powys   Map 03 SO21

Corner House Tea Room
1 Bank Buildings
Beaufort Street
Tel (0873) 810234

A white-painted corner building alongside the A40 in the centre of Crickhowell, with fresh décor, modern furniture and fresh flowers. A good range of home-baked cakes and scones is available with a choice of Earl Grey and lemon tea. Sandwiches and light meals such as toasted sandwiches, jacket potatoes and lasagna are also served.

Pot of tea and one cake average 75p
Light lunches

CRINAN   Strathclyde   Map 10 NR79

Crinan Coffee Shop
Tel (054683) 261

Delightfully situated beside the western basin of the Crinan Canal, the former canal horse stables have been attractively converted. The self-service counter displays a delicious array of baking from the nearby hotel kitchens: doughnuts, cakes and scones, and some savoury items too, such as quiche, sausage rolls and open sandwiches. Homemade ice cream is also popular. Some speciality teas are available.

Pot of tea 55p–65p
Open Easter–Oct, every day, 9am–5pm

CULLEN   Grampian   Map 15 NJ56

The Tea Cozy
8–10 The Square
Tel (0542) 40638

Small neatly laid out teashop in a corner site of central Cullen. Simple but pleasant, plates and pictures adorn the walls and there is a display of dried flowers in the window. A small selection of homemade scones, biscuits and cakes is served. A choice of blends is available and tea is served in stainless steel teapots.

Pot of tea 50p
Open Jan–Dec, every day 10am–5pm (6pm in summer)

CWMDUAD   Dyfed   Map 02 SN33

Neuadd Wen
Tel (0267) 87438

All meals are served in the restaurant of this guest house on the A484 between Carmarthen and Cardigan in a lovely wooded valley, including morning coffee and afternoon tea with a selection of teacakes, scones and cakes.

Pot of tea and one cake average 75p, cream tea £1.50
Open Wed–Mon
Lunches and evening meals
1   3

CYNWYL ELFED   Dyfed   Map 02 SN32

The Old Corn Mill
Tel (0267) 87610

Beside the A474, overlooking the Duad River between Cynwyl Elfed and Cwmduad, stands an 18th-century mill whose comfortable, cheerfully decorated premises now house a licensed restaurant and tearooms offering a good range of home-cooked food. Hot snacks and sandwiches are available, as well as cream teas and a selection of individual items including Welsh cakes, bara brith, pies, cheesecake and gateaux. Tea can be taken on the lawn in warmer weather, and there is a children's play area.

Pot of tea 45p, set teas £1.50–£2
Open every day

DALBEATTIE   Dumfries & Galloway   Map 10 NX86

Coffee and Things
32 High Street
Tel (0556) 611033

Smartly decorated teashop offering a civilised environment with leaf tea served in china pots and Wedgwood crockery. There is a display of china for sale and a small shop at the rear selling bric-à-brac. Lunches are served between 12 and 2pm and there is a small range of good homemade cakes, scones and biscuits. Indian, Ceylon and China teas are available.

Pot of tea 50p
Open mid Mar–Dec, Tue–Sat, 10am–5pm
Lunch 12 noon–2pm

DALBEATTIE   Dumfries & Galloway   Map 10 NX86

The Gift Gallery
14 High Street
Tel (0556) 610404

Small neatly laid out tea and coffee shop, serving snacks and a small range of homebaked scones, biscuits and puddings such as lemon meringue pie. Tea is made in a stainless steel pot. Service is friendly and efficient.

Pot of tea and one cake average 75p
Open Jan–Dec, Mon–Sat, 8am–5pm
Snacks

DARESBURY   Cheshire   Map 07 SJ58

Lord Daresbury Hotel
Tel (0925) 67331

The foyer-lounge of this modern hotel offers freshly-prepared sandwiches and homemade cakes and pastries throughout the day, more substantial meals being available in either of the two restaurants within the complex. There is also a small shop selling novelties, many linked with Lewis Carroll of *Alice in Wonderland* fame, who lived and is buried in the village.

Pot of tea and one cake average £1.40
Open every day

DARLINGTON   Co Durham   Map 08 NZ21

Brambles Tea and Coffee Shoppe and Mews Restaurant
Wellington Court Mews
Grange Road
Tel (0325) 485271

Set in an area of fashionable shops and eating places, and distinguished by colourful flower tubs and baskets, this attractive mews restaurant offers seating outside during warmer weather – not only at ground level, but also on an upstairs balcony. As well as cream teas and delicious cakes, guests can enjoy a selection of sandwiches ranging from egg to tuna scramble, accompanied by a choice of tea blends.

Pot of tea and one cake £1.95, set tea £1.85
Open Mon–Sat
Light meals, vegetarian dishes.

DARTINGTON   Devon   Map 03 SX76

Dartington Cider Press Centre
Shinners Bridge
Tel (0803) 864171

A unique Visitors' Centre which was once the home of Dartington Cider houses some of the country's leading craft work and an extensive collection of Dartington Crystal glassware. A good range of farm foods, plants and herbs, pottery, knitwear, and unusual ethnic/ traditional crafts and toys is on sale. Visitors can either enjoy a Devon cream tea and homemade cakes at Muggins or a more health-conscious snack at Cranks, both restaurants also offering pizzas, pasties and pies, all freshly prepared on the premises (Cranks including low-cholesterol and vegetarian options).

Pot of tea and one cake £1.20, set tea £1.50
Open every day in summer, closed Sun in winter

DARTMEET   Devon   Map 03 SX67

Brimpts Farm
Tel (03643) 250

China or English tea accompanies a choice of sandwiches, teacakes, crumpets, home-baked cakes and scones with clotted cream and jam in the farmhouse or pretty little tea garden of this 70-acre farm in pleasant rural surroundings.

Pot of tea and one cake average £1.60
Open every day

DARTMOUTH   Devon   Map 03 SX85

Cranfords
29 Fairfax Place
Tel (0803) 832328

Just around the corner from the small harbour, Cranfords is a pleasant café/tearoom serving morning coffee, hot lunches and snacks as well as afternoon tea. Sandwiches and toasted sandwiches are available and there is a fine window display of home-baked cakes and scones. A choice of Earl Grey and Darjeering tea is offered.

Pot of tea and one cake average £1.50, Devon cream tea £2.25
Lunches and snacks, licensed
Open every day (5 days in winter)

DEDHAM   Essex   Map 05 TM03

The Essex Rose Teahouse
Royal Square
Tel (0206) 323101

This fine building was once a Master Weaver's house and still retains many of the original beams. Personally directed by the Bower family, it is often busy, but well worth a visit for the delicious home baking, served by the friendly staff. The mouthwatering cakes include lemon torte, chocolate layer cake and toasted teacakes on a cold winter's day.

Pot of tea and one cake average £1.30, set teas £2.40–£2.60
Open all year (except Dec 25–27), every day, 9am–6pm

DELAMERE   Cheshire   Map 07 SJ67

Romany Tearoom
Chester Road
Delamere Forest
Tel (0606) 882032

A charming little tearoom featuring white wrought iron patio furniture and intricate model Romany caravans. Situated in a caravan sales complex together with a large accessory shop alongside the A556 close to Delamere Forest. Mouthwatering homemade cakes, scones and gâteaux are served at the counter, and savouries such as sandwiches, pasties, lasagne and moussaka.

Pot of tea 40p
Open Jan–Dec (except Christmas and New Year), every day, 10am–5pm

DINAS MAWDDWY   Gwynedd   Map 06 SH81

The Old Station Coffee Shop
Tel (06504) 261

Situated in the old railway station, with pine tables and chairs, the coffee shop is self-service with a super display of homemade cakes and scones. There are large cakes for sale and take-away picnic food. Light lunches include homemade soups, pizzas, quiche, sandwiches and salads. Several blends of tea, including herbal, are available and are served in stainless steel pots. Smoking is not permitted, and children's pushchairs cannot be accommodated, although invalid chairs are welcome if space allows.

Pot of tea and one cake average £1, set tea £2
Open mid Mar–mid Nov and Dec 27 for 10 days, every day 9.30am–5pm
Light lunches
Licensed

DINGWALL   Highland   Map 14 NH55

Tudor Coffee Shoppe
25–27 High Street
Tel (0349) 64631

A bright, clean coffee shop on the first floor of The Bargain Box, a knitwear and craft shop in the High Street. A wide range of home-baked gâteaux and cakes are temptingly displayed and service is helpful and friendly. Homemade soups, salads and sandwiches are also available and a choice of tea blends is offered.

Pot of tea and one cake average £1.30
Open Mon–Sat 9.30am–5pm

1   3

DODDWOOD UNDER SKIDDAW   Cumbria   Map 11 NY22

The Old Sawmill
(Near Keswick)
Tel (07687) 74317

The Old Sawmill was built in 1880 to prepare the larches felled on the Mirehouse estate, and was still in use until 1970. On the walls are tools and pictures from the Mill's past, and the original machinery, still in place, is now a feature of this fascinating tearoom. The Manor house is open to the public and there are many walks through the woods. No smoking is permitted.

Pot of tea and one cake average 88p, cream tea £1.25
Open three weeks before Easter–Oct 31, every day, 10am–5.30pm
Snack lunches available

DOLGELLAU   Gwynedd   Map 06 SH71

Clywedog Tea Garden
Dolserau
Tel (0341) 423428

A stone-built house dating back to 1700 located near Torrent Walks, two miles east of the town, serves an à la carte menu of freshly-filled sandwiches with home-baked scones, fruit loaves and almond slices both in a cottage-style tearoom and in its riverside garden.

Pot of tea 70p, set tea £1.50
Open Sun–Fri, 11am–6pm

DOLGELLAU   Gwynedd   Map 06 SH71

Yr Hen Efail
Tel (0341) 422977

Yr Hen Efail means 'old smithy' and this small licensed restaurant is located in an old smithy by the large public car park near the river. The restaurant is plain and simple, offering a range of meals throughout the day at reasonable prices. Good homemade fruit pies are also served.

Pot of tea and one cake average £1.10
Open mid Feb–mid Jan every day (also Mon during winter), 9am–10pm
Meals served all day

1   2   3

DOLPHINTON   Strathclyde   Map 11 NT14

Beechwood Tearoom
Tel (0968) 82285

Small roadside tearoom, clean and neat inside with solid fuel stove and pictures displayed available for sale. One can also buy homemade jam and marmalade. Tea is served with a small selection of homemade cakes, biscuits and scones.

Pot of tea and one cake average £1.10, set teas £2.50–£3.25, high teas £5–£5.50
Open every day, 10am–6pm

DORCHESTER   Dorset   Map 03 SY69

Potter In
19 Durngate Street
Tel (0305) 68649

Small 17th century house with seating on two floors, pine tables and chairs and a well stocked counter of homemade wholemeal cakes and pastries. Twelve blends of tea, including herbal, are offered. Service is helpful and friendly, vegetarians are catered for and smoking is not permitted.

Cream tea £1.65
Open all year Mon–Sat,
10am–5pm
Lunch

DORKING   Surrey   Map 04 TQ14

Burford Bridge Hotel
Boxhill
Tel (0306) 884561

A charming hotel set amidst beautiful gardens on the bank of the River Mole and edging onto Boxhill Country Park. Tea is served in the comfortable lounge with sandwiches, scones, pastries and biscuits. A choice of Indian and China tea blends is available.

Pot of tea and one cake average £2.25, cream tea £4.25, set tea £7.25
Open all year, every day, 24 hours a day, afternoon tea served 3pm–5.30pm

DOWALLY   Tayside   Map 14 NO04

Dowally Craft Centre, Pottery and Restaurant
Tel (03502) 604

A purpose-built pottery and craft shop beside the A9 about seven miles south of Pitlochry, ideally situated for the holidaymaker en route to the Highlands. Upstairs, a spotlessly clean, stylishly modern restaurant provides a selection of meals and snacks which includes sandwiches and filled rolls, home-baked scones, pancakes, carrot cake, fruit slices, small cakes and gâteaux, with a selection of tea blends.

Pot of tea and one cake £1
Open every day

DOWNHAM MARKET   Norfolk   Map 05 TF60

Crown Hotel
Bridge Street
Tel (0366) 382322

The flintstone and timbered interior of the Stables Grill and Buttery, furnished with panelled settles and polished tables, provides a friendly atmosphere in which to enjoy a variety of hot meals and snacks or an afternoon tea menu of sandwiches, teacakes, scones, cakes and gâteaux served with Indian or Earl Grey tea. Additional seating is available in the courtyard during the summer months.

Pot of tea and one cake average £1.20
Open every day
Hot meals and snacks
1 3

DREWSTEIGNTON   Devon   Map 03 SX79

Castle Drogo Restaurant
Tel Chagford (06473) 3306

This quality restaurant/tearoom forms part of the austere castle (owned by the National Trust – entrance fee payable). Tastefully appointed and comfortable, with courteous service by uniformed waitresses, it features an inventive menu of homemade food, the three set teas on offer including a tempting selection of such items as scones, flapjacks and chocolate, fruit or carrot cake, with a choice of tea blends.

Pot of tea 60p, set teas £2.10–£3.95
Open Apr–Oct Sat–Thu 2.30–5.30pm (4.45pm Oct)

DROITWICH   Hereford & Worcester   Map 03 SO86

Château Impney Hotel
Tel (0905) 774411

A late 19th-century replica of a French château standing in 65 acres of landscape grounds, Château Impney provides an opportunity to relax over afternoon tea in truly elegant surroundings. There is attentive service by professional staff, who can offer a good selection of cakes, scones and gâteaux – all made here.

Pot of tea £1.25
Open all year, every day,
2.30–6pm (for tea)
Meals available
[1] [2] [3]

DROITWICH   Hereford & Worcester   Map 03 SO86

Raven Hotel
St Andrews Street
Tel (0905) 772224

Convenient for the centre of Droitwich, the Raven has a very pleasant and comfortable lounge in which to enjoy afternoon tea. Tea is served with professional propriety by attentive staff, and a good selection of cakes, gâteaux and scones are all homemade.

Pot of tea £1.25
Open all year, every day,
2.30–6pm (for tea)
Meals available
[1] [2] [3]

DRYBURGH   Borders   Map 12 NT53

Dryburgh Abbey Hotel
Tel (0835) 22261

A charming red sandstone house situated in its own delightful grounds and gardens alongside the River Tweed and by the famous Abbey. The comfortable lounge is a perfect setting for afternoon tea. Homebaked cakes, scones and sandwiches are served.

Set tea £3.45
Open all year, every day,
8am–midnight
[1] [2] [3]

DRYMEN   Central   Map 11 NS48

Drymen Pottery
The Square
Tel (0360) 60458

This small gift shop, selling locally-made pottery, now features a new restaurant area to the rear in addition to its cosy little tearoom (reserved for non-smokers), and there is also terrace seating. Gâteaux and a good range of traybakes are available, and scones can be served with jam and cream, while a choice of tea blends includes Earl Grey, Assam, Darjeeling and lemon.

Pot of tea and one cake
£1.30, set tea £1.90
Open every day 9.30am–
5.30pm
[1] [2] [3]

DUDLEY   West Midlands   Map 07 SO98

Druckers
Unit L78
Merry Hill Centre
Brierley Hill
Tel (0384) 481301

A patisserie within the new Merry Hill Shopping Centre offers savoury items such as filled croissants and individual quiches as well as the large display of cakes and pastries made at its own bakery. This modern, stylish, self-service cafe is predictably popular with weary shoppers.

Pot of tea and one cake
average £1.50
Open Mon–Sat 9am–7pm

DUFFTOWN   Speyside   Map 15 NJ34

Taste of Speyside
10 Balvenie Street
Tel (0340) 20860

This is a 'Taste of Scotland' restaurant, tartan carpeted with large round wooden tables. Excellent homemade cakes, scones and biscuits are available with specialities such as heather honey and malt whisky cheesecake. Our inspector particularly enjoyed the whisky cake. Pancakes are made to order and a choice of tea blends is offered.

Pot of tea and one cake average £1.20
Open Mar–Oct, every day 11am–6pm
Good lunches are served, à la carte dinners served 6–9pm

DULVERTON   Somerset   Map 03 SS92

Ashwick House
Tel (0398) 23868

Standing on the edge of Exmoor, this charming house is set in six acres of beautiful grounds overlooking the River Barle valley. Afternoon tea, served in fine bone china, can be taken in one of the three comfortable lounges – where fires burn invitingly during the colder months – or on the terrace with its fine views across the surrounding countryside. All the food is homemade and the range of teas usually includes some rarer blends for the connoisseur, such as Imperial Gold China tea. The service is friendly and efficient and owners, the Sherwood family, are often on hand to welcome their visitors.

Tea and biscuits 75p, set tea £1.75
Open all year, every day, 3–5.30pm

DULVERTON   Somerset   Map 03 SS92

Carnarvon Arms Hotel
Tel (0398) 23302

An early Victorian hotel situated on the edge of Exmoor. There are a number of comfortable lounges and a garden where one might take tea. Blazing log fires in winter, fresh flowers and deep armchairs all contribute to the enjoyment of memorable homemade cakes, scones, biscuits, jam and Somerset clotted cream. Herb tea and Earl Grey are offered as alternatives to the standard blend.

Pot of tea and one cake average £1.60, set tea £2.50–£3.50
Open all year (ex 3 wks Feb), every day, 3.30pm–5.30pm

1   3

DULVERTON   Somerset   Map 03 SS92

Tarr Farm
Tarr Steps
Tel (064385) 383

A 15th/16th-century farmhouse overlooking Tarr Steps – the longest and most ancient stone clapper bridge in the country – offers a blackboard menu of savoury snacks, salads, sandwiches and generous portions of delicious homemade cakes either in the garden or in three interconnecting tearooms. Earl Grey tea provides an alternative to Indian and either can be served with lemon if preferred.

Pot of tea and one cake average £1.20, set tea £2.60
Open Mar–Nov, every day
Snacks

DUMFRIES   Dumfries & Galloway   Map 11 NX97

**The Old Bank
Restaurant**
94 Irish Street
Tel (0387) 53499

A former bank now converted to an elegant and comfortable restaurant serving morning coffee, light lunches and afternoon teas. There is a large selection of tempting homemade scones, cakes and speciality puddings – the toffee banana pie being particularly good! A choice of tea blends is served in stainless steel pots.

Pot of tea 60p
Open all year (ex 2 wks Christmas), Tue–Sat, 10am–5pm
Light lunches

DUMFRIES   Dumfries & Galloway   Map 11 NX97

Oliver's Coffee Shop
135 High Street
Tel (0387) 61381

Friendly, self-service High Street franchise. Homemade, though rather commercial looking cakes, scones and sandwiches are served. A choice of tea blends is offered, and tea is served with a pottery teapot and mug, individual jugs of milk and sugar sachets.

Pot of tea 55p
Open all year every day, 8am–5pm

DUNBLANE   Central   Map 11 NN70

Cromlix House
Kinbuck
Tel (0786) 822125

This distinguished country house has lost none of its atmosphere in the transition from family seat to hotel. Situated close to the village of Kinbuck, off the B 8033, 3 miles north east of Dunblane, the hotel still forms part of the 5,000 acre estate. The public rooms are comfortable, containing many fine antiques and paintings, and log fires blazing in the grates in colder months create a homely atmosphere. Afternoon tea may either be taken in the Morning Room or in the recently restored Edwardian conservatory. All the scones, biscuits and jams in the set tea are homemade, and served by polite, young staff.

Afternoon tea £5
Open all year (except 2 weeks Feb), every day, 2–5pm

DUNKELD   Tayside   Map 11 NO04

**Country Fare Coffee
House & Restaurant**
20 Atholl Street
Tel (03502) 231

Smart, and conveniently situated on the main street, Country Fare is popular with both locals and visitors. This is a branch of the restaurant at Aberfeldy where everything apart from the wine and soft drinks is homemade, and goods are delivered daily to Dunkeld.

Pot of tea and one cake average £1
Open Mon–Sat
Light meals

DUNKELD   Tayside   Map 11 NO04

**Stakis Dunkeld
House Hotel**
Tel (03502) 771

A smartly refurbished hotel which is part of a leisure and time share complex. The hotel stands on the banks of the Tay in 280 acres of grounds. Teas are served in the comfortable foyer-lounge. The selection offered ranges from tea and biscuits to open sandwiches, and the set tea comprises sandwiches, homemade scones and cakes. A range of tea blends is offered.

Tea and biscuits £1.50, set afternoon tea £7.50
Open all year, every day, 9.30am–5.30pm, afternoon tea is served 3pm–5.30pm

1 2 3 &

DUNSTER   Somerset   Map 03 SS94

The Tea Shoppe
3 High Street
Tel (0643) 821304

Built in 1495 the Tea Shoppe is the only brick faced building in the High Street. The interior is olde worlde style with polished tables and lots of plants. The display counter is said to have come from Dunster Castle. Homemade cakes include carrot cake, Dunster tutti frutti, Somerset cider cake and Bramley apple cake. Herb, Indian and China teas are served.

Tea 50p–60p, scone tea £1.80, Dunster cream tea £2
Open Mar–Oct and 22 Dec–1 Jan, Mon–Sun, 9.30am–6pm (open weekends Nov–22 Dec)

DURHAM   Co Durham   Map 12 NZ24

Bowes Brasserie
Royal County Swallow
Hotel
Old Elvet
Tel 091–386 6821

A comfortable venue with friendly service where a small choice of teas is available. Tea is well presented in a china teapot with lots of hot water. Sandwiches, cheese scones, sweet scones, cream cakes and Danish pastries are served.

Pot of tea 90p–95p, set afternoon tea £4
Open Jan–Dec, every day, 10am–9.30pm, afternoon break menu served 3.30pm–5.30pm
Lunch and dinner

1 2 3 &

DURHAM   Co Durham   Map 12 NZ24

Galley Cafe
19A Silver Street

Steps down from a short alley – along the river bank known locally as 'Broken Walls' and close to the castle – lead into a friendly little two-storey café whose upstairs room is furnished with pine tables and benches. Sandwiches, quiche, scones and cakes (some home-baked) are accompanied by a good selection of tea blends which includes mixed fruit, rose hip, camomile, peppermint and nettle blends as well as Queen Mary, Earl Grey, Assam, jasmin, keemun, orange pecoe and lapsang. Taylors roasted coffee is also available.

Pot of tea and one cake £1.10
Open Mon–Sat

DURHAM   Co Durham   Map 12 NZ24

Lisann's
11 Elvet Bridge
Tel 091–383 0352

An attractive basement coffee lounge with pretty tablecloths below the owners' bow-windowed confectionary shop specialising in Continental chocolates. In addition to the homemade cakes and scones, mouthwatering quiche, toasted sandwiches, jacket potatoes and hot chocolate fudge cake are served. A choice of tea blends is offered.

Pot of tea and one cake average £1.45, cream tea £2.45
Open Mon–Sat (Sun pm in high season)
Light lunches

DURHAM   Co Durham   Map 12 NZ24

Treats
27–28 Silver Street
Tel 091–384 5620

A first-floor, self-service tearoom off the pedestrian walkway in the city centre. Treats offers a good selection of homemade goodies such as lemon meringue pie, Dutch apple pie, chocolate nut crunch and rum fudge log. There are also scones, pastries, savoury flans, filled rolls and sandwiches. Standard blend, Earl Grey and English Breakfast teas are available.

Pot of tea 43p
Open Jan–Dec, Mon–Fri, 9am–5pm, Sat 9am–4.30pm
Light lunches

EAGLESHAM   Strathclyde   Map 11 NS55

Wishing Well
63 Montgomery Street
Tel (03553) 2774

A friendly popular teashop where homebaking is the speciality. The converted cottages make for a homely atmosphere with a real fire, plain painted walls and pictures for sale. There is a wide selection of homebaked scones, teabreads and cakes – all very tempting and at reasonable prices. While there is no choice of tea blends, tea is well presented in traditional teapots with bone china crockery.

Pot of tea and one cake average £1.25, set teas £1.20–£2.20
Open all year (except last fortnight Oct) Tue–Sun, 10am–5pm

EARDISLAND   Herefordshire   Map 03 SO45

Eardisland Tearooms and Garden
Church Lane
Tel (05447) 226

A pretty cottage in the picturesque Tudor village. Tea is served in the conservatory with additional seating in the attractive garden when weather permits. The cottage is also a gift and craft shop with an abundance of tourist information. Homemade cakes are served from attractive crockery. Light snacks are available and picnic food is sold to take out.

Pot of tea 45p, set tea £1.60
Open all year, every day, 11am–6pm (or dusk)
Snack meals
[1]

EASDALE (SEIL, ISLE OF)   Strathclyde   Map 10 NM71

The Harbour Tearoom and Country Shop
Tel (08523) 349

Set in an island connected to the mainland by a small bridge – the only one to span the Atlantic! – this simple but friendly tearoom beside the harbour incorporates a craft and country fashion shop. Home baking provides a range of cakes which includes cherry, ginger, iced sponges, fruit slices, apple and fruit tarts, shortbread and various scones; Earl Grey tea is offered as an alternative to Indian.

Pot of tea and one cake £1
Open Apr–Oct, every day
[1] [2]

EASINGWOLD   North Yorkshire   Map 08 SE56

Truffles
Snowdon House
Spring Street
Tel (0347) 22342

Situated in the centre of this picturesque Yorkshire village, the tearoom is part of a delicatessen shop. The proprietors also specialise in outside catering. A large selection of pastries and cakes are served in the pretty pine-furnished room. Hot dishes of the day and sandwiches are also available. A choice of five tea blends is offered and tea is made in stainless steel pots.

Pot of tea 50p–75p, set afternoon tea £2.95
Open all year, Mon–Sat, 9am–5.30pm Tue–Thu, 9.30am–5pm Mon and Sat

EASTBOURNE   East Sussex   Map 05 TV69

Chatsworth Coffee Lounge
5 Chatsworth Walk
Cornfield Road
Tel (0323) 26169

Conveniently situated for shopping, this is a popular contemporary coffee shop with a good selection of filter coffees and choice of teas. Snack meals include Welsh rarebit, ploughmans lunch and fresh sandwiches. An assortment of cakes, biscuits and teabreads is also served by efficient uniformed staff.

Tea and cake £1.50
Open all year, Mon–Sat, 8.30am–4.30pm
Snack meals

EASTBOURNE   East Sussex   Map 05 TV69

Wish Tower Hotel
King Edward's Parade
Tel (0323) 412912

Pleasantly furnished split-level hotel lounge with chandelier and gilt lighting, sofas and easy chairs, conveniently situated opposite the Wish Tower, museum and sea, close to the town centre with ample parking close by. Tea is served between 3.30 and 5.30pm offering a choice of tea blends, toast, fruitcake and gâteau or a set cream tea. A range of sandwiches is available all day.

Pot of tea and one cake average £1.85, Sussex cream tea £2.25
Open every day
$\boxed{1}$ $\boxed{2}$ $\boxed{3}$

ECCLESHALL   Stafordshire   Map 07 SJ82

St George Hotel
Castle Street
Tel (0785) 850300

A busy town centre hotel with green and white façade and olde worlde interior: exposed beams, inglenook fireplace and polished brass tables. Morning coffee and afternoon tea are served throughout the day in the bar area or, in the summer, one may sit outside. Scones, gâteaux and teacakes are served, and a choice of tea blends is available.

Pot of tea 45p, set afternoon tea £2
Open all year, every day, 10.30am–11pm
$\boxed{1}$ $\boxed{2}$ $\boxed{3}$

EDDLESTON   Borders   Map 11 NT24

The Scots Pine
Cottage Bank
Tel (07213) 365

A single storey building situated on the A703 just north of the village and five miles from Peebles. Homemade cakes, fruit slices, toffee shortbread and apple pie are featured on the menu as well as hot and cold meals and vegetarian dishes. The set tea comprises cakes, scones and sandwiches.

Pot of tea and one cake average 78p, set tea £2.10 (£1.35 without sandwiches), high tea £4.50
Open all year, every day, 9am–5pm
Lunches

EDINBURGH   Lothian   Map 11 NT27

Caledonian Hotel
Princes Street
Tel 031-225 2433

Built on the site of the old Caledonian Railway Station, this distinguished building now houses a superb hotel. Traditional afternoon tea here is served in the large and gracious lounge by smart, professional and friendly staff. A good variety of well-prepared cakes, freshly-cut sandwiches and scones is available.

Pot of tea and one cake average £2.75, set tea from £6.50 and à la carte
Open all year, every day, 3–5.30pm (for afternoon tea)
Meals available

[1] [2] [3]

EDINBURGH   Lothian   Map 11 NT27

Melrose Room, The Roxburghe Hotel
Charlotte Square
Tel 031–225 3921

Part of an elegant Georgian hotel – with access both from it and directly from the street – this buttery-style restaurant serves food throughout the day in comfortable surroundings. As well as the Roxburghe Traditional Afternoon Tea, which comprises cucumber and egg-and-cress sandwiches, crumpets, homemade scones with jam and cream and freshly baked pastries, there is an à la carte selection of sandwiches, scones, biscuits and cakes, and a choice of tea blends is offered.

Pot of tea £1.20, set tea £4.75
Open every day

[1] [2] [3]

ELIE   Fife   Map 12 NO40

Gillespie's
41 High Street
Tel (0333) 330117

This small, cosy and attractive tearoom behind a High Street gift shop serves a limited but entirely home-baked range of scones (fruit, plain and wholemeal) and cakes; sandwiches are freshly made, and Earl Grey tea is available as well as Indian.

Pot of tea and one cake average £1
Open Thu–Tue

ELLESMERE   Shropshire   Map 07 SJ33

Tudor Cottage Teashop
31 Scotland Street
Tel (0691) 623228

Tea is served in the front room of this half-timbered Tudor cottage which has a wealth of charm and character. There is a large inglenook fireplace, exposed beams and an abundance of brass and bric-à-brac. Cinnamon toast, crumpets, scones and homemade cakes are available and leaf tea is made in an eathenware pot with china crockery and a strainer provided. Eleven blends of tea are offered.

Pot of tea 45p, set teas £2
Open all year, Tue & Thu–Sun 9am–7pm
Hot and cold snack meals

ELPHIN   Highland   Map 14 NC21

Elphin Tea Room
Near Lairg
Tel (085486) 214

Situated beside the A835 with spectacular views of the rugged Sutherland mountains, and where eagles can often be seen circling the high hill behind the building, this former croft house has been sympathetically renovated and converted to create this popular little tearoom. It offers a range of delicious home baking, all-day snacks and light meals.

Cup of tea and one cake average 75p
Open Easter–Oct every day
Light meals and snacks

ELY   Cambridgeshire   Map 05 TL58

Steeplegate
16–18 High Street
Tel (0353) 664731

These air-conditioned tearooms are situated above a craft shop and divided into smoking and non-smoking parts. It is a characterful building with sloping floors and bare tables. Homebaking is a feature of the menu which offers a selection of biscuits, cakes, gâteaux, cheesecakes, scones and teacakes. A choice of tea blends is available.

Pot of tea and one cake average £1.35, set tea £1.25–£2.00, scone 75p
Open all year (except Bank Holidays and week following Christmas), Wed–Sat and Mon, 10am–5pm

---

ELY   Cambridgeshire   Map 05 TL58

Tea For Two
8 St Marys Street
Tel (0353) 665011

On the main street with leaded window exterior, the décor of this teashop is simple with pink clothed tables, pine wheelbacked chairs and pink and grey china. There is a display shelf with a range of homemade cakes, pastries, scones, shortbread, apple pie and gingerbread men. Well-flavoured tea is served and a variety of blends is offered.

Tea 70p, set tea £2.95
Open all year, every day, 10am–6pm

ERWOOD   Powys   Map 03 SO14

**Erwood Station
Craft Centre**
Erwood Station
Llandeilo Graban
Tel (0982) 560 674

A small craft shop in the old station with woodturning demonstrations. There is an old engine and carriages, a picnic area and river walk close by. Teas are served on the old platform under a canopy with Welsh cakes, scones, fruitcake and pastries; simple fare but fresh and good. Herb teas are available.

Pot of tea and one cake average 70p
Open Feb–Dec daylight hours
1 3

ESHOLT   West Yorkshire   Map 07 SE14

Ashwood
The Old Hall
Church Lane
Tel (0274) 597866

Fans of *Emmerdale Farm* will love this little teashop set in the village where the series is filmed. The walls are adorned with pictures of the actors and 'Emmerdale' souvenirs are on sale. It is a charming stone building in a really lovely setting providing a good cup of tea with freshly-made sandwiches and homemade cakes. The tea garden and toilets are in the farmyard of the oldest inhabited house in Bradford.

Pot of tea and one cake average £1
Open Apr–Oct every day 10am–7pm (Sun only in winter)

ETTINGTON   Warwickshire   Map 04 SP24

School House
Banbury Road
Tel (0789) 151

An attractive stone-built house by the old school in the centre of the village. Tea is served in the pretty lounge where crafts are displayed for sale. The tearoom is furnished in pine with Nottingham lace cloths and delicate china. A range of homebaked cakes, fruit pies, scones and shortbread is available and tea is presented in the traditional way with loose leaves and hot water.

Cream tea £1.75, set tea £2.50
Open all year, Tue–Sat, 10am–5.30pm (5pm winter), Sun 2pm–5.30pm (5pm winter)
Light lunches

EVESHAM   Hereford & Worcester   Map 04 SP04

Diamonds
53 High Street
Tel (0386) 2293

This restaurant has a shop front type exterior, simple décor: plain walls with prints, clothed tables and a counter area with a small display of homemade cakes and scones. There is a full menu including some snack items, served by friendly, welcoming staff.

Tea 50p, set tea £1.60
Open all year, Mon–Sat, 9am–5.30pm
Lunch and dinner
1 2 3

EXETER   Devon   Map 03 SX99

Tinleys of Exeter
Cathedral Close
Tel (0392) 72865

This listed building, thought to be Exeter's oldest tearoom, stands in a delightful position opposite the Cathedral. It was built on the site of the Michael's Gate and remains of the original inner city wall can still be seen on the ground floor. The cosy, beamed tearoom adjoins the Harvester Bakery where the delicious bread and cakes, as well as dishes for the first floor restaurant, are made. There is a wide selection of pastries, toasts and tea breads as well as the set Devon cream tea, and also a continental breakfast, available all day!

Pot of tea from 60p, cream tea £2.00
Open all year, Mon–Sat, 8.30am–6.00pm
Hot meals in restaurant
1 3

EYAM   Derbyshire   Map 07 SK27

Eyam Tea Rooms
The Square
Tel (0433) 31274

Situated opposite the Bull Ring, the building dating back to 1650, this is a popular place with ramblers, cyclists and tourists. Scones are made every two hours in the open-plan kitchen and sandwiches, salads, apple pie and gâteau are available along with a choice of 23 tea blends, including speciality fruit teas. There is a set cream tea and a fruit tea comprising fruitcake, Wensleydale cheese, fresh fruit and Chinese walnuts.

Pot of tea and one cake average £1.40, set teas £2.50
Open Feb–Oct Tue–Sun

Acorns Coffee Shop
Aldiss Department
Store
Market Place
Tel (0328) 864554

A split level coffee shop in the second floor of the department store. Not suitable for the disabled as the stairs are numerous. A pink carpet with pine furniture creates a cosy atmosphere. Light snacks and meals are available all day, and cakes and pastries are all homemade. A choice of tea blends is offered.

Pot of tea 50p
Open all year (except Christmas), Mon–Sat, 9.15am–4.30pm
Lunch

**Pensthorpe
Waterfowl Trust**
Norwich Road
Tel (0328) 851465

After many years of work this park was finally opened in 1988. As well as the wildfowl to see, the old flint farm buildings have been restored to create an exhibition hall, gift shop and tearoom. A good selection of homemade cakes, pastries and light snacks is available on a self-service basis. Smoking is not permitted.

Cakes 40p, scone with jam and cream 70p
Open Easter–Dec, every day, 10am–6pm
Lunches
&

Tricia's Tea Rooms
5 Cattle Market Street
Tel (0328) 855004

This pretty teashop is well worth seeking out in a small street behind the market. The atmosphere is warm and cheerful, and owners David and Tricia Evsden are always on hand should you need assistance in choosing from the excellent range of teas, all naturally flavoured. The tempting array of homemade cakes is beautifully presented on fine china. No smoking is permitted.

Pot of tea 55p
Open all year, except Christmas, every day 9am–5.30pm
Light lunches served all day

**Kind Kyttock's
Kitchen**
Cross Wynd
Tel (0337) 57477

Situated in an historic former vicarage close to the Falkland Palace, this characteristic tearoom takes its name from the heroine of a poem by Scots poet, William Dunbar. Kind Kyttock settled in Falkland and one of her virtues was serving refreshments to weary travellers. The ballad is printed in full inside the menu. The tearoom is on two floors, decorated with paintings and ornaments and features several loudly ticking clocks – all showing the wrong time! There is a good range of loose leaf tea and an extensive menu of homemade cakes and shortbreads, including Scot's pancakes, Isle of Rhum gingerbread and Campbell fudge cake. The licensed restaurant also serves light meals.

Special tea 80p, cream tea £3.00
Open Feb–Christmas Eve, Tue–Sat, 10.30am–5.30pm
Snacks and light lunches

FALMOUTH   Cornwall & Isles of Scilly   Map 02 SW83

de Wynns
55 Church Street
Tel (0326) 319259

Traditional style teashop overlooking the harbour with heavy print wallpaper, wooden tables, bow backed chairs, settles and benches. There are many antique pieces and objects of interest. Food is served from attractive willow patterned plates. Mostly homemade cakes, scones and teabreads are served. Lunches, toasted sandwiches and snack foods are available.

Cup of tea 40p, set tea £1.70
Open all year, Mon–Sat, 10am–5pm
Lunches

FALMOUTH   Cornwall & Isles of Scilly   Map 02 SW83

Cavendish Coffee House
12 Market Street
Tel (0326) 319438
Opposite Marks and Spencers

A pleasant coffee house with exposed beams, soft lighting, light oak chairs and pretty table cloths. There is a comprehensive menu and a fine display of homemade cakes and pastries in the window. Eight tea varieties are offered, served in china pots with milk or lemon.

Pot of tea 50p–55p, cream tea £2.25
Open all year, every day, 9am–5.30pm
Light lunches

FALMOUTH   Cornwall & Isles of Scilly   Map 02 SW83

Penmere Manor Hotel
Mongleath Road
Tel (0326) 211411

This delightful country house hotel, set among well-tended gardens and woodland in a residential area of the town, serves afternoon tea in its Fountain Bar and Terrace Lounge – or on the terrace itself in fine weather. A range of home-baked biscuits and gâteaux accompanies Earl Grey or Indian tea.

Set teas £1.20–£2.75
Open every day
No coach parties
[1] [2] [3]

FARNHAM   Surrey   Map 04 SU84

The Bush Hotel
The Borough
Tel (0252) 715237

Tea is served in the open lounge area with coffee tables and attractive décor in keeping with the traditional style of the hotel. A selection of tea varieties is offered and a range of pastries, cakes and scones is served by courteous staff.

Tea 90p
Open Jan–Dec, every day, 10am–10pm, afternoon tea served 2pm–6pm
[1] [2] [3]

Cromwells Chocolatiers
Lion and Lamb Yard
(off West Street)

This tiny café is set in one of the old buildings surrounding a delightful cobbled yard now converted into a quality shopping precinct. Hanging baskets and wrought iron tables and chairs outside create a pleasant corner in which to enjoy a cup of tea and a slice of gâteau on a summer's day, and there are six tables inside the shop – a simple, white-painted room with French Impressionist prints and a floral frieze. Run by a firm of speciality chocolate makers (try the wicked hot chocolate with cream and flakes of real Belgian chocolate) the shop offers a limited menu of outstandingly good gâteaux and patisserie, with a choice of speciality teas.

Pot of tea and one cake average £2
Open Mon–Sat 9am–5pm (shop to 5.30pm)

The Garden Restaurant
The Redgrave Theatre
Brightwells, East Street
Tel (0252) 716601

A pleasant airy restaurant located inside the Redgrave theatre overlooking the gardens, with fresh décor and pretty lace table cloths. A choice of teas is offered with homemade scones and cakes, gâteaux and teacakes.

Pot of tea 40p
Open all year, Mon–Sat (half day Mon), 10am–8pm, tea served 3pm–5pm

Lion and Lamb Coffee Shop
Lion and Lamb Yard
(off West Street)

The interior of this old, bow-windowed building features exposed beams and white-painted walls on which pictures are displayed for sale. Floral crockery and teapots are complemented by polished wood tables, while additional patio-style seating is provided at the edges of the cobbled courtyard outside. As well as a good range of conventional sandwiches, visitors can sample 'The Lion's Share' (half a French stick with salad/meat/cheese) or 'The Lion and Lamb Toastie' of ham and cheese, followed, perhaps, by homemade scones or treacle tart, fruit bread, pastries or gâteaux.

Pot of tea and one cake average £1.75, cream tea £2.40
Open Mon–Fri 10am–5pm, Sat 9.30am–5pm

FARNHAM   Surrey   Map 04 SU84

Manor Restaurant
Manor Craft Centre
Wood Lane
Seale
Tel (02518) 3333

A series of converted stables houses not only this attractive restaurant but also the workshops of a woodturner and a glassblower (who can be watched at their work at certain times) and a maker of stained glass; there is a craft shop in an adjacent building. You can eat outside, in what was the old stable yard, or in a room whose exposed stone walls and old beams have been preserved unspoiled to retain the character of the original building. Biscuits, traybakes, sponges, cheesecakes and gâteaux are all prepared on the premises, as are the sandwiches and savoury snacks which are available all day, and a choice of tea blends is offered.

Pot of tea and one cake average £1.20, cream tea £2.25
Open Tue–Sat 10am–6pm, Sun 11am–6pm
Table d'hote country style dinners
1 3

FARNHAM   Surrey   Map 04 SU84

**The Squirrels'
Pantry Coffee Shop**
Forest Lodge Garden Centre
Holt Pound
Tel (0420) 23275

This conservatory-style coffee shop – part of a sizable garden centre set back from the A325 about two miles south of Farnham – offers seating at white plastic tables interspersed with indoor floral displays; its large windows overlook the attractive landscaped grounds, while French windows open onto a patio area which is used for eating during the summer months. Salads and hot or cold snacks are available all day, as well as a selection of sandwiches, scones, teacakes and cakes ranging from doughnuts and Danish pastries to éclairs and gâteaux.

Pot of tea and one cake average £1.35, cream tea £1.85
Open every day 10am–5pm
Hot and cold snacks

FAVERSHAM   Kent   Map 05 TR06

Shelleys Restaurant and Tea Rooms
1 Market Place
Tel (0795) 531570

In a charming corner house overlooking the historic Guildhall in the pedestrianised centre of this picturesque town, meals are served in a long room with a central fireplace and beamed ceiling. Hanging plants surround the windows, there are pictures on the walls, and the tables have dusky pink linen cloths covered by cream lace and topped with glass, complementing the attractive, good quality, china. Open sandwiches and a selection of cakes including teacakes, scones, shortbread, Danish pastries, fruitcake and chocolate fudge cake are accompanied by a good range of speciality teas. Salads and omelettes are also available.

Pot of tea and one cake £1.25
Open Mon–Fri 10am–4.30pm, Sat 9.30am–5pm, also Fri and Sat 7pm–late (last orders 10pm)

FENWICK   Strathclyde   Map 10 NS44

The Carpenter
3 Stewarton Road
Tel (05606) 262

Just yards from the junction of the Stewarton road with the busy A77, and providing an ideal break on a journey, this cosy little country coffee shop on the edge of the village also offers a small but varied range of gifts for sale. Service is friendly and personal, the selection of mainly homemade cakes includes scones, millionaires' shortbread, carrot cake, passion cake, gingerbread and meringues, while Earl Grey, Darjeeling and Lemon tea provide an alternative to the standard blend. Filled rolls, sandwiches, light lunches and snacks are also available.

Pot of tea and one cake £1.10
Open every day, Mon–Sat 10am–4.30pm, Sun 1–4.30pm

FETTERCAIRN   Grampian   Map 15 NO67

The Fettercairn Tea Room
Tel (05614) 271

The interior of this small, homely tearoom – situated at the centre of the village, just off the main square – is fresh and clean, its plain white walls adorned with a collection of framed prints and pictures which are generally available for purchase. A range of home-baked cakes tempts visitors with such delights as plain, fruit and treacle scones, shortbread, Eyemouth tart, whisky cake, colony cake, coffee buns and melting moments, while snacks include homemade soup with crusty bread and butter, pies and quiche. Though tea is served by the cup, a second cup 'on the house' is guaranteed, with Assam and Darjeeling as an alternative to the standard blend.

Pot of tea and one cake 95p
Open every day (closed Tue in winter)

FLAMBOROUGH   Humberside   Map 08 TA27

Copperfields Restaurant
Chapel Street
Tel (0262) 850495

A small homely restaurant serving morning coffee, lunches and afternoon tea, the latter available between 3.30 and 5pm. A range of simple, fresh homemade fare is available: teacakes, scones, gâteaux and puddings with freshly-made sandwiches. The Afternoon Treat set tea is a particular favourite: fresh crab or ham sandwich, scones, jam and cream, gâteau or trifle and tea.

Pot of tea and one cake average £1.70, set tea £3.35
Open every day 9am–7pm
Lunches

FOCHABERS   Grampian   Map 15 NJ35

The Gallery
85 High Street
Tel (0343) 820981

Small coffee shop area to rear of a gift shop, simply furnished with wooden tables and stools, and additional seating in the garden. Paintings are hung for sale. A selection of cakes, biscuits and scones is served with a choice of tea blends, good homecooked snacks and lunches also being available. Smoking is not permitted.

Pot of tea and one cake average 70p
Open all year, every day, 9am–5pm
1 2

FOCHABERS   Grampian   Map 15 NJ35

Spey Restaurant
Visitor Centre
Baxters of Speyside
Tel (0343) 820393

New bright, spacious self-service restaurant, part of the Baxters Visitor Centre. Lunches and high teas are served, and a selection of homemade scones, teabreads, biscuits and cakes are available. Baxters pancakes are cooked to order.

Pot of tea 40p
Open 24 Mar–27 Oct, Mon–Fri, 10am–4.30pm, Easter weekend, Sat–Sun 13 May–10 Sep (Sat 11am–5.30pm, Sun 12.30pm–4.30pm)

FOLKINGHAM   Lincolnshire   Map 08 TF13

Quaintways
17 Market Place
Tel (05297) 416

A lovely little teashop in an interesting village, full of local history. The proprietress provides friendly and attentive service. Light lunches and afternoon teas are served with a choice of tea blends and a good range of home baking.

Pot of tea 45p–50p, set teas £1.75–£2.75
Open Apr–Sep, Thu–Sun, noon–5pm
Lunches

FORRES   Grampian   Map 14 NJ06

Brodie Countryfare
Brodie
Tel (03094) 555

An imaginative complex not far from Brodie Castle includes a craft and gift shop, a dress shop featuring designer knitwear and a farm produce outlet, as well as this bright, clean self-service restaurant with its attractive modern décor and pine fittings. Teatime fare includes filled rolls, sandwiches (plain and toasted), scones, pancakes, a range of homemade cakes and bakes, and such delectable desserts as apple strudel, Mississippi mud pie and fresh strawberry meringue; Assam, Darjeeling, Earl Grey and lemon tea are offered as alternatives to the standard blend. Hot and cold snacks are available throughout the day, with more substantial chef's specials at lunch time.

Pot of tea 45p
Open every day

FORRES   Grampian   Map 14 NJ06

Busters Bistro
39 High Street
Tel (0309) 75541

Bright, lively bistro with art deco theme and pine tables and chairs. There is a small range of homemade scones, teabreads and cakes, and tea is served in a stainless steel pot.

Pot of tea 45p, cream tea £1.45
Open all year, every day, 9.30am–11pm

FORT WILLIAM   Highland   Map 14 NN17

La Creme
Governor's House
The Parade
Tel (0397) 4217

This stylish coffee shop and patisserie, set well back from the main street, occupies a renovated stone house with its own car park. It is tastefully decorated in designer style, oval iron-pedestalled tables with marble-effect tops being paired with striking, black-upholstered brass tubular chairs. Smartly dressed waitresses provide table service once you have made your choice from a display of items ranging from scones with cream and jam to cream cakes and gâteaux. Speciality leaf teas complement the standard blend sachets, and sandwiches, filled rolls and soup are also available.

Pot of tea and one cake
£1.20
Open 10am–5pm

FOWEY   Cornwall & Isles of Scilly   Map 02 SX15

The Brasserie
1 Lostwithiel Street
Tel (0726) 832649

This restaurant/bistro, decorated in 20s style with brown furnishings and white linen, fresh flowers and a piano (for jazz), serves food all day but has a separate tea menu. A variety of home-baked cakes and pastries is served, and filled open French sticks – fresh crab being particularly good. A good choice of tea blends is offered, including herbal. A seat at the rear terrace offers a good view of the estuary.

Pot of tea and one cake
average £2.70, set tea
£2.20
Open every day, all day
except short break late
pm, afternoon tea 2–5pm
Lunches, evening meals
[1] [3]

FOWEY   Cornwall & Isles of Scilly   Map 02 SX15

Frenchman's Creek
Town Quay
Tel (072683) 2431

A small licensed restaurant in seafaring style, conveniently situated right on the quayside, it is open daily for morning coffee, light lunches, snacks and cream teas. Its homemade apple pie, buttered scones and toasted teacakes are particularly to be recommended, and full table service is provided.

Pot of tea and one cake £1,
set tea £1.95
Open Spring Bank
Holiday–Oct every day

FRAMPTON   Dorset   Map 03 SY69

Gatehouse
7 Dorchester Road
Tel (0300) 20280

Village post office with tea shop, part of which dates from the 17th century. It is a small, cosy room with pine furniture, plants and pictures, where scones, cakes and pastries are served by the friendly proprietress. Smoking is not permitted.

Teas £1.10–£1.80
Open Jan–Dec, Tue–Sat,
9am–5.30pm

FRASERBURGH   Grampian   Map 15 NJ96

**Ritchie's Coffee
Shop**
30 Cross Street
Tel (0346) 2774

Attractive, freshly decorated and clean coffee shop. Although a simple operation it offers good home baking in pleasant surroundings – a scarce commodity in this north-east corner of Scotland. No smoking is permitted.

Pot of tea 55p
Open Jan–Dec, Mon–Tue and Thu–Sat, 9am–4.30pm

FRENSHAM   Surrey   Map 04 SU84

The Mariners Hotel
Millbridge
Tel (025125) 2050/4745

A much-extended country inn, charmingly set overlooking the River Wey, serves afternoon tea in either its formal dining room or the more relaxed surroundings of the foyer lounge and bar. In summer, however, the obvious place to eat is in one of the garden or patio seating areas. The menu is a flexible one, including a choice of gâteaux, the day's desserts, and sandwiches to order.

Pot of tea and one cake average £2.25
Open every day, refreshments available during normal hotel hours

☐1 ☐2 ☐3

FULNECK   West Yorkshire   Map 08 SE23

Fulneck Restaurant
54 Fulneck
Pudsey
Tel (0532) 564069

It would be hard to better the range of tea blends (including three herbal) available at an attractive teashop; the house leaf tea is served from large caddies and can also be purchased by the quarter pound. Housed in the village shop of this delightful Moravian settlement, a well furnished dining area being situated behind the tuck shop, it offers a good range of scones, sponges and cakes.

Pot of tea and one cake £1, set teas £1.95–£2.10
Open Mon 9.30am–2pm, Tue–Sat 9.35am–5pm

☐1 ☐2

GALASHIELS   Borders   Map 12 NT43

Sanders Restaurant
94A High Street
Tel (0896) 56055

A charming little restaurant, once a tailoring workshop which is reflected in the pictures on the walls. The atmosphere is warm and friendly, and whether you sample the traditional afternoon tea, high tea or a hot meal you will know that it is all good home cooking.

Pot of tea 30p, set tea £2.50
Open Jan–Dec, every day, 10am–9.30pm weekdays (ex Mon 10am–3pm), 4pm–7pm Sun
Lunch, high tea, supper, evening meals

☐1 ☐3

GARVE   Highland   Map 14 NH36

Achanalt House
Achanalt
Tel (09974) 283

Set amid magnificent scenery between Garve and Achnasheen, a converted roadside bothy dating from 1750 displays an interesting array of farming implements and tools on its whitewashed stone walls. Visitors can enjoy sandwiches and a small range of good, homemade cakes, scones and biscuits with English or Earl Grey tea – colourful knitted tea cosies providing a homely touch.

Pot of tea and one cake average £1.20
Open Tue–Sun, 10.30am–5.30pm

GATEHOUSE OF FLEET   Dumfries & Galloway   Map 11 NX55

Bobbin Coffee Shop
36 High Street
Tel (05574) 229

The dining room of a listed guesthouse. A light, airy room to the rear of the High Street property. Very homely with a selection of very good home baking, sandwiches (plain and toasted) and homemade soup. Smoking is not permitted.

Pot of tea 48p
Open Jan–Dec, Tue–Sat,
10.15am–2.15pm
(10.15am–3.15pm July–
Aug)
☐1 ☐3

GATEHOUSE OF FLEET   Dumfries & Galloway   Map 11 NX55

Murray Arms
Anne Street
DG7 2HY
Tel (05574) 207

Here, teas are served in the comfortable surroundings of the Lunky Hole Food Bar, visitors making their own selection from a mouthwatering array of home-baked scones, biscuits, fruit pies, cakes and gâteaux; sandwich fillings range from cheese to smoked salmon, and a range of hot and cold snacks is available throughout the day – the comprehensive menu being geared to supplying whatever might be requested.

Pot of tea and one cake
average £1
Open every day
Hot and cold snacks
☐1 ☐2 ☐3

GLASGOW   Strathclyde   Map 11 NS56

Bradfords
245 Sauchiehall Street
Tel 041–332 1008

A smart tearoom over the baker's shop of the same name in the pedestrian precinct section of Sauchiehall Street. The set afternoon tea is popular: sandwiches, a selection of traybakes or cut cake and the choice of a fresh cream cake, served from a traditional stand, with various teas (all sachet) available. Baked goods are all from the company's bakery and may be bought from the shop downstairs.

Pot of tea and one cake
average £1.25, set tea
£3.75
Open Mon–Sat 8.30am–
5.30pm

GLASGOW   Strathclyde   Map 11 NS56

The Willow Tea Room
217 Sauchiehall Street
Tel 041–332 0521

This building which once housed the famous Willow Tearoom (1904) has been restored to the original designs of architect Charles Rennie Mackintosh and is furnished with contemporary tables and chairs also of his design. The delightful décor is complemented by the smart black and white uniforms of the waitresses who serve hot snacks, scones, cakes and pastries, or a set afternoon tea (with China or Herbal blends if preferred). The tearoom is situated on the first floor and entry is through the small shop below.

Cup of tea 50p, afternoon
tea £3.55
Open all year, Mon–Sat,
9.30am–4.30pm (closed
bank holidays)
Light lunches available

GLASTONBURY   Somerset   Map 03 ST53

**The Willows
Tearooms**
Shapwick Road
Westhay
Tel (04586) 389

Par of the Willows Peat Company which also includes a garden centre and visitor centre with displays of the story of peat. The tearoom is pretty with bright green furniture and oil cloths and there is additional seating in the garden. There is a Light Bite menu with vegetarian dishes and traditional afternoon tea fare, all fresh and homemade.

Cream tea £1.95
Open all year (ex Christmas and New Year), every day 10am–6pm (5pm in winter)
Light meals
1 3

GLENCOE   Highland   Map 14 NN15

Crafts & Things
Old Croft of
Tighphuirst
Tel (08552) 325

This small coffee shop adjoins a craft shop occupying traditional highland cottages just off the main road on the western side of the village. It has a flagstone floor and tables clad with pretty plastic cloths and posies of flowers. A small selection of local baking is available from the self-service counter, including scones, shortbread, gingerbread and chocolate cake, as well as filled rolls.

Pot of tea and one cake average £1.20
Open Apr–Sep 9.30am–5pm
1 3

GLENRIDDING   Cumbria   Map 11 NY31

**Kilners Coffee
House**
CA11 0PB
Tel (07684) 82228

This small coffee house and tearoom adjoining the Glenridding Hotel has been known as Kilners since Victorian days; close to the steamer pier (departure point for regular cruises on Ullswater), it offers a variety of refreshments which includes salads, quiche, freshly-made sandwiches, scones and cakes (some of which are home-baked), accompanied by Earl Grey, Ceylon or Indian tea.

Pot of tea and one cake average £1.40
Open every day

GLOUCESTER   Gloucestershire   Map 03 SO82

Pickwick's Pastries
19 St John's Lane
Tel (0452) 500755

Cornish cream teas are the speciality of a small café set off Northgate Street in the city centre, furnished with bentwood chairs and tables covered by pretty oilcloth, and displaying a large selection of fresh pastries, cakes and chocolates. Scones, sweet and savoury pancakes, a good range of sandwiches and hot or cold meals are also available, with Earl Grey or lemon tea as an alternative to the standard blend.

Pot of tea and one cake average £1, set tea £1.50–£3
Open Mon–Sat 9am–5pm

GLOUCESTER   Gloucestershire   Map 03 SO82

**Seasons Restaurant
& Teahouse**
5A College Court, off
Westgate Street
Tel (0452) 307060

Situated in a narrow lane off a main street and adjacent to St Michaels Gate, this is a large, light tearoom with feature windows, clothed tables and wooden furniture. Lunch is served, with a good selection of vegetarian dishes and light snacks. A choice of homebaked scones, cakes, Continental pastries and American desserts is offered, and a variety of tea blends.

Pot of tea and one cake average £1.40
Open all year, Mon–Fri, 10am–5.30pm, Sat 9am–5.30pm
Lunch

GLOUCESTER   Gloucestershire   Map 03 SO82

Undercroft Restaurant
Church House
College Coreen
Tel (0452) 307164

A particularly interesting restaurant, entered through the cathedral cloisters and retaining such original features as a quarry-tiled floor and exposed beams, it is furnished with polished wood tables with fresh flowers and rattan chairs. The extensive range of food available is one hundred per cent homemade, including a good choice of hot, cold and vegetarian dishes, featuring treats such as scones with cream and jam, shortbread and a selection of cakes, accompanied by English breakfast, Earl Grey, Assam or camomile tea.

Pot of tea and one cake average £1.15
Open Mon–Sat 10am–5pm, Sun 12 noon–5pm

GOSFORTH   Cumbria   Map 11 NY00

The Lakeland Habit
Tel (09405) 232

An open staircase from a newsagent and an outdoor clothing shop leads to this attractive and comfortable tearoom – a converted warehouse which retains its original pulley and hoist. Tempting choices include cakes, gâteaux, cheesecakes, sandwiches and scones with Cumberland rum butter. Good quality teas (choice of blends) are served by friendly staff – an excellent place to stop.

Pot of tea 50p–55p, traditional high tea £2.75
Open all year, every day, 9.30am–5.30pm (Sun 6pm in season)
1 3

GRANGE-IN-BORROWDALE   Cumbria   Map 11 NY32

Grange Bridge Cottage Tea Shop
Keswick
Tel (0596) 8420

Set beside the bridge in this beautiful village, with seating available outside on summer days, a charming little cottage tearoom offers light hot and cold meals and ice creams as well as a good range of sandwiches (made to order), scones, traditional and speciality cakes. Although no special tea blends are used, the local water produces tea which tastes particularly good.

Pot of tea and one cake average £1.25
Open Apr–Jun Tue–Sun and bank holiday Mons, Jul–Oct every day

GRANGE-OVER-SANDS   Cumbria   Map 07 SD47

The Cedar Tree
Yewbarrow Terrace
Tel (05395) 32511

Situated behind a gift shop with a Victorian pavement canopy, almost opposite the railway station, this small teashop features displays of colourful teacloths, cheese boards and trays on its walls. The range of set teas includes a Cumberland tea with rum butter, or you can choose from a good selection of sandwiches, followed, perhaps, by scones or chocolate gâteau and cream; China tea is available, as well as Luckipole.

Pot of tea and one cake, average 95p, afternoon tea 80p–£2.45
Open all year, every day, 9.30am–5pm
Lunches available (with a dish of the day)

GRANTHAM   Lincolnshire   Map 08 SK93

Catlins
11 High Street
Tel (0476) 590345

This is an historic building worthy of note. Built in 1560, much of the original facework and interior beams are still to be seen. In 1740 Grantham Gingerbread was first made in a bakery to the rear and is still served today made to the original recipe. A range of cakes, scones, teacakes and sandwiches is served by friendly staff and an extensive à la carte menu (with a good choice of snacks) is available all day.

Pot of tea 45p, cream tea
£2.00
Open Jan–Dec, Mon–Sat,
9am–5pm
 1 3

GRANTHAM   Lincolnshire   Map 08 SK93

Knightingales
Guildhall Street
Tel (0476) 79243

A small, friendly self-service establishment, popular throughout the day for morning coffee, light lunches and afternoon tea. All home baking, specialising in wholefood and vegetarian dishes. The carrot and cinnamon cake enjoyed by our inspector is a particular favourite, but scones, fruit and nut bars, date slices and gingerbread are also tempting. There is a comprehensive choice of speciality teas.

Pot of tea and one cake
average £1
Open all year (ex bank
holidays), Mon–Sat, 9am–
4.30pm

GRANTOWN-ON-SPEY   Highland   Map 14 NJ02

**Coffee & Ice Cream
Parlour**
32–35 High Street
Tel (0479) 2001

Despite the name, this establishment offers much more than ice cream and coffee. As well as a range of hot dishes and salads, a good selection of leaf teas can be enjoyed with home baking and quality gâteaux. Tea is made in china teapots and served with fresh milk.

Pot of tea 40p–60p, cakes
from 50p
Open Feb–Dec, Mon–Sat,
9am–5pm or 7pm
Lunch

GRASMERE   Cumbria   Map 11 NY30

**The Dove Cottage
Tea Shop and
Restaurant**
Town End
Tel (09665) 268

This attractive, beamed teashop – part of Dove Cottage and the Wordsworth Museum, owned by the Wordsworth Trust – serves afternoon tea in a spacious lounge with comfortable armchairs and settees; on sunny days there is also seating under parasols on the patio. A wide choice of open sandwiches including such delicacies as smoked salmon and herrings in Madeira is on offer, together with scones, shortbread, banana bread, fruitcake and gâteaux, or you may prefer something from a selection of hot dishes and vegetarian fare. Assam, Darjeeling, Earl Grey, orange pekoe and herbal teas are available.

Pot of tea and one cake
average £1.60
Open every day

GRASMERE   Cumbria   Map 11 NY30

Merry Kettle
College Street
Tel (09665) 790

Situated at the centre of the village, overlooking the small green, a tearoom with patio and other outdoor seating not only serves an enjoyable cup of tea with scones, chocolate/caramel slices and gâteaux baked on the premises but also features homemade soups, jacket potatoes and a hot dish of the day, as well as a good range of sandwiches.

Pot of tea and one cake average £1.40
Open every day
Light meals

GRASMERE   Cumbria   Map 11 NY30

The Wild Daffodil Tea Shop
Stock Lane
Tel (09665) 770

Situated at the rear of a Gift and Body Shop this is a spacious tearoom with pine tables and chairs, quilted place mats, dried flowers and a display of preserves and copper pans. A wide range of sandwiches, pastries, cakes and scones is served, along with homemade soup, quiche and salads, and a choice of tea blends.

Pot of tea and one cake average £1.25
Open every day
Light lunches

GRAYSHOTT   Surrey   Map 04 SU83

Brambles
7 The Square
Tel Hindhead (0428) 606022

Newly-opened in a square off the road through the village, this charming, softly-lit café features briar-patterned wallpaper with pleasant pictures, fresh flowers on glass-topped tables and fluted bone china in a floral design. A choice of tea blends is available. Sandwiches are made to order, and scones and cakes are all homemade – as is the range of snacks and savouries that can be served at any time.

Pot of tea and one cake average £1.50
Open Mon–Sat 9am–5.30pm
Snacks

GREAT BARTON   Suffolk   Map 05 TL86

Suffolk Barn
Fornham Road Farm
Tel (028487) 317

A barn in a rural location, housing an interesting collection of crafts, wild flowers, herbs and plants, offers sandwiches, savouries and a wide selection of cakes which are home-baked to such traditional recipes as Passion cake, Dorset Yum Yum and Chelsea Buns. Indian, Earl Grey, rosehip and herbal teas are served.

Pot of tea and one cake average £1.10
Open Wed–Sun
1 3

GREAT BIRCHAM   Norfolk   Map 09 TF73

Bircham Windmill
Tel (048523) 393

The self-service tearooms are part of a small complex comprising the windmill, bakery and stables. Homemade cakes are served with a fresh pot of tea. Traditionally baked loaves are also for sale along with a range of gift items.

Pot of tea 45p, cream tea £1.75
Open 20 May–20 Sep, Sun–Fri, from Easter Wed and Sun

GREAT DRIFFIELD   Humberside   Map 08 TA06

The Tea Exchange
37 Exchange Street
Tel (0377) 241180

A fully restored, comfortably appointed town centre house (adjacent to the main council car park off Eastgate) offers friendly service and a good range of Taylors Yorkshire teas (including Earl Grey, Assam, lapsang, orange peko, lemon and a more unusual decaffeinated blend) to accompany a selection of cakes and pastries – homemade rich fruitcake and wholemeal scones being particularly popular. On warmer days teas can be served in a fully enclosed courtyard at the rear of the shop.

Pot of tea and one cake average £1.10
Open every day

GREAT YARMOUTH   Norfolk   Map 05 TG50

Cliff Hotel
Gorleston
Tel (0493) 662179

A licensed three-star hotel with a large car park serves tea in an elegant lounge where comfortable armchairs and sofas are grouped round low tables. Afternoon tea consists of sandwiches, followed by home-baked scones and cakes, while tea blends include Ceylon, lapsang souchong, Earl Grey and Darjeeling, with iced lemon in warm weather. A short à la carte menu of light savouries and snacks is also available.

Pot of tea and one cake average £1.35, set tea from £2.75
Open every day
1 2 3

GRIMSBY   Humberside   Map 08 TA20

The Larder
39 Bethlehem Street
Tel (0472) 361867

On two floors behind a provisions shop (coffee and tea a speciality), this coffee and teashop is inviting and comfortable with large round tables and matching wheelback chairs. Lunches are served, and a selection of sandwiches, homebaked cakes, pastries and gateaux, with an extensive range of teas and coffees.

Pot of tea and one cake average £1.75
Open Jan–Dec, Mon–Sat 9am–4.30pm
Lunches

Le Boulevard Café
The Friary Centre

At upper street level in the Friary Centre, separated from surrounding shops and pedestrians only by cords looped elegantly between pillars, this café's layout mimics the pavement setting of its namesakes. Food, too, is Continental in style, including filled baguettes, croissants and a selection of patisserie – though English expectations are fulfilled by a range of tea blends and the set afternoon tea of scones, cream and strawberry jam. Hot and cold snacks and savouries are available throughout the day.

Pot of tea and one cake average £1.70, cream tea £1.95
Open Mon–Sat 9am–5pm
Hot and cold snacks

The Danish Kitchen Restaurant
2–3 Phoenix Court
Tel (0483) 572041

Within earshot of the traffic at the bottom of the city's High Street, but set in a tranquil pedestrianised precinct with tables and chairs outside, this restaurant reflects a Danish influence not only in the posters and pictures decking its walls but also in an extensive use of light-coloured wood to create separate areas within the overall space. A wide range of sandwiches and filled jacket potatoes, available at separate outlets, supplements the salads, hot and cold snacks, scones, teacakes, doughnuts, Danish pastries and gâteaux offered with a choice of tea blends at the main self-service counter.

Pot of tea and one cake average £1.35
Open Mon–Fri 9am–5pm, Sat 9am–5.30pm
Hot and cold snacks

Kings Shades Coffee House
20 Tunsgate
Tel (0483) 56718

This small, subtly-lit and discreetly decorated coffee shop/restaurant stands in a quiet street only a hundred yards from the city centre. Eating areas on two floors – the higher being designated 'no smoking' – are furnished with mock-wood tables and wicker chairs or padded bench seating; pleasant brown crockery is provided, and there are fresh flowers on the tables. A wide range of set teas is augmented by a good choice of sandwiches (with interesting vegetarian options), scones, teacakes and Continental patisserie, as well as an equally extensive range of tea blends.

Pot of tea and one cake average £2.15, set teas, £2.60–£5.50
Open Mon–Sat 2.30–5.30pm for afternoon tea

National Trust Tearoom
Loseley Park Farms
Tel (0483) 57881

Once a tithe barn on this estate well-known for its dairy herds, the tearoom reflects these origins in oak floors, wooden tables and chairs and neutral-coloured curtains on wooden rings and rods; popular with walkers, it provides a particular staging point for those following the Pilgrims' Way. Scones, pastries, cakes and biscuits are all homemade, as is the range of hot and cold snacks (including soup) available throughout the day. Earl Grey, lapsang, peppermint, rosehip and camomile tea offer an alternative to the standard blend.

Pot of tea and one cake average £1, cream tea £2
Open Jun–Sep, Wed–Sat 11am–5pm
Hot and cold snacks

Next Cafe
White Lion Walk
Tel (0483) 579942

A light, airy contemporary establishment located in a shopping arcade within the Next store. Scones, cakes, gâteaux and pastries are served with a selection of tea blends.

Pot of tea 55p, afternoon tea £2.20
Open all year, Mon–Sat, 8.30am–5pm

GUILDFORD   Surrey   Map 04 SU94

The Roof Garden Food Centre
The Friary Centre

On the top floor of the Friary Centre a collection of separate self-service outlets serves jacket potatoes, doughnuts, hot dogs, wholefoods, Chinese dishes and traditional English fare. Fontana's Patisserie offers home-baked scones cakes and pastries. Whatever your choice of eating style, meals are served in a series of patio-like settings, divided up by imitation box hedges and trees.

Pot of tea and one cake average £1.25
Open Mon–Thu 8.30am–5pm, Fri–Sat 8.30am–5.30pm

GWEEK   Cornwall & Isles of Scilly   Map 02 SW72

Gweek Tea Gardens
Tel (032622) 635

A listed period cottage in the creek-side village famed for its seal sanctuary. Children are welcome here where the theme is unmistakingly The Lord Of The Rings. The tearoom is simply furnished and decorated with Hobbit paraphernalia. Ideal budget eating for the family, with hot and cold meals, homemade scones, cakes and pastries.

Pot of tea and one cake average 90p, cream tea £1.60
Open Apr–Sep, every day, 9am–8pm
Hot meals

HADDINGTON   Lothian   Map 12 NT57

Peter Potter Gallery
10 The Sands (off Church Street)
Tel (062082) 2080

A popular rendezvous for locals, this 'no smoking' teashop serves a delicious array of home-baked cakes including lemon cake, peacan pies, date crumble, flapjacks, scones and croissants. Tea is served in local pottery teapots with a choice of speciality blends and herbal infusions. The gallery and bookshop offer additional interest.

Pot of tea 45p, cakes 25p–60p
Open all year, Mon–Sat, 10am–5pm, Thu 10am–2pm, closed Sun (closes at 4pm Nov–Mar)
Light lunches 12 noon–2pm

HADLEIGH   Suffolk   Map 05 TM04

Odds and Ends
131 High Street
Tel (0473) 822032

This delightful teashop, with the appearance and atmosphere of a private house, has a lovely old cast-iron fireplace and an old copper boiler. Good home cooking provides inexpensive, tasty meals, and a tempting display of cakes includes date and walnut, chocolate and fruit cakes. Tea is served in functional brown teapots in keeping with the surroundings.

Set tea £2–£2.60
Open Apr–Oct, 10am–5pm, Nov–Apr 10am–2.30pm, closed Tue
Lunch

HALIFAX   West Yorkshire   Map 07 SE02

Spinnies Coffee Shop
23 Woolshops
Tel (0422) 349377

This bright and cheerful tea/coffee shop, is set above a shop selling hand-made chocolates and greetings cards. Glass-topped tables with pink cloths, attractive crockery and piped music create a pleasant background for the enjoyment of a selection of sandwiches, homemade scones, toast, crumpets, various cakes and gâteaux, accompanied by a choice of tea blends; soup and jacket potatoes are also available.

Pot of tea and one cake £1.60, set tea £1.60
Open Sun 10am–4pm, Mon 10am–5pm, Tue–Sat 9am–5pm

HALLAND　East Sussex　Map 05 TQ41

The Coffee Shop
Halland Forge Hotel
Tel (082584) 456

Situated on the A22 with excellent car parking facilities, this modern fully-licensed coffee shop has a cafeteria-style buffet and self-service counter. Homemade Sussex cream teas, buttered scones, iced sponges and freshly made sandwiches are available.

Pot of tea and one cake average £1, set tea £1.65
Open Tue–Sat 7.30am–9.30pm, Sun and Mon 8am–6pm
Breakfast, morning coffee, lunch

HAMBLE　Hampshire　Map 04 SU40

The Village Tea Rooms
High Street
Tel (0703) 455683

Two years ago Mr Jenkin, the proprietor, left the *QE2* as shops manager and turned his hand to converting this former rope makers/coffin makers into a cosy tearoom. The old building, full of character, dates from about 1640. There is a variety of tempting cakes, and a selection of tea blends, as well as friendly, courteous service.

Set teas £1.65–£2.25
Open all year, Mon–Fri 9am–5.30pm (5pm in winter), Sat–Sun 9am–7pm (6pm in winter)

HANBURY　Hereford & Worcester　Map 07 SO96

The Jinney Ring Restaurant
Tel (052784) 653

Scones and a choice of twelve different cookies and cakes (including banana bread and cider loaf), served by pleasant staff, are accompanied by a traditional pot of tea with a choice of speciality blends; full meals and snacks are also available.

Pot of tea and one cake average £1.30, set tea £3.50
Open all year, Wed–Sat 10.30am–5pm, Sun 2pm–5.30pm
Lunch

HARLECH　Gwynedd　Map 06 SH53

Bwtri Bach
Stryd Fawr

Situated close to the Castle, Bwtri Bach forms part of a delicatessen in the village centre. The large stone fireplace, stone floor and pretty tablecloths provide a pleasant setting for afternoon tea. Tempting homemade cakes, scones and rolls, displayed on an old shop counter, are served by friendly staff. There is a good range of Welsh cheeses for sale.

Pot of tea and one cake average £1, cream tea £1.25
Open all year, Mon–Sat 9.30am–4.30pm, closed Wed pm and Suns in winter

HARLECH　Gwynedd　Map 06 SH53

The Plas
High Street
Tel (0766) 780204

Enjoying one of the finest views in Harlech, the café (part of a restaurant, crafts and gallery complex) is decorated in conservatory style with a grassed terrace for summer use. Traditional pots of tea, pastries, scones and a range of cakes (some homemade) are served by efficient staff.

Pot of tea 55p, cakes and pastries 50p–80p
Open all year, daily, 9am–8pm
Lunch, dinner

Betty's Café Tea Rooms
1 Parliament Street
Tel (0423) 502746

Overlooking Montpellier Gardens, Betty's, founded by a Swiss confectioner in 1919, is famous throughout Yorkshire and beyond. There are three further branches of the tearooms (see entries under Ilkley, Northallerton and York). No visitor to Harrogate should miss this experience. Everything is freshly baked in the firm's own bakery, using a unique combination of Swiss and traditional Yorkshire recipes, and you will simply be spoilt for choice. For a real Yorkshire treat, though, you could try one of Betty's special rich fruit cakes with a slice of Wensleydale cheese as an accompaniment. The range of tea blends leaves nothing to be desired. In the evenings there are café concerts.

Pot of tea from £1.25, cream tea £3.48
Open all year, every day, 9am–9pm
Hot meals also served
[1] [3]

Emma's Tea Rooms and Restaurant
1 Valley Drive
Tel (0423) 560311

This tastefully decorated tearoom and restaurant is in an attractive Victorian building opposite Valley Gardens. The very good quality food is cooked on the premises by husband and wife team Mr and Mrs Irving. They offer sandwiches ranging from egg and cress to smoked salmon; cakes; locally made ice-cream, and light meals such as Fishermans's Pie with granary bread and salad. Speciality and herbal teas are available.

Pot of tea and one cake average £1.90
Open Tue–Sat 10am–5pm, Sun 10am–5.30pm
Light lunches

Loves Restaurant
9 Westminster Arcade
Parliament Street
Tel (0423) 506663

Opening onto the first floor of a fashionable Victorian-style shopping arcade whose restored wrought ironwork suggests an 'al fresco' atmosphere, this restaurant offers a traditional afternoon tea menu of sandwiches, toast, and cakes, pastries and scones produced by a local bakery; an extensive range of tea blends is available, and customers looking for a more substantial meal can choose from daily specials such as scrambled egg and smoked salmon or vegetable samosas and salad.

Pot of tea and one cake average £1.80
Open Mon–Sat
Hot snacks

HARROGATE North Yorkshire Map 08 SE35

Next Espresso Bar
Next
Tel (0423) 531122

A modern-style coffee bar on the first floor of the Next clothes and accessories shop offers not only Espresso and Capuccino coffee but also a wide range of traditional tea blends, together with a selection of cakes and gâteaux, freshly filled rolls, croissants or potatoes and a daily changing hot dish such as lasagne. Customers are seated either at tables or on stools at the Espresso bar itself, and there is a no-smoking area.

Pot of tea and one cake average £1.20
Open Mon–Sat
Snacks

HARROGATE North Yorkshire Map 08 SE35

Nidd Hall
Nidd
Tel (0423) 771598

A fine country manor set in 23 acres of attractive grounds. Tea is served in the elegant lounge or library by attentive staff, and tables are fully set with linen cloths and napkins. Scones, fruitcake and gâteau are all baked on the premises and sandwiches are available, and a set tea (with or without a glass of champagne or sherry). In summer additional items such as quiche and smoked haddock are served.

Pot of tea and one cake average £3.25, set teas £4.75–£5.75
Open every day

HARTINGTON Derbyshire Map 07 SK16

Beresford Tea Rooms
Tel (0298) 84418)

A friendly little establishment at the heart of the village, popular with both walkers and tourists, creates a relaxed and welcoming atmosphere with soft piped music and a good display of the works of local artists. Sandwiches are freshly made and cakes are home-baked – scones and meringues being particularly popular – while Earl Grey or Darjeeling tea can be provided on request.

Pot of tea and one cake 95p
Open 1 Apr–31 Oct, every day
Snack lunches

HARVINGTON Hereford & Worcester Map 07 SO87

Moatside Licensed Restaurant & Tearoom
Harvington Hall
Tel (0562) 267

Three miles south-east of Kidderminster, just off the A448, Harvington Hall is part medieval, but mostly built about 1580, and after a tour of the Hall the Moatside Tearoom is the ideal place to stop for tea. A tempting range of cakes, scones and sandwiches is served with a choice of tea blends, and full lunches are also available.

Pot of tea and one cake average £1, set teas £1.55–£2.75
Open Mar–Sep every day
Lunches

HARWICH Essex Map 05 TM23

Sworda House Tea Room
78 West Street
Tel (0255) 552575

These tearooms occupy 350-year-old premises once used as an armoury for the soldiers defending the harbour. In the cosy, intimate atmosphere of its wooden-beamed, pine-furnished interior customers can enjoy a wide range of sandwiches and an extensive selection of home-baked cakes, pastries and scones with a good choice of tea blends.

Pot of tea and one cake average £1
Open every day 11.30am–9pm
Light lunches

HASLEMERE   Surrey   Map 04 SU93

Darnleys Restaurant
High Street
Tel (0428) 3048

Set back from the pavement at the bottom of the town's main street, its exterior made attractive by hanging baskets, this café offers tables outside in warmer weather. The interior – in traditional English teashop style, with polished tables and chairs – displays a blackboard menu and an interesting collection of hats in diverse styles; in its pleasant atmosphere customers can enjoy a particularly good pot of Indian, Earl Grey or China tea with sandwiches, toast, teacakes, scones and a selection of cakes (some of which are homemade). Hot snacks are also available throughout the day.

Pot of tea and one cake average £1.35, set teas £2.50–£2.75
Open every day 9.30am–5pm
Hot snacks

HATHERSAGE   Derbyshire   Map 08 SK28

Corner Cupboard Café
Main Road
Tel (0433) 50770

Bow windows look out onto the main street, and at the rear there is a garden for teas in summer. In the upstairs room there is a permanent White Elephant stall, with the proceeds going to a local charity. Home-baked treats include Auntie Pat's Cake – a confection of sponge, raspberries, double cream and butter cream – and there is a choice of tea blends.

Pot of tea and one cake average £1.50, set tea £2.50–£4, full afternoon tea £2.30
Open every day, Mon–Fri 10am–5pm, Sat 9.30am–6pm, Sun 9am–6.30pm
Breakfast and light lunch also served

HAVERFORDWEST   Dyfed   Map 02 SM91

Rendezvous Coffee Shop
Ocky White
Department Store
7 Bridge Street
Tel (0437) 2781

A clean, modern coffee shop situated in a department store. The self-service counter offers doughnuts, custard slices, assorted pastries, sandwiches and a salad bar. There is a choice of traditional or lemon tea.

Pot of tea and pastry £1.20
Open all year, Mon–Sat, 9am–5.30pm
3

HAWKCHURCH   Devon   Map 03 ST30

Fairwater Head Country House Hotel
Tel (02977) 349

Set in beautiful gardens with glorious views, this warm and friendly country house hotel offers traditional afternoon tea served either on the patio or in the garden lounge. Dorset and West Country recipes provide the basis for home-baked fruit cakes, flapjacks, carrot cake and shortbread; there is a choice of tea blends.

Set tea £1.50
Open Feb–Oct, daily, 2.30pm–5.30pm

HAWORTH   West Yorkshire   Map 07 SE03

Cobbled Way
60 Main Street
Tel (0535) 42735

At the top of the cobbled main street of Haworth – famous for its association with the Brontës – a pretty little tearoom with lace cloths on its tables offers home-baked scones, pies and cake, a wide range of sandwiches and snacks and a good selection of tea blends. Cosy surroundings and friendly service combine to create a pleasant atmosphere.

Pot of tea and one cake £1.10, set teas £1.60–£2.10
Open every day (ex Tue in winter) 9.30am–5.30pm

HAWORTH   West Yorkshire   Map 07 SE03

Emma's
82 Main Street
Tel (0535) 42499

A charming, attractively furnished Victorian-style teashop at the top of the cobbled main street. There is a sideboard display of very good homemade cakes including passion cake, chocolate, honey and carrot cake, Bakewell tart, gâteaux and scones. A selection of tea blends is served from Queensgate bone china, and there is a range of sandwiches.

Pot of tea and one cake average £2, set tea £2.80
Open every day 9.30am–6.30pm

HAYDOCK   Merseyside   Map 07 SJ59

Haydock Thistle Hotel
Penny Lane
Tel (0942) 272000

A large modern hotel with an attractive Georgian-style façade and courtyard gardens, just off junction 23 of the M6, close to Haydock Park racecourse. Afternoon tea with sandwiches, gâteau, scones, homemade pastry and a selection of tea blends is served in the elegant lounge or on the terrace facing the gardens.

Pot of tea and one cake average £3, set tea £5.95
Open every day
1 2 3

HAY-ON-WYE   Powys   Map 03 SO24

Swan Hotel
Church Street
Tel (0497) 821177

Afternoon tea with sandwiches, scones, toasted teacakes and a choice of Indian or Earl Grey tea is served in the elegant lounge or comfortable bar-lounge of this lovely Georgian hotel. Every hotel service is available.

Pot of tea and one cake average £1.50, cream tea £1.50
Open every day
1 2 3

HEACHAM   Norfolk   Map 09 TF63

Norfolk Lavender
Caley Mill
Tel (0485) 70384

Stop for tea here to enjoy home-baked cakes and cream teas amid a field of scented lavender at England's only lavender farm, and home of the National Collection of Lavender. The Miller's Cottage Tea Room with its oak beams gives friendly individual service.

Pot of tea 50p, cream tea £1.10
Open all year, daily 10am–5pm, during winter in gift shop, closed for Christmas holiday

HEBDEN BRIDGE   West Yorkshire   Map 07 SD92

Corrina-a-Maying Tea Rooms
6 Hollins Place
off St George's Square
Tel (0422) 843855

A delightful little tearoom over a wool shop in the centre of town. Bright, fresh and cosy, with pretty floral tablecloths, a good range of teas and coffees is available and a choice of tasty home baking including Grantham gingerbread biscuits, apricot and walnut teabread and Boston brownies. No smoking is permitted; baby feeding and changing facilities on request.

Pot of tea and one cake average £1.50, set tea £3
Open Mon & Wed–Sat 10am–5pm
Lunches, hot and cold snacks

HELSTON   Cornwall & Isles of Scilly   Map 02 SW62

Burncoose Cottage
Cury Cross
TR12 7QT
Tel (0326) 240747

The colourful cottage garden of an old Cornish farmhouse between Helston and Mullion (signposted off the main Lizard road) offers the ideal setting in which to relax over a cream tea with home-baked scones and cake. Seating is on benches – with alternative provision in an outbuilding for inclement weather – and a pair of peafowl and the occasional hen wander among customers as they eat.

Cream tea £2 (half portion for children £1)
Open May–Oct every day

HELSTON   Cornwall & Isles of Scilly   Map 02 SW62

The Handy Shop
Sithney
Tel (03265) 573545

This simply furnished tearoom is behind a Cornish stone cottage just one mile from the Helston to Penzance road. Mrs Langford has served tea and homemade cakes here for 19 years, and the atmosphere is very friendly and chatty. Scones, rock cakes, lemon sponge and iced fancies are just some of the cakes available.

Plain tea £1.15, cream tea £1.45
Open Easter–Sep, daily, 9am–6pm

HENLEY-IN-ARDEN   Warwickshire   Map 07 SP16

Henley Café
97 High Street
B95 5AT
Tel (056479) 2135

This bow-fronted café on the main street offers a wide range of hot and cold meals as well as a good selection of home-baked cakes and pastries in an attractive room where pretty clothed tables and bentwood chairs are set off by beams, exposed stone walls and a quarry-tiled floor.

Pot of tea and one cake average £1.45, cream tea £1.95
Open Tue, Wed and Fri–Sun

HENLEY-ON-THAMES   Oxfordshire   Map 04 SU78

Red Lion Hotel
Hart Street
Tel (0491) 572161

Henley's famous Red Lion Hotel stands at one end of the old arched bridge over the River Thames. Traditional afternoon and cream teas are served in a comfortable lounge by professional staff. Sandwiches, teacakes, scones and pastries are all good, and the pots of tea are well flavoured, with a choice of Indian, Ceylon, Darjeeling or Earl Grey.

Pot of tea and one cake average £3.25, set teas £3.75–£7.50
Open every day, 3pm–6pm
1 2 3

HEREFORD   Hereford & Worcester   Map 03 SO54

The Cottage Pine Craft Shop and Tea Rooms
2 Bridge Street
Tel (0432) 263815

A small, friendly and relaxed tearoom at the rear of a gift and craft shop close to the Cathedral offers both set teas and a tempting range of light snacks, sponges, scones and biscuits. Darjeeling, Earl Grey and Assam tea are available.

Pot of tea and one cake average 85p, set teas £1.50–£2.55
Open Mon–Sat

HIGH LEGH   Cheshire   Map 07 SJ78

High Legh Garden Centre
Near Knutsford
Tel (092575) 6991

Part of a garden centre where knowledgeable staff advise on a massive range of indoor and outdoor plants, this conservatory-style self-service restaurant offers sandwiches and a wide selection of cakes, pies and pastries which, though not home-baked, provide a tempting accompaniment to a good cup of tea (English Breakfast or Earl Grey available). Hot snacks and light lunches are also served.

Pot of tea and one cake average £1.05
Open every day

HOLKHAM   Norfolk   Map 09 TF84

Ancient House Tea Room
Coast Road
Wells-next-the-Sea
Tel (0302) 711285

A traditional flintstone house – part of the Holkham Estate, but privately run – serves homemade snacks, savouries, pastries and cakes with a range of tea blends in both a simply-furnished tearoom and an attractive garden. Gifts and pottery are sold in the adjacent shop, and car parking space is provided.

Pot of tea and one cake average £1.05, cream tea £2
Open every day 10.30am–5pm

HOLLINGBOURNE   Kent   Map 05 TQ85

Great Danes Hotel
Tel (0622) 30022

The Garden Cafe, located on the busy A20, offers meals from 11am–7pm; afternoon tea – served between 3 and 6pm – comprises a choice of sandwiches, scones with jam and cream, the gâteau of the day and a selection of fine tea blends; a children's menu is available on request.

Set tea £3
Open every day, 3–6pm for tea

HOLMFIRTH   West Yorkshire   Map 07 SE11

Hubbards
5 Victoria Square
Tel (0484) 684529

A small, Victorian-style teashop, tucked away in a courtyard, stands at the heart of 'Last of the Summer Wine' country – Sid's Cafe being just across the road. With its blackleaded grate and plain walls hung with plates and dog prints, it offers a warm, cosy atmosphere in which to enjoy either a set tea or snacks, sandwiches and homemade cakes. A range of tea blends is served in attractive bone china cups.

Pot of tea and one cake average £2, set teas £1.50–£3.25
Open every day, 11am–5pm

HOLMFIRTH   West Yorkshire   Map 07 SE10

The Wrinkled Stocking Tea Room
Huddersfield Road
Tel (0484) 681408

Fans of 'Last of the Summer Wine' will love this attractive little teashop which stands next to 'Norah's House', its walls adorned with photographs and cartoons of the series' stars. As well as two set teas, the menu offers a good selection of snacks, salads and sandwiches, together with such temptations as warm chocolate fudge cake with chocolate sauce and fresh cream, and there is a choice of tea blends.

Pot of tea 55–75p, set teas £1.60–£2.80
Open every day, summer 10am–5.30pm, winter 10am–5pm

HOLT   Norfolk   Map 09 TG03

The Mews
Chapel Yard
Tel (0263) 713968

Teas and light snacks are served in this friendly, small café just off the main high street. Sandwiches and a fine selection of quality hand-made cakes and pastries are available, as well as cream teas (with a good pot of tea) throughout the day, there is a take-away service.

Pot of tea 55p–65p, cream tea £1.50
Open all year, Mon–Sat (except Thu out of season), 9.30am–5pm
Take-away service, fully licensed

HORLEY   Surrey   Map 04 TQ24

The Chequers Thistle
Brighton Road
Tel (0293) 786992

This Tudor coaching inn, now a friendly hotel, serves traditional tea (with a choice of blends) in the pleasant buttery and by the fireside in the foyer lounge. Homemade sandwiches, quiches and gâteaux are also available.

Pot of tea and biscuits £1.10
Open all year, daily, 11am–10.30pm
[1] [2] [3]

HORNING   Norfolk   Map 09 TG31

Staithe Cottage Tea and Craft Shoppe
Lower Street
Tel (0692) 630915

This delightful thatched and white-painted cottage, set next to a craft shop by the River Bure, features an open terraced area surrounded by shrubberies. Its immaculate interior – simply but comfortably furnished – displays an array of seventeen different scones, cakes and gâteaux, while a blackboard menu offers snacks and savouries; a range of tea blends is available.

Pot of tea and one cake average 95p
Open every day (except Tue and Wed in winter)
Snacks

HORSHAM ST FAITH   Norfolk   Map 09 TG21

Elm Farm Chalet
Tel (0603) 898366

A substantial guest house, picturesquely located at the centre of the village, serves tea in the comfort of a spacious dining room formally set out with linen-clothed tables. Both set afternoon tea and an à la carte selection of items are available, the latter including homemade desserts from the trolley, and there is a range of tea blends.

Pot of tea 75p, set teas £1.50–£2.75
Open Mon–Sat, 10am–5pm
[1] [2] [3]

HOVETON   Norfolk   Map 09 TG31

Wroxham Barns
Tunstead Road
Tel (0603) 783762

A collection of traditional barns set in ten acres of parkland provide a fine rural crafts centre at the heart of which stands a comfortably and attractively furnished tearoom providing lunches and homemade teas. Snacks and savouries are available, as well as sandwiches, scones, cakes, pastries and gâteaux – all prepared on the premises and accompanied by Earl Grey, lemon, herbal or Indian tea.

Pot of tea and one cake average £1.20, cream tea £2.50
Open daily

HOWDEN   Humberside   Map 08 SE72

Bridgegate House
15 Bridgegate
Tel (0430) 431010

Situated at the rear of a wholefood shop, this is a small, no smoking tearoom with a tiled floor and simple rough cast walls. Our inspector was amazed at the range of appetising, homemade wholefood cakes and pastries which were available. The tea is freshly made with a choice of blends and herbal infusions.

Pot of tea from 65p, cakes from 55p
Open all year except for two weeks in Apr and Aug, Mon–Sat, 9am–4.30pm
Breakfast, morning coffee, light vegetarian lunches

HOYLAKE   Merseyside   Map 07 SJ28

Rengrae's Coffee Shop
Unit 4
The Wirral Horn Arcade
Tel 051–608 2668

Situated at the end of an arcade of shops off the main street, a small, pretty coffee shop with converted sewing machine tables offers an enjoyable range of home bakery: scones, fairy cakes, Bakewell tart and millionaires' shortbread, for example, and a limited choice of speciality tea blends. Light snacks are also available, and a selection of ground coffees is offered for sale.

Pot of tea and one cake average £1.20
Open Mon–Sat (except Wed pm)
Snacks

HUDDERSFIELD   West Yorkshire   Map 07 SE11

Choosey's Tea and Coffee House
King Street
Tel (0484) 518823

Set above a specialist tea and coffee shop in the centre of the town, this simply-decorated establishment predictably offers a good range of tea blends with its sandwiches, gâteaux and homemade scones. Jacket potatoes, salads and toasties are also available.

Pot of tea 55–70p, cream tea £1.50
Open Mon–Sat, 9am–5pm

HULL   Humberside   Map 08 TA02

Chambers Restaurant
Carmichaels
George Street
Tel (0482) 23439

Part of Carmichaels, a well-known quality store, this formal but friendly restaurant with a relaxed atmosphere offers traditional menus for morning coffee, luncheon and afternoon tea, this last accompanying freshly-prepared sandwiches, teacakes, muffins, fruit loaf, scones and gâteaux with a range of speciality tea blends.

Pot of tea and one cake average £1.50, cream tea £3.50
Open Mon–Sat
Lunches

HUNGERFORD   Berkshire   Map 04 SU36

The Bear Hotel
Charnham Street
Tel (0488) 682512

The cosy Kennet Bar of this 13th-century roadside inn is an ideal place in which to enjoy fresh homemade cakes – including fruit loaf, apple scones and gingerbread – and either a pot of tea or a cup of coffee. In the summer afternoon tea can be served on the terrace.

Pot of tea 85p, cream tea £2.50
Open all year, daily, 3.30pm–5.30pm
1 2 3

HUNGERFORD   Berkshire   Map 04 SU36

The Tutti Pole
3 High Street
Tel (0488) 682515

Named after an ancient local custom, this teashop has a tempting display of homemade cakes and biscuits which are also on sale to take home. Chocolate crunch, caramel squares and coffee and walnut cake are just some of the choices. A variety of tea blends and coffee is available.

Pot of tea 55p–75p, cream tea £1.95, cakes and biscuits 22p–52p
Open all year, Mon–Fri 9.30am–5.30pm, Sat 9am–6pm, Sun 10am–6pm, usually closed Christmas–New Year
♿

HUNSTANTON   Norfolk   Map 09 TF64

The Copper Kettle
25 High Street
Tel (08453) 34663

This smart, bright and cheery coffee lounge/tea rooms in the centre of town serves a good selection of teas, including a substantial afternoon tea of sandwiches, scone and cream, cake, biscuits and a pot of tea.

Pot of tea 45p, set teas £1.80–£2.75
Open all year, daily, 10am–5pm (4.30pm in winter), closed Mon in winter

HUNSTRETE   Avon   Map 03 ST66

Hunstrete House Hotel
Tel (0761) 490490

This country house hotel, with its outstanding gardens and 92-acre park, makes the tradition of English afternoon tea an experience to remember – guests enjoying the comfort of its luxurious lounges warmed by log fires in winter, or overlooking the croquet lawn outside in warmer weather. Tempting sandwiches are followed by scones with clotted cream and homemade jam, then a choice of freshly-baked pastries, cakes and gâteaux, all accompanied by Indian, China, Ceylon or Earl Grey tea.

Set teas £2.50–£10
Open every day, 3.30–5.30pm for tea
1 3

HUNTINGDON   Cambridgeshire   Map 04 TL27

The Gallery
Newton Court
Hartford
Tel (0480) 412622

A light and attractively furnished tearoom, part of a small courtyard complex in the town centre, offers comfortable seating and matching tablecloths and curtains. The teatime menu lists an à la carte range of scones, teacakes, cakes, pastries and gâteaux, most of which are made on the premises, as well as the set cream tea, and there is a choice of tea blends.

Pot of tea 55p, cream tea £1.95
Open Mon–Sat

HUNTINGDON   Cambridgeshire   Map 04 TL27

Old Bridge Hotel
Tel (0480) 52681

A large terrace lounge furnished with comfortable sofas and chairs is the setting for afternoon tea at this hotel on the banks of the River Ouse. The range of cakes and pastries on display includes tarts, shortbread, scones and fruit cake and summer fruits in season. The tea is well-made and includes a choice of speciality blends.

Pot of tea £1.05, scones and tea £2.25
Open all year, daily, 2.30pm–6.00pm
[1] [2] [3]

HURLEY   Berkshire   Map 04 SU88

Ye Olde Bell Hotel
High Street
Tel (0628) 825881

One of the oldest inns in England, tracing its history back to about 1136, and retaining much of its original character, offers tea in the small, beamed cocktail lounge or, weather permitting, on a well-maintained and attractive garden terrace. The standard set tea comprises a pot of tea or coffee and fresh fruit scones served with jam and cream, but the chef's homemade desserts and patisserie can also by sampled.

Set tea £2.95
Open for tea 3.50–5.30pm
[1] [2] [3]

ILKLEY   West Yorkshire   Map 07 SE14

The Bay Tree
7 Wells Road
Tel (0943) 601793

This cosy little pine-furnished teashop, located behind a fine wholefood shop in the centre of the town, offers for sale the array of ceramics which adorn its walls. A choice of tea blends (including several herbals) accompanies a good range of sandwiches and homemade cakes, biscuits and desserts, while special hot dishes of the day are displayed on a blackboard menu.

Pot of tea and one cake average £1.75
Open every day 10am–6pm

ILKLEY   West Yorkshire   Map 07 SE14

Betty's Café Tea Rooms
32–34 The Grove
Tel (0943) 608029

A traditionally-styled tearoom with stained glass windows and potted plants. Not only does Betty's provide fine teas, but also a good range of light hot dishes, sandwiches, salads, and of course lovely cakes and pastries made in their own Harrogate bakery using Swiss and Yorkshire recipes. Staff are very smart, polite and efficient. See entries for Harrogate, Northallerton, York.

Pot of tea from £1.25, cream tea £3.48
Open all year, daily (including most Bank Holidays) Mon–Thu 9am–7pm, Fri–Sun 9am–9pm
Hot meals, salads
[1] [3]

ILKLEY   West Yorkshire   Map 07 SE14

Muffins
14A Brook Street
Tel (0943) 603040

A good range of hot snacks, muffins and homemade scones and cakes is served by friendly staff in the pleasant atmosphere of a bright, fresh, pine-furnished tearoom in the town centre; customers have a choice of tea blends, and magazines are provided for their enjoyment.

Pot of tea 60–70p
Open every day 9am–5pm

INGLETON   North Yorkshire   Map 07 SD67

Vinery Coffee Shop
The Pines Country
House Hotel
Tel (05242) 41252

This attractive conservatory coffee shop – part of The Pines Guest House – stands beside the A65 just north of Ingleton. Beneath the vine from which it takes its name, or on an attractive patio terrace in fine weather, customers can enjoy not only sandwiches and a range of homebaked scones and cakes but also salads, soups, omelettes and hot snacks such as spaghetti bolognese.

Pot of tea and one cake
average £1.60
Open every day 10am–
5pm
Light meals and snacks

IPSWICH   Suffolk   Map 05 TM14

Boodles Trading Co
Dial Lane
Tel (0473) 254241

This small first floor gallery-style teahouse is situated in a listed building in a narrow lane in the town centre. Light toasted snacks, pies, pastries and cakes are available and a choice of eight good quality teas are served in white earthenware teapots with matching milk jug and crockery.

Pot of tea 50p
Open all year, Mon–Sat,
9.15am–4.45pm
Snacks

ISLAY, ISLE OF   Strathclyde   Map 10 NR16

Croft Kitchen
Port Charlotte
Tel (049685) 208

The grounds of this bright, spacious tearoom on the edge of the village lead down to a small sand and shingle beach, and customers enjoy fine views when it is warm enough to sit outside. Everything is homemade – the mouthwatering aroma of freshly-baked scones, biscuits or sponges often filling the air – and the generously sized servings are reasonably priced. A range of crafts and gifts is also available.

Pot of tea and one cake
average £1
Open Apr–Oct

KEIGHLEY   West Yorkshire   Map 08 SE04

**East Riddlesden Hall
Teashop**
East Riddlesden

Located in the historic East Riddlesden Hall with its exposed stone walls and timber-framed roof, this spotlessly clean, value-for-money teashop occupies a spacious room furnished with settees and stick back chairs. A truly English tea complements home-baked scones, parkin, Bakewell tart and gâteaux with a range of tea blends which includes Assam, Darjeeling, Earl Grey and Ceylon.

Pot of tea and one cake
£1.40
Open Wed, Thu 2–5pm,
Sat, Sun 11am–5pm
(longer hours in Jul &
Aug)

KEITH   Grampian   Map 15 NJ45

Lunch Box Coffee Shop
121 Mid Street
Tel (05422) 2194

This newly decorated coffee shop above a bakers in the main street offers a range of homemade scones, Danish pastries, doughnuts and cakes, and the tea is freshly made. This is a popular place at lunchtime.

Pot of tea 40p
Open all year, Mon–Sat,
10am–4pm
Light lunches

KEITH   Grampian   Map 15 NJ45

The Cottage
142A Mid Street
Tel (05422) 7942

This fairly simple cottage-style restaurant in a side street off the main shopping area offers a small selection of homemade scones, biscuits and cakes and freshly made tea.

Pot of tea 30p
Open all year, daily, 9am–
4.30pm

KELTY   Fife   Map 11 NT19

The Butterchurn
Cocklaw Farm
Tel (0383) 830169/
831614

Only minutes from junction four of the M90, yet enjoying panoramic country views, this quaint converted farm building offers a most impressive selection of home-baked country fare, including carrot cake, coffee gâteaux, chocolate cake, apple pie and meringues. Traditional or wholemeal scones are served with cream and special-recipe homemade preserves, sandwiches are freshly prepared, and savoury pies or quiche with salad provide a more substantial meal. Seating is available in the garden, while farmyard animals, a pets' corner and a play area keep children happily amused.

Pot of tea and one cake average 90p
Open 1 Apr–4 Nov, every day, 10am–5.30pm
Light meals

KENDAL   Cumbria   Map 07 SD59

Mr Bumble's
The Westmorland
Centre
Tel (0539) 740358

This Dickensian coffee house in the Westmorland Shopping Centre is one of a small group of such dotted about the north of England; occupying a series of rooms, and extending onto a patio area in fine weather, it is easily recognised by its distinctive green-and-white striped awnings. As well as the set 'Dreamy Cream Tea', it offers a range of 'Waistcoat Fillers' (scones, crumpets, muffins and cakes 'from the Dingley Dell Bakehouse'), 'Mr Micawber's Toasties' and 'Workhouse Gruel' (homemade soup of the day); half portions of most items are available for children. Earl Grey and lemon tea offer an alternative to the standard blend.

Pot of tea 40p
Open Mon–Sat

KENDAL   Cumbria   Map 07 SD59

Lakeland Hampers Tea Room
14 New Shambles
Tel (0539) 730036

An attractive little tearoom in a narrow lane off Market Square serving full afternoon tea with a round of sandwiches, a scone with jam and cream and a choice of cakes, plus homemade light meals (quiche, soup, baked potatoes), and some delicious desserts and ice creams. There is a selection of tea blends including herbal and decaffeinated. The shop sells hampers filled with local eatables.

Pot of tea and one cake average £1.10, set tea £2.75
Open Mon–Sat
Light meals

KENDAL   Cumbria   Map 07 SD59

The Union Jack
15 Kirkland
Tel (0539) 722458

This little café – easily distinguished by its Union Jack façade – stands close to both Abbot Hall Art Gallery and a public car park. Clean and friendly, with an attractive stone fireplace in one corner, it provides the ideal setting in which to enjoy a well made cup of tea, chosen from a good range of blends, with home-baked scones and cakes. Light snacks, and meals for children under five, are also available.

Pot of tea and one cake average £1
Open all year, Mon–Sat

KERSEY   Suffolk   Map 05 TM04

The Bell Inn
The Street
Tel (0473) 823229

This delightfully characterful, heavily-beamed inn is set in a beautiful village renowned for the water 'splash' which crosses the main street. Enjoy afternoon or cream tea in the convivial surroundings of the traditionally furnished restaurant, bars or patio area.

Pot of tea and one cake average £1.20, cream tea £2.50, afternoon tea (to order)
Open every day
À la carte restaurant and bar meals also served

The Bay Tree
1 Wordsworth Street
Tel (07687) 73313

A three-roomed teashop and restaurant with one room set aside for non-smokers, situated on the Penrith Road (A591) at its junction with Wordsworth Street. Fourteen varieties of leaf tea are available and traditional afternoon teas are served in addition to an all-day breakfast and other light dishes including giant Yorkshire puddings with onions and gravy.

Pot of tea and one cake average £1, set tea £2.50
Open every day (closed Wed & Thu Nov–Easter)
Light meals, licensed

Bryson's Tearoom
38–42 Main Street
Tel (07687) 72257

A comfortable and spacious tearoom with solid pine tables and chairs, set above the family bakery which supplies the varied selection of cakes. Two set teas – the Lakeland cream tea with rum butter, and the Cumberland Farmhouse tea are available, and traditional tea is served in attractive china. Smoking is not permitted.

Pot of tea 45p–55p, set teas £2.20 and £2.40
Open Mar–Dec, Mon–Sat, 8.30am–5.30pm
Breakfast, lunch, dinner

The Honey Pot
6 New Street
Packhorse Court
Tel (07687) 74974

A well proportioned coffee shop in the fashionable redeveloped court with glass-topped tables covering attractive arrangements of dried flowers. A wide variety of good quality teas and coffees is available together with homemade cakes, gâteaux and light meals.

Pot of tea and one cake average £1.40, set tea £3.50
Open every day
Light meals

The Rembrandt
25 Station Street
Tel (07687) 72008

Cheery young waitresses serve a good array of homemade cakes and pastries and two set afternoon teas, each with four homemade preserves – lemon curd, plum, strawberry and blackcurrant. This neat unpretentious tearoom also serves meals.

Pot of tea 50p, set tea £2.50
Open all year, daily, 10am–10pm (Nov–Feb 10am–7.30pm)
Lunch, dinner, vegetarian meals

Stakis Lodore Swiss Hotel
Borrowdale
On the B5289 3 miles outside Keswick

A well-established hotel, built of Lakeland slate and commanding fine views over Derwentwater and the surrounding fells. An enjoyable afternoon tea is served in a comfortable, spacious lounge with period-style furniture and large windows. The set tea consists of a choice of sandwiches, scones, teacakes, and fresh cream gâteaux, but an à la carte selection of items is also available, and a good range of speciality tea blends.

Pot of tea and one cake average £2.30, set tea £5.90
Open all year, every day
1 2 3

KESWICK   Cumbria   Map 11 NY22

The Wild Strawberry
54 Main Street
Tel (07687) 74399

An attractive tearoom and gallery with stone walls, flagstone floors and exposed beams. A range of coffee and tea blends, including fruit teas and infusions is available, and homemade cakes, scones and sandwiches. Light meals are also served, such as vegetarian soup, quiches and toasted sandwiches. Smoking is not permitted.

Pot of tea and one cake average £1.50
Open Thu–Tue (closed 6 weeks Jan & Feb)
Snacks

KEW   Surrey   Map 05 TQ17

Newens – The Original Maids of Honour
288 Kew Road
Tel 081-940 2752

In this neat, unpretentious tearoom cheerful young waitresses serve a good range of home-baked cakes and pastries – specialities including Cumberland Nicky, Sticky Toffee Pudding, Bread and Butter Pudding and Lemon Meringue Pie. Afternoon teas (served all day) offer fresh scones with four homemade preserves, a choice of sandwich and salad, and tea or coffee.

Pot of tea and one cake average £2, set cream tea £3.75
Open all year, 10am–5.30pm, afternoon tea from 2.45pm, closed Sun and Mon afternoon

KILCHRENAN   Strathclyde   Map 10 NN02

Ardanaiseig Hotel
Kilchrenan by Taynuilt
Tel (08663) 333

One of Scotland's most famous gardens, noted for its azaleas and rhododendrons, surrounds this fine country-house hotel on the shores of Loch Awe. Visitors to the gardens may round off their afternoon by taking tea in the lovely drawing room overlooking the lawns and the loch. A full afternoon tea, with cucumber sandwiches, scones, cream and raspberry jam, finished by freshly baked cakes, is served with great charm by attentive young staff. To drink, there is a choice of Assam, Earl Grey, Darjeeling or Lapsang Souchong.

Tea and biscuits £1.75, cream tea £2.75, full afternoon tea £3.75
Open mid Apr–late Oct, every day, 3–5pm
1 2 3

KILDRUMMY   Grampian   Map 15 NJ41

Mossat Restaurant
Bridge of Mossat
Tel (09755) 71355

There is a country feel to this restaurant with its beams and floral table cloths, part of a popular gift shop/ garden centre. Waitresses serve freshly made tea and a small range of homemade scones, cakes and biscuits.

Pot of tea 45p
Open Mar–Oct, daily, 10am–6.30pm (Nov–Feb Sat–Sun 10am–6.30pm)
 1 3

KILKHAMPTON   Cornwall & Isles of Scilly   Map 02 SS21

The Coffee House
2 Lower Square
Tel (02882) 484

Beside the A39 Bideford to Bude Road, in the village square, stands a small, informal tea and coffee shop furnished in simple refectory style, with emulsioned walls and a quarry tiled floor. Here, or in the little tea garden with its benches and hanging baskets, customers can enjoy a cream tea or individual items from a range of open sandwiches, scones and cakes, all homemade and served with a choice of tea blends.

Pot of tea and one cake average £1.20, set teas from £1.85
Open all year, every day, 9am–10.30pm
Snacks, vegetarian & children's meals

KILLIN   Central   Map 11 NN53

The Mustard Pot
Main Street
Tel (05672) 503

A quaint craft shop and cosy tearoom, created by the conversion of a former railway house, offers a wide range of light snacks and baked goods. At nicely appointed tables with crisp linen against a background of craft exhibits, visitors can enjoy their choice of speciality or herbal tea from good quality bone china. As well as such typically teatime items as sandwiches, oatcakes, cakes and gâteaux.

Pot of tea and one cake average £1.05
Open May–Sep, Mon–Sat 10am–5.30pm, Sun 2.30–5.30pm

KINCRAIG   Highland   Map 14 NH80

Ossian Teashop
Ossian Hotel

A small country hotel has converted an outbuilding into a neat little tearoom with natural stone walls and pine furniture. The tea is freshly made and nicely presented in pottery teapots and the range of homemade cakes and pastries includes Yorkshire cheesecakes, scones and jam, meringues and millionaire shortbread.

Pot of tea 75p and £1.25, cakes 20p–£1
Open Feb–Oct, daily, 10am–6pm
3

KING'S LYNN   Norfolk   Map 09 TF62

Crofters
Kings Lynn Arts Centre
King Street
Tel (0553) 773134

This basement café/restaurant has a Continental atmosphere. Date and orange cake, coffee fondant sponge and caramel slices are just a few of the many cakes and pastries on display. The tea is served in a traditional teapot by pleasant waitresses.

Pot of tea and one cake average £1.30
Open all year, Mon–Sat, 9.30am–5pm
Light snacks, lunch

KING'S LYNN   Norfolk   Map 09 TF62

Duke's Head
Tuesday Market Place
Tel (0553) 774996

A modern coffee shop on the front of the centrally situated Duke's Head Hotel. Gâteaux, Danish pastries and scones, prepared by a local bakery, are served with a traditional pot of well-flavoured tea.

Cream tea £2.50
Open all year, daily, 9am–10.30pm
Morning coffee, light snacks
1 2 3

KING'S LYNN   Norfolk   Map 09 TF62

Knights Hill Hotel
South Wooton
Tel (0553) 675566

Dating back to 1588 and originally a hunting lodge, this three-star hotel at the A148/A149 junction offers an à la carte range of freshly prepared sandwiches, scones, cakes and pies, together with a display of pastries which, though not homemade, are good quality; Earl Grey, Darjeeling and lemon tea are available. Table service is professional and prompt and there are excellent car parking facilities.

Pot of tea and one cake average £1.50
Open all year, every day

KINGTON   Hereford & Worcester   Map 03 SO35

Church House
Lyonshall (two miles from Kington at junction of A44/A480)
Tel (05448) 350

Church House is a small, Georgian, country guesthouse standing in its own grounds in the beautiful Herefordshire countryside. The interior is decorated in the Edwardian style and authentically furnished to make a truly delightful setting for afternoon tea. A wide variety of freshly made scones, cakes and different blends of tea is always available, and beautifully served. A full Edwardian afternoon tea with finger sandwiches can be ordered in advance. The nearby Church House craft shop displays an enticing range of Edwardian-style needlecraft and other giftware. No smoking is permitted.

Pot of tea 60p, cream tea £1.30, full Edwardian tea (advance order only) £2.85
Open Mar–Oct, every day, 10am–12 noon and 3–5.30pm for tea
No smoking in the tearoom
&

KINGUSSIE   Highland   Map 14 NH70

Retro Tea Room
54 High Street

A forties theme has been created at this wood-clad tearoom – even the music being contemporary; walls are adorned with memorabilia of the period, and converted sewing machines provide the tables where visitors can enjoy sandwiches, scones and tasty homemade cakes with a range of speciality tea blends. Soup is also available.

Pot of tea and one cake average £1.20
Open all year, Mon–Sat 10am–5pm, Sun 12 noon–5pm

KINROSS   Tayside   Map 11 NO10

Grase and Claret Restaurant
Heathery Road (just west of the M90)
Tel (0577) 64212

This cosy little restaurant enjoys an attractive outlook across a lake. The home-baking could include apple and almond cake, scones and chocolate gâteaux and although the selection is not large, the quality is first class. The tea is well made, with a choice of blends and herbal infusions. Homemade fudge and preserves are for sale.

Pot of tea 40p–60p, cakes 20p–£1.20
Open Mar–Dec, 9am–9pm (teas served until 4.30pm)
Lunch, dinner

KIRKBY LONSDALE   Cumbria   Map 07 SD67

Royal Hotel
Market Square
Tel (05242) 71217

A visit to the old market town would not be complete without traditional afternoon tea in 'The Nook' at this erstwhile coaching inn. Sandwiches, teacakes, and homemade scones and cakes – served on cake stands in the time-honoured fashion – are accompanied by a good choice of tea blends, and a more substantial high tea is available after 5.30pm.

Pot of tea and one cake average £1.95, set tea £4.50
Open every day
1 3

KIRKBY STEPHEN   Cumbria   Map 12 NY70

Cobblestones Tea Room
40 Market Street
Tel (0930) 71586

An attractive little café and tea room with hanging flower baskets, situated at the centre of the town but providing car parking space immediately outside its premises, features beams, stone walls and an abundance of pot plants. Scones, teacakes, home-baked sponges and a selection of fresh cream cakes are available, together with a wide selection of sandwiches, salads and hot snacks.

Pot of tea and one cake average 80p
Open all year, every day

KIRKCUDBRIGHT   Dumfries & Galloway   Map 11 NX65

The Belfry
39 St Mary Street
Tel (0557) 30861

A combined antique and coffee shop on a corner site in the main street. Scones, tea breads, and cakes (some homemade) are available and the tea is served in a traditional teapot with beautiful Limoges fine china cups and saucers.

Pot of tea and one cake average £1.10
Open Mar–Dec, Mon–Sat 10am–5pm, Sun 1pm–5pm
1 3

KNOWLE   Devon   Map 02 SS43

Jenny Wren's Cottage
Near Braunton
Tel (0271) 812429

This delightful fairytale cottage with its own car park stands beside the main Barnstaple-Ilfracombe road; dating back to the 16th century, it features exposed beams and an inglenook fireplace, its charm enhanced by pretty wallpapers, flower arrangements, antique furniture and many beautiful pieces of china. Understandably popular, with a reputation for excellent home-baked fare, it offers a choice of quality set teas.

Set teas £1.95–£2.40
Open Sun–Fri 3–6.30pm

KNUTSFORD   Cheshire   Map 07 SJ77

Courtyard Coffee House
Rear, 92 King Street
Tel (0565) 53974

A little alleyway running off the lower shopping street gives access to a coffee shop and the first Penny Farthing museum, set behind a furniture shop in a converted barn with conservatory extension. During the summer months customers can also eat at tables in a cobbled courtyard with bright floral displays. Three set afternoon tea menus are offered, as well as a table d'hôte selection of freshly-made sandwiches, homemade scones and such tempting cakes as hot gingerbread and almond and marsala flan, with China tea if preferred.

Pot of tea and one cake average, £1.85, set tea £3.10–£4.30
Open Mon–Sat

KNUTSFORD   Cheshire   Map 07 SJ77

Jane's Coffee Shop
117a King Street
Tel (0565) 51898

More than just a coffee shop, this small café in the main shopping street offers four set afternoon teas and an à la carte selection of locally baked cakes and pastries which includes such delectable items as brandy snaps filled with whipped cream and chocolate layer cake flavoured with neat brandy; a choice of speciality tea blends is served with either milk or lemon.

Pot of tea and one cake average £1.50, set tea £1.60–£4.50
Open every day

LACOCK   Wiltshire   Map 03 ST96

King John's Hunting Lodge
Tel (0249) 73313

The oldest house in the town, dating from the 1200s, provides a cosy atmosphere for afternoon tea, with polished tables, wooden chairs and a fire in winter. All the cakes and scones are baked on the premises and there is usually a choice of lemon, chocolate, coffee, carrot and fruitcake. Scones are served with clotted Jersey cream, strawberry preserve or local honey. A choice of loose tea blends is offered.

Pot of tea and one cake average £1.50, set tea £2.50
Open Mar–Oct, every day, 3pm until ready to close

LADOCK   Cornwall & Isles of Scilly   Map 02 SW85

Bissick Old Mill
Near Truro
Tel (0726) 882557

Tucked away off the main road in colourful, well-tended gardens and having its own car park, a slate-roofed stone mill building dating back 300 years serves tea at four round tables set with pretty floral crockery in a slate-floored dining room. The sideboard bears an array of such temptations as home-baked carrot or apple cake, chocolate fudge squares and Bakewell tart, and guests can choose between Indian, Assam or Earl Grey tea. Iron tables and chairs are set out on the terrace for warmer afternoons.

Pot of tea and one cake average £1.20, set teas £1.95–£2.50
Open all year, every day Light meals, bed and breakfast and self-catering cottage
[1] [3]

LAGGAN   Highland   Map 14 NN69

Kiln Room Coffee Shop
Caoldair Pottery
(Nr Laggan Bridge on the A889 Dalwhinnie road)
Tel (05284) 231

This pleasant coffee and tea shop is part of a small pottery and as you would expect, the teapots, cups and saucers are made here, as are the excellent homemade cakes, available in a large selection which includes coffee, chocolate, apple, spice and carrot cake. Laggan is set in beautiful countryside, with the Monadhliath Mountains to the north, and not far from the Highland Wildlife Park, so the pottery is a convenient port of call for anyone touring the area, and for those looking for an individual souvenir to take home, there is pottery on sale in the showroom.

Pot of tea and one cake average £1.20
Open Easter–Oct every day 9am–6pm
[1] [3]

LANARK   Strathclyde   Map 11 NS84

Daisies
18 Broomgate
Tel (0555) 65209

This bright, smart little tearoom is tucked away along a side street, but conveniently close to the car park at the bottom of the town's main street. An ever-changing selection of home baking includes such items as herb scones, tiffin, meringues and fruit pies. Earl Grey and lemon teas are available and light meals are also served.

Pot of tea and one cake average 85p
Open Mon–Sat 9am–5pm
Light meals

LAND'S END   Cornwall & Isles of Scilly   Map 02 SW42

The Old Manor House
Sennen
Tel (0736) 871280

The original Land's End Hotel, built around 1790, has a huge inglenook fireplace. The atmosphere is homely and meals are served all day by the jovial proprietors, Mr and Mrs Sedgwick. Homemade scones, carrot cake and traditional Cornish hevva cake are served for tea, with a choice of speciality teas including mixed fruit and mango.

Pot of tea and one cake average £1.10
Open all year (except Christmas), every day, 2pm–5pm (for tea)
[1] [3]

LANGHAM   Norfolk   Map 09 TG04

Langham Glass
Tel (0328) 830511

A gift shop, the glass marketing centre and a viewing area where visitors can watch skilled craftsmen at work at close quarters are also housed in the collection of flintstone outbuildings that surround this simply furnished tearoom. Its short menu offers a tasty range of sandwiches, savouries and snacks as well as scones, cakes, pastries and ice cream, with a good choice of tea blends.

Pot of tea and one cake average £1.05, set tea £2
Open all year, every day

LANGHOLM   Dumfries & Galloway   Map 11 NY38

Th'Auld Acquaintance
89 High Street
Tel (03873) 80573

Small and chintzy, with wood-panelled walls and cheerful red carpeting and table mats, this restaurant on two levels offers both high and afternoon teas. Freshly-made sandwiches – white and wholemeal bread with prawns, gammon ham or beef, for example – are popular, together with home-baked scones served with cream and jam; Earl Grey Darjeeling and Assam teas are available.

Pot of tea and one cake average 75p
Open Thu–Tue
Morning coffee, lunch, evening meal

LAVENHAM   Suffolk   Map 05 TL94

The Old Tea Shop
45–46 Church Street
Tel (0787) 247248

Thatched, timbered, and featuring leaded windows and an enormous inglenook fireplace, this character house opposite the church offers seven different set teas and a wide selection of snacks, desserts, ice creams, sandwiches and home-baked cakes, together with a choice of speciality tea blends; there is also a small but well-stocked gift shop.

Pot of tea and one cake £1.40, set teas £1.60–£2.50
Open all year Tue–Sun
Lunches

LAVENHAM   Suffolk   Map 05 TL94

The Swan
High Street
Tel (0787) 247477

Lavenham is probably one of the best surviving examples of a medieval town, and the Swan Hotel is an amalgamation of several old houses, including the Wool Hall. The lovely setting is further enhanced by a harpsichord recital on Saturday and Sunday. Cream tea is served with a choice of tea blends, or full afternoon tea comprising finger sandwiches, bridge rolls, scones and a selection of homemade cakes.

Pot of tea and one cake average £2.30, cream tea £4.50, full afternoon tea £6.95
Open all year, every day, tea served 3pm–5.30pm
Only full afternoon tea served on Sunday

LAVENHAM   Suffolk   Map 05 TL94

Tickle Manor Tearoom
17 High Street
Tel (0787) 248216/
248438

A pair of feet and a feather is the sign outside this 16th-century timber-framed house on the high street of this lovely Suffolk town. Cream teas, carrot or banana cake and many other good value items are available, as well as more substantial meals. Some speciality teas are offered and tea is served in a Port Meirion pot. Smoking is not permitted.

Pot of tea and one cake average £2.25, cream tea £2.85
Open all year (except 24–28 Dec), everyday, 10am–6pm

LEA   Derbyshire   Map 08 SK35

Lea Gardens
Matlock

Visitors to Lea Gardens – a unique collection of Rhododendrons, Azaleas and Alpine screes which is ablaze with colour during its short flowering season – can enjoy a varied selection of home-made cakes and biscuits in a teashop in the plant sales area; tea blends available include Earl Grey and herbal, and service is both friendly and helpful. A charge is made for entry to the gardens, but admission to the teashop is free.

Pot of tea and one cake average 90p
Open 20 Mar–mid Jul, every day, 10am–5.30pm

LEAMINGTON SPA (ROYAL)   Warwickshire   Map 04 SP36

Regency Fare Restaurant
86 Regent Street
Tel (0926) 425570

This establishment has moved two doors down the street and has exactly reproduced the shop interior in Regency style. Popular with locals, the restaurant has a reputation for good home cooking. Breakfast, coffee, light lunches and afternoon tea are served. Pancakes and strawberry cream sponges are particular favourites. Standard blend, plus Earl Grey and herb tea are offered, served in china crockery.

Pot of tea 52p, set teas £1.85–£3
Open all year, Mon–Sat (except bank holidays), 9am–5.30pm
Lunches
[1] [2] [3]

LEAMINGTON SPA (ROYAL)   Warwickshire   Map 04 SP36

Roosters
37–39 Oxford Street
Tel (0926) 426881

An open plan delicatessen/bistro, the delicatessen offers a fine selection of cheeses from a stock list of 400. The bistro area has an open cold display, cabinet and blackboard menu from which to choose. Friendly staff will recommend the popular chocolate brandy cake and apple pie. Light lunches, snacks, afternoon tea and evening meals are served. A choice of speciality teas is available.

Pot of tea 50p, cream tea £1.50
Open all year, Mon–Sat and Sun lunch, 9am–10pm
Lunch, dinner

LECHLADE   Gloucestershire   Map 03 SU29

Katie's Tearoom and Gift Shop
Marlborough House
High Street
Tel (0367) 52273

This is a small, cosy Cotswold tearoom, to the rear of the gift shop, furnished in cottage style. Morning coffee and afternoon tea are served with homemade teacakes, scones, cakes and pastries, soups and sandwiches, and traditional English puddings and sweets. A choice of tea blends is available served with quality bone china. Smoking is not permitted.

Pot of tea 55p, Cotswold cream tea £2.10
Open all year, every day, 9.30am–6pm
Times vary according to season

LEEDS   West Yorkshire   Map 08 SE33

The Georgian Tea Room
Waterloo Antiques Centre
Crown Street
Tel (0532) 444187/ 423194

This charming little tearoom on the second floor of the Waterloo Antiques Centre – over 40 shops in the ancient White Cloth Hall – is brightly decorated in pink and green with fresh flowers on its lace-clothed tables. Worth seeking out for its excellent scones and good range of home-made cakes, it also offers sandwiches, salads and snacks together with a choice of tea blends and very good coffee.

Pot of tea and one cake average £1
Open all year, Tue–Sat 10am–5pm

LEICESTER   Leicestershire   Map 04 SK50

Peacock Alley
62–64 High Street
Tel (0533) 539093

This is a light, spacious 1920s-style establishment with palm trees, pastel décor, circular clothed tables and bentwood chairs. Recently extended, Peacock Alley is now open some evenings. Homemade cakes, gâteaux and scones, savoury pies, hot meals and snacks are served. A choice of 45 tea blends is offered and tea is well presented in white pots with strainers.

Pot of tea 65p, cream tea £2.20
Open all year, every day, 10am–8.30pm
Lunch, dinner
1 3

LEOMINSTER   Hereford & Worcester   Map 03 SO45

The Lower Hundred Craft Workshop
Kimbolton (just off the A49, north of Leominster)
Tel (058472) 240

This converted stone barn now houses a craft workshop, sale room and a pleasant little no smoking tearoom. Homemade cakes, a good cup of tea and friendly service can be enjoyed in pleasant surroundings.

Cup of tea 32p
Open Apr–Oct, daily, 10am–5.30pm, Nov daily 10am–5pm, Dec Sat and Sun 10am–5pm

LEWES   East Sussex   Map 05 TQ41

The Coffee Shop
White Hart Hotel
High Street
Tel (0273) 473794

A small coffee shop is within this historic hotel. The building has Tudor origins and there are beams, wood panelling and low ceilings. Cane armchairs are clustered in fours and there is friendly waitress service. Homemade scones and gâteaux are served with a choice of standard blend or Earl Grey tea.

Set tea £1.60–£3.20
Open all year, every day, 10am–10pm
1 2 3

LEWIS, ISLE OF   Western Isles   Map 13 NB23

Callanish Tearoom
18 Callanish
Tel (085172) 373

A red-brick house near the Callanish Stones has been converted to provide a craft shop and a pleasant, spotlessly-clean teashop serving a small range of homemade cakes with Earl Grey, Indian or herbal tea.

Pot of tea and one cake average 80p
Open May–Sep, Mon–Sat, 11am–5pm

LEWIS, ISLE OF   Western Isles   Map 13 NA65

Harbour View
Callicvol
Tel (0851 81) 735

What must be Britain's most north-westerly tearoom – originally a boat builder's house dating from 1800 – serves a selection of fine teas, sandwiches and excellent homemade cakes on neatly-clothed tables in a charming little room with a stone floor and a real fire; a small display of local produce and crafts is also offered for sale.

Pot of tea and one cake average £1.20, set tea £2
Open Easter–Oct Mon–Sat

LEYBURN   North Yorkshire   Map 07 SE19

Clyde House Tea Room
5 Railway Road
Tel (0969) 23941

Pretty, cottage-style tearooms on the southern edge of this busy little town's market square offer Darjeeling, Assam or Earl Grey tea (loose leaf) with hot snacks, salads, sandwiches, scones, fruit loaves and a selection of mainly home-baked cakes. An adjacent restaurant, open on Thursday, Friday and Saturday evenings, serves a traditional range of freshly-cooked meals.

Pot of tea and one cake average £1.25, set tea £2.60
Open Tue–Sat
Hot and cold snacks
3 (£10 minimum)

LIFTON   Devon   Map 02 SX38

Thatched Cottage
Sprytown
Tel (0566) 84224

Just one hundred yards from the A30, between Oakhampton and Launceston, a delightful thatched cottage in two-and-a-half-acre grounds offers afternoon tea in either of its two attractive restaurants, in the lounge and in the gardens. In this relaxed, friendly atmosphere, guests can enjoy a Devon cream tea, or sandwiches ranging from chicken to smoked halibut with homemade scones (served warm) and cakes; the selection of teas includes herbal and fruit blends as well as standard, China and Earl Grey.

Pot of tea and one cake average £1.20, set teas £1.20–£2.25
Open all year, every day, 8.30am–9.30pm
Lunches, à la carte/table d'hôte dinners
Accommodations in 4 annexe bedrooms
1 2 3

LIMPLEY STOKE   Wiltshire   Map 03 ST76

The Cliffe Hotel
Crowe Hill
Tel (0225) 723871

This small country house hotel, set high above the Avon Valley with views of wooded countryside, offers tea in its attractive lounge; a limited range of individual items is available as well as the cream and full afternoon teas, and a range of tea blends is served.

Pot of tea and one cake average £2, set teas £1.75–£6
Open every day
1 2 3

LINCOLN   Lincolnshire   Map 07 SK97

Bishops Table
7 Eastgate Street
Tel (0522) 26442/
511280

This newly opened establishment is part of the Hair, Beauty and Leisure Salon, owned and supervised by Elizabeth Freedman, for use by regular clients and visitors to Lincoln. In the style of the Stuarts, the Bishops Table offers a salad bar, light meals and traditional afternoon teas, carefully presented with bone china.

Pot of tea 55p
Open all year, every day,
10am–4pm
Light meals
1 3

LINCOLN   Lincolnshire   Map 07 SK97

Whites of Lincoln
The Jews House
15 The Strait
Steep Hill
Tel (0522) 524851

A fine little restaurant which has been continuously occupied as a house for over 800 years – the longest in Europe. It is comfortably furnished with antiques, and because of its size and style children, unfortunately, are not allowed. Lunch is served until 2pm, then afternoon tea with quality flans, scones and teacakes, but the undoubted favourite is the spectacular Charlotte Royale.

Pot of tea 60p, special tea
£1.30
Open Feb–Dec, every day
high season, 6 days winter,
12 noon–5pm and
7.30pm–8.45pm
Lunch
1 3

LITTLE WALSINGHAM   Norfolk   Map 09 TF93

Sue Ryder Coffee Shop
High Street
Tel (0328) 820622

Part of the Sue Ryder charitable organisation, standing adjacent to the Sue Ryder Gift Shop in a red-brick terrace on the High Street, this simply furnished coffee shop offers an attractive display of scones, cakes and pastries, a set tea being available if booked in advance, with an à la carte menu of more substantial items.

Pot of tea and one cake £1,
set tea £2
Open all year, every day,
9.30am–5.30pm

LITTLE WALSINGHAM   Norfolk   Map 09 TF93

Swallows
15 High Street
Tel (0328) 820555

A restaurant at the heart of this picturesque village which was once the pilgrim centre of England, parts of its flintstone construction dating back to the 16th century. Meals and snacks are served throughout the day, the set afternoon tea comprising scones with buttered crumpets or teacakes and a pot of tea chosen from a range of a dozen blends; sandwiches (made to order) are also available.

Pot of tea and one cake
85p, set teas £2–
£2.35
Open Feb–Dec, every day,
7.45am–8pm

LIVERPOOL   Merseyside   Map 07 SJ39

The Britannia Adelphi
Ranelagh Place
Tel 051–709 7200

The Grand Lounge – aptly named, with its ballroom dimensions, marble pillars and chandeliers – is the setting for tea at this long-established hotel. Indian, lapsang, Earl Grey or lemon tea accompany freshly-prepared sandwiches and homemade scones and pastries, the three set menus representing particularly good value for money to the senior citizens for whom a concession is made from Monday to Friday.

Pot of tea and one cake
average £2.10, set teas
£2.75–£5.25
Open every day

LIVERPOOL Merseyside Map 07 SJ39

The Gallery Coffee Shop
Tate Gallery
Albert Dock
Tel 051 – 709 3223 ext 2211

This self service coffee shop is situated on the mezzanine floor of the Tate Gallery in the recreated Albert Dock complex. Scones, shortbread, cheesecake and gâteaux are baked on the premises, and savoury options include oatcakes with Lancashire cheese, quiche, homemade soup and imaginative salads which use fresh herbs; hot and cold main course 'specials' are also available.

Pot of tea and one cake average £1.10
Open all year except Christmas Day, Boxing Day and New Years Day, Tue – Sun, 11am – 6.45pm

LIVERPOOL Merseyside Map 07 SJ39

Liverpool Cathedral Refectory
St James' Road
Tel 051 – 709 3160

Housed in the Welsford Porch, on the north side of Britain's largest cathedral, and reached through the bookshop, a modern self-service refectory – its wooden tables attractively arranged beside the massive stone pillars – serves a choice of speciality teas with a delicious range of home-baked cakes, biscuits, pies and scones. Light snacks are also available at lunch time.

Pot of tea and one cake average £1
Open every day
Light lunches

LIVERPOOL Merseyside Map 07 SJ39

Lucy's Coffee Shop
Unit 11, Britannia Pavilion
Albert Dock
Tel 051 – 709 5277

A busy, glass-fronted coffee/tea shop in Victorian style, housed in the Albert Dock complex's award-winning Britannia Pavilion, displays a wide range of homemade cakes, scones, pastries and gâteaux on a large wooden dresser; freshly made sandwiches and light snacks are also available, and there is a choice of tea blends.

Pot of tea and one cake average £1.25
Open every day

LIVERPOOL Merseyside Map 07 SJ39

Waterfront Café
Albert Dock
Tel 051 – 207 0001

This little café in the former pilotage building forms part of the Merseyside Maritime Museum, which itself is incorporated into the Albert Dock complex with its many activities and areas of interest. Scones and cakes are served, with sandwiches, salads, soup, quiche and baked potatoes. Tea is served in red plastic pots.

Pot of tea 40p, cakes 35p – 85p
Open Easter – Oct, daily (except Christmas, New Year and Good Fri), 10.30am – 5.30pm (last admission 4.30pm)
Light meals

LLANARMOM DYFFRYN CEIRIOG Clwyd Map 07 SJ13

Hand Hotel
Tel (069 176) 666

A charming hotel in a lovely setting; tea here is served in the lounge where a welcoming log fire burns in winter or in fine weather one may sit outside. Homemade biscuits, toasted teacakes and scones are available with a choice of tea blends.

Pot of tea 70p, cream tea £1.65
Open mid Mar – Jan, every day, 8am – 10pm

LLANBEDR   Gwynedd   Map 06 SH52

Maes Artro Village
Tel (034123) 467

This purpose-built tea/coffee shop, with additional patio seating beside a lily pond, forms part of an extensive complex (entrance £2 adults, £1.50 OAP'S and children) whose attractions include an aquarium, village and RAF museums, craft and souvenir shops, nature walks and a children's playground. Hot snack meals and sandwiches are available, as well as scones, bara brith and assorted cakes.

Pot of tea and one cake average £1.10
Open Easter–Oct, every day 10am–5.30pm
Hot snacks

LLANDEILO   Dyfed   Map 02 SN62

Brynawel Guest House
19 New Road
Tel (0558) 822925

This modern, all-day restaurant, part of the adjoining guest house, features wood panelling, polished tables and a serving bar offering a good range of freshly made sandwiches, pastries and fresh cream cakes; tea blends include Breakfast Special, Afternoon Brew, Ceylon and Earl Grey. A la carte and children's menus are also available, providing snacks and light meals, and a traditional Sunday lunch.

Pot of tea and one cake average 90p, cream tea £1.50
Open all year, every day
Evening meals (à la carte)
1 3

LLANDEILO   Dyfed   Map 02 SN62

Café Royal Patisserie
King Street
Tel (0558) 822908

This small café near the church has polished floorboards, linen covered tables and a cosy atmosphere. A wide choice of tea blends is offered along with homemade eclairs, meringues, gâteaux and pastries. Snacks such as pizzas and pies are also served.

Pot of tea and one cake £1.25
Open all year, Mon–Sat, 8.30am–5.30pm, daily
Snack meals

LLANDEILO   Dyfed   Map 02 SN62

Cawdor Arms Hotel
Tel (0558) 823500

A comfortable Georgian house hotel, the Cawdor Arms offers a lounge service where one may enjoy tea with scones, jam and cream in elegant surroundings.

Tea 80p
Open all year, every day
1 3

LLANDEILO   Dyfed   Map 02 SN62

Plough Inn
Rhosmaen
Tel (0558) 823431

An inn beside the A40 a mile from Llandeilo serves afternoon tea in the first-floor lounge which looks out over the park designed by Capability Brown. As an alternative to the set cream and Welsh teas, guests can select individual items from a range of scones, teacakes and pastries, with Earl Grey or Darjeeling available as well as the standard tea blend.

Pot of tea and one cake £2, set tea £2.50
Open all year, every day

LLANDEILO Dyfed   Map 02 SN62

Trapp Art and Crafts Centre
Tel (0269) 850362

Part of the crafts centre, this is a clean, bright, well maintained tearoom on two floors with waitress service. Homemade scones, shortbread, bara brith and gingerbread are served, and there is a choice of standard blend, Earl Grey or lemon tea.

Pot of tea and scone 80p
Open Nov–Christmas,
Mar–Easter, 11am–
5.30pm, Easter–Oct every day 11am–5.30pm (Jul–Aug to 7pm)
Lunches

LLANDOVERY Dyfed   Map 03 SN73

The Coffee House
High Street

A small café with plastic covered tablecloths and wheel-back chairs. Homemade cakes, scones, Welsh cakes and sandwiches are served from a small counter, and home-cooked hot dishes such as lasagne, jacket potatoes and ham quiche.

Cup of tea and scone 75p
Open all year

LLANDRILLO Clwyd   Map 06 SJ03

Tyddnllan Country House
Tel (049084) 264

This delightful country house hotel, privately owned and personally run, stands on the edge of the village. In the tranquillity of its pleasant, comfortable lounge – or in the garden if weather permits – you can sample freshly made sandwiches, a range of home-baked scones, cakes and biscuits, cream teas and a choice of tea blends.

Pot of tea and one cake average £2.50
Open every day 3–5pm for afternoon tea

LLANDRINDOD WELLS Powys   Map 03 SO06

Aspidistra Restaurant
Station Cresent
Tel (0597) 822949

Set at the centre of this spa town, a restaurant with pretty oilcloth table coverings and modern seating offers soup, jacket potatoes and a good range of snacks as well as sandwiches, toasted teacakes, scones and pastries. Earl Grey, Darjeeling and herbal teas are available as an alternative to the standard blend.

Pot of tea and one cake average 80p
Open Mon–Sat, 10am–5pm, Sun 11.30am–4.30pm

LLANDUDNO Gwynedd   Map 06 SH78

Habit Tearooms
12 Mustyn Street
Tel (0492) 75043

A green fronted shop on the main street. The green theme is continued inside with polished pine tables, high-backed cane chairs, prints and pot plants. There is a good display of homemade cakes and scones, and China, Indian, Earl Grey and lemon teas are served loose leaf in the pot with a strainer.

Pot of tea and one cake average £1.10
Open all year, every day, 10m–5.30pm, closed Sun Nov–Mar

LLANDUDNO   Gwynedd   Map 06 SH78

St Tudno Hotel
North Parade
Tel (0492) 874411

The St Tudno is a charming sea-front hotel, run by very hospitable owners who are always on hand to welcome you. The hotel restaurant has a very high reputation for its food and its excellent standards are demonstrated in the delicious scones, meringues, flans and pastries or freshly made sandwiches. There is a wide choice of tea blends, including some fruit-flavoured teas, which make an interesting change from the normal range. The lounges are beautifully furnished and you can be sure of a comfortable and relaxing atmosphere.

Pot of tea and one cake average £2.85, set tea £4.50, sandwiches from £1.50
Open every day, except for first two weeks of January, 7.30am–midnight
1 2 3

LLANDUDNO   Gwynedd   Map 06 SH78

Sandbach
78A Mustyn Street
Tel (0492) 76522

A delightful little teashop, situated on the first floor of a charming shop selling handmade chocolates and sweets. The pretty teashop is an area displaying greetings cards, handmade glass and pictures. A selection of cakes, pastries and biscuits is served from the trolley, and there are teacakes and ices. Hot and cold snacks and lunches are available, and a good range of teas and freshly ground coffees.

Pot of tea 55p, Welsh afternoon tea £2.65
Open all year, Mon–Sat, 9.30am–5.15pm
Lunch

LLANFAIR KILGEDDIN   Gwent   Map 03 SO30

Oaklands
Tel (0873) 840218/
880584

Set in attractive lawns and woodland, just off the B4235 Usk to Abergavenny road, tea is served outside in good weather and indoors at other times. Ploughman's, quiche and sandwiches are available, along with scones, apple pie, bara brith, Welsh cakes and sponges.

Pot of tea and one cake average £1
Open every day

LLANFAIR PWLLGWYNGYLL   Gwynedd   Map 06 SH57

Sidings Restaurant and Coffee Shop, James Pringle Woollen Mill
Station Site
Tel (0248) 717171

Situated next to the station with the very long name, the Sidings is in the large quality-clothing shop. The self-service restaurant is split-level with a tiled floor, polished wooden tables and matching chairs with padded seats. Hot lunches, salads and teas are served, with a good selection of cakes and a choice of six tea blends.

Pot of tea 52p
Open all year, every day except Christmas Day and Boxing Day, 9am–5.30pm (10.30am–5pm Sun)
Lunch

LLANGEFNI   Gwynedd   Map 06 SH47

The Whole Thing
5 Field Street
Tel (0248) 724832

This bright, fresh little wholefood restaurant and coffee shop is situated over a popular wholefood shop. The décor is simple but pleasant in a country style, with plain walls and carpets, pine furniture and pictures for sale. A really excellent display of home baking, including flapjacks and carrot cake, is offered, and a choice of teas is available. There is a daily blackboard menu for wholefood, wholesome hot dishes such as lentil, carrot and coriander soup and pasta vegetable bake. Smoking is not permitted.

Open all year, Mon–Fri, 9am–5.30pm
Lunch

LLANGURIG   Powys   Map 06 SN98

The Old Vicarage
Tel (05515) 280

A small guest house standing beside the road from Llangurig to LLanidloes – shortly to be left in a cul-de-sac when this road is re-routed – offers a tea-time menu of sandwiches, scones, Welsh cakes, bara brith and a choice of cakes, all home-baked, with a good selection of tea blends. Teas are served in a pleasant lounge, or on the lawn in good weather.

Pot of tea and one cake average £1.10
Open Wed–Mon

LLANRHAEADR   Clwyd   Map 06 SJ06

The Lodge
Tel (074578) 370

This former lodge on the main A525 has been converted into an exclusive ladies' clothing shop and teashop. Light lunches and homemade cakes, including carrot cake, sponges and cheesecakes, are available and there is also a small dispenser bar. Standard blend, lemon and China tea is served with Hornsea pottery.

Pot of tea and one cake average £1
Open all year, Mon–Sat (except bank holidays), 9.30am–5.30pm, Mar–end Sep, 10am–5pm Oct–Mar
Light lunches
1 3

LLANRWST   Gwynedd   Map 06 SH86

The Old Tannery
Willow Street
Tel (0492) 640185

Part of an antique shop and kitchen display, old tables, church pews and chairs are situated among antique furniture, clocks and pot plants, creating a pleasant atmosphere enhanced by friendly service. Homemade cakes and scones are served with pizzas, various snacks and sandwiches.

Pot of tea and one cake average 90p
Open all year, every day, 9am–5pm
Snack meals
3

LLANRWST   Gwynedd   Map 06 SH86

Tu Hwnt I'r Bont
Tel (0492) 640138

In this delightful, stonebuilt 15th century court house, situated on the river bank next to the bridge where the B5106 meets the A470, cottage-style ground-floor tearooms with low beamed ceilings and inglenook fireplaces offer home-baked scones, bara brith and sandwich cake, with a choice of tea blends. The first floor of the building is occupied by a shop selling books, craft items and bric-à-brac.

Pot of tea and one cake average £1.10, set teas £1.10–£3
Open Easter–end Sep, Tue–Sun 10.30am–5.30pm

LLANTWIT MAJOR   South Glamorgan   Map SS96

Major Café
East Street
Tel (0446) 7942922

This small self-service café is a few steps up from the entrance at street level. The menu offers mainly hot meals and snacks, but homemade Welsh cakes, fancy cakes, apple pie, gâteaux and cheesecakes are also served.

Pot of tea and one cake average 70p
Open all year except Christmas Day, Boxing Day and New Years Day, Mon–Sat, 9am–5.30pm, Sun 11am–5pm
Lunches

LLANTWIT MAJOR   South Glamorgan   Map 03 SS96

West House Hotel
West Street
Tel (0446) 792406

Set afternoon teas, or individual items accompanied by coffee or tea (Indian/Earl Grey), are served in the very modern conservatory-lounge or equally comfortable bar-lounge of this hotel which offers a full range of facilities.

Pot of tea and one cake average £2.05, set tea £2.95
Open every day
1 2 3

LLANWDDYN   Powys   Map 06 SJ01

Lake Vyrnwy Hotel
Tel (069173) 692

A high quality hotel with excellent views of Lake Vyrnwy serves an afternoon tea menu including scones with jam and cream, bara brith and gâteaux in its elegant lounge or bars; full hotel services are available.

Pot of tea and one cake average £1.80
Open every day
1 2 3

LLANWRTYD WELLS   Powys   Map 03 SN84

Cambrian Woollen Mill
Tel (05913) 211

This simply furnished tearoom stands above the shop attached to an authentic woollen mill (tours conducted at set times), and at its self-service counter guests can take their pick from homemade Welsh cakes, biscuits and cakes.

Pot of tea and one cake average 65p
Open summer Mon–Fri, 8.15am–5.15pm, winter Sat 8.15am–1.15pm
1 3

LLYSWEN   Powys   Map 03 SO13

Llangoed Hall
Tel (0874) 754525

Formal afternoon teas are served in a choice of three lounges at a splendid country house, very tastefully converted to hotel use, set in the lovely Wye Valley beside the A470 just north of the village. Sandwiches, scones, biscuits and cakes are of excellent quality, the range of teas available includes China, Earl Grey and herbal blends, and service is friendly. There is terrace seating when the weather permits.

Pot of tea and one cake average £2.50, set tea £6.50
Open all year, every day
[1] [2] [3]

LLYSWEN   Powys   Map 03 SO13

The Pottery
Tel (0874) 754388

Part of the pottery and shop that stand at the centre of the village (alongside the A438 at its junction with the A470), a tearoom furnished with pine chairs and modern round tables attractively decked with fresh flowers offers standard or Earl Grey tea accompanied by a range of cakes, toasted teacakes, Welsh cakes and scones.

Pot of tea and one cake average 85p
Open Wed–Mon
[1] [3]

LLYS-Y-FRÂN   Dyfed   Map 02 SN02

Llys-Y-Frân Centre
Llys-y-Frân Reservoir and Dam
Tel (09913) 273

A good range of meals, snacks, cream teas, scones, pastries and cakes – together with a good pot of tea – are served in this completely modern, spacious and well-furnished restaurant which forms part of the shops and complex overlooking the reservoir with its extensive fishing facilities and other leisure activities. The centre is situated three miles north-east of the Clarbeston road.

Pot of tea and one cake average £1.40
Open Easter–Oct, every day 10am–dark

LOCHEARNHEAD   Central   Map 11 NN52

The Golden Larches
Balquidder Station
Tel (05673) 262

A purpose-built restaurant with pine tables and chairs stands beside the A84 two miles south of the town, opposite what used to be Balquidder Station. Though hot dishes and snacks predominate, cream teas are available, together with an appetising selection of such home-baked items as shortbread, pies and cakes – including the intriguing Mars Bar cake! The traditional Scottish high tea consists of a hot main course with toast and a pot of tea, followed by scones and cakes.

Pot of tea and one cake average £1, set tea £1.60
Open mid Mar–Oct, every day 10am–8pm
Hot meals and snacks

LOCHGILPHEAD   Strathclyde   Map 10 NR88

The Smiddy
Smithy Lane
Tel (0546) 3606

This little gem is tucked away in a lane behind the main shopping area. Once the smithy stables, it is now a popular cottage-style coffee shop and licensed bistro. Only fresh, whole, natural food is served, with vegetarian dishes and seafood featuring strongly. The superb home baking includes florentines, peanut butter slices, and oatmeal toffee cake, but the moist passion cake is particularly recommended. A choice of leaf teas, including herbal, is available. Smoking is not permitted.

Pot of tea and one cake average £1.15
Open all year, every day, summer Mon–Sat 10am–10pm, Sun noon–8pm, winter Mon–Thu 10am–5.30pm, Fri–Sat 10am–10pm
Lunch, dinner
3

LOCHINVER   Highland   Map 14 NC02

Achins Book & Coffee Shop
Inverkirkaig
Tel (05714) 262

A timber-built book, craft and coffee shop three and a half miles south west of Lochinver, the interior is cheery with plain white walls adorned with prints and craft goods and furnished in pine. A selection of mostly home-baked produce is served along with hot meals such as baked potatoes, homemade soup and a speciality nut roast. Filled rolls are also available, and there is a choice of tea and herbal infusions.

Pot of tea and one cake from 75p
Open Mon–Sat
Light meals

LONDON NW3

Holiday Inn
128 King Henry's Road
Swiss Cottage
Tel 071–722 7711

A busy modern, cosmopolitan hotel where tea is served by pleasant, helpful staff in the comfortable lounge. A good selection of gâteaux, cheesecakes and sandwiches is available, and a choice of tea blends is offered.

Pot of tea £1.50, set afternoon tea £7.50
Open all year, every day, 10am–10.30pm, tea served 3pm–5pm
1 2 3 &

LONDON SW1

The Chinoiserie,
Hyatt Carlton Tower
Cadogan Place
Tel 071–235 5411

This luxurious, modern, five star hotel just off Sloane Street is well placed to revive you after shopping either in Knightsbridge or in Chelsea. Afternoon tea is served in its delightful Chinoiserie Lounge, which is famous for its spectacular arrangements of fresh flowers. As a background to the ritual of afternoon tea, harp music plays softly in the afternoons. Speciality teas include some quite unusual ones – China rose petal, Russian caravan, Japan cherry, China black, jasmine, gunpowder, as well as Darjeeling, Earl Grey and mint. Sandwiches, scones and pastries are served by friendly waiters and waitresses.

Pot of tea and one cake average £7, set tea £10.50
Open daily for tea 3–5.30pm
[1] [2] [3]

LONDON SW1

Hyde Park Hotel
Knightsbridge
Tel 071–235 2000

Views over Hyde Park from the delightful Park Room Restaurant help you to relax over the delicious afternoon teas served in this traditional English hotel. Pastries, scones and gâteaux may be accompanied by a choice of teas – Darjeeling, Assam, Earl Grey, Lapsang Souchong – or infusions, for example, spice, imperial, vanilla, all served in excellent silver and fine china.

Set tea £10.50
Open every day 4–6pm
[1] [2] [3]

LONDON SW1

Stafford Hotel
St James's Place
Tel 071–493 0111

Sister to the famous Ritz Hotel, and only a few minutes' walk away in St James's, the Stafford is a peaceful haven just off Piccadilly and close to Green Park. Afternoon tea is served in the elegant lounge, and the choice of teas, besides Indian or China, includes mint and various herbal blends. The set afternoon tea begins with a selection of dainty finger sandwiches, followed by toasted scones with jam and cream, and ends with a choice of homemade patisseries. The service is highly professional, which, together with the fine china and luxurious setting, helps to create a soothing atmosphere in which to relax after a busy day.

Full afternoon tea £8
Open daily 3–5.30pm

[1] [2] [3]

LONDON SW19

Cannizaro House
West Side
Wimbledon Common
Tel 071–879 1464

Standing in gardens on the edge of Wimbledon Common, this is a most attractive, historic building, beautifully transformed into a luxurious hotel. The elegant drawing room, with its comfortable chairs, antiques and paintings, is the elegant setting for afternoon teas, with homemade scones, fruit cake, strawberry tartlets, shortbread and a range of excellent patisseries and sandwich triangles. A good choice of tea varieties includes China White Point, jasmine, Assam, Darjeeling, Earl Grey, mango and passion fruit, and they are nicely served in china pots by an efficient staff.

Afternoon teas £5.50–£8.50
Open all year, every day, 3pm–5.30pm
1 2 3 &

LONDON W1

Britannia Inter-Continental
Grosvenor Square
Tel 071–629 9400

A modern comfortable lounge is the setting for afternoon tea in this popular and luxurious hotel overlooking Grosvenor Square. A range of tea blends is available to accompany the selection of sandwiches, homemade scones, cakes and gâteaux.

Pot of tea £1.75, afternoon tea £7.95
Open all year, every day, 3pm–5.30pm
1 2 3

LONDON W1

Browns Hotel
Albermarle and Dover Streets
Tel 071–493 6020

This most English of hotels now spans 12 houses, and preservation orders ensure that their appearance and decorative detail are preserved amid the luxury shops and galleries of Mayfair. Inside, oak panelling and stained glass contribute to the calm and discreet atmosphere. Tea is served in the lounge in 'Hathaway Rose' bone china and you can choose from a wide range of Indian, China and herbal teas. Refreshments, brought by the professional, cheerful staff, comprise sandwiches, brown bread and butter and preserves, toasted, buttered scones with clotted cream, and delectable homemade cakes and pastries.

Set tea £10.50
Open every day 3–6pm
Gentlemen are requested to wear a jacket and tie
1 2 3

Churchill Hotel
Portman Square
Tel 071–486 5800

This modern hotel has a sunken lounge where a harpist entertains and fresh flowers are displayed amid glittering chandeliers. Full afternoon tea is served, comprising finger sandwiches, homemade fruit scone with Devonshire cream and strawberry jam, and assorted pastries. Loose-leaf tea is well served and a choice of blends is offered.

Pot of tea £2, set tea from £9.75 (£6 for children under 10 years)
Open all year, every day, 3pm–5.30pm
1 2 3

Claridges Hotel
Brook Street
Tel 071–629 8860

One of London's most famous hotels, Claridges serves its afternoon teas with style, as befits a distinguished hotel, accustomed to catering for the needs of guests who may be members of royal houses, stars of stage and screen, or international business tycoons. The setting for tea is the lounge foyer, which leads off the impressive marbled and pillared entrance hall. Service, by tail-coated staff, is excellent; the tea, whether you take Earl Grey, Assam, Lapsang Souchong or one of the various herbal infusions is fresh and well flavoured, the scones, French pastries and gâteaux are as delicious as one would expect from the chefs here.

Set tea £9
Open every day, 4–5.15pm
1 2 3

Cumberland Hotel
Marble Arch
Tel 071–262 1234

The hotel is nicely placed to attract weary Oxford Street shoppers, being close to Marble Arch. Traditional afternoon tea is served in the comfortable lounge, or a coffee shop provides lighter refreshments. Both lounge and coffee shop have table service.

Pot of tea and one cake average £4.75, set tea in lounge from £6
Open 3pm–5.30pm for afternoon tea, beverages, pastries and gâteaux available 7am–6pm
1 2 3

Grafton Hotel
Tottenham Court Road
Tel 071–388 4131

Conveniently situated at the northern end of Tottenham Court Road, this is a lively hotel, its spacious lounge has comfortable armchairs and sofas and is decorated with numerous pictures. Pleasant waitresses serve a choice of tea blends with biscuits or accompanying a full afternoon tea of sandwiches, scones and cakes.

Tea and biscuits £1.20, set tea £7
Open all year, every day, 3pm–5pm

LONDON W1

Inn on the Park
Hamilton Terrace,
Park Lane
Tel 071–499 0888

Many people would rate this as the best modern hotel in London. The marble-floored entrance hall, with its beautiful fresh flowers leads into the foyer lounge where very pleasant waitresses take your order for tea as you settle into the comfortable armchairs. There are two set teas, and speciality tea blends include gunpowder and Queen Mary's. Scones, French pastries and gâteaux are all freshly made and delicious.

Set teas £9 and £10
Open every day 3–6pm
1️⃣ 2️⃣ 3️⃣ ♿

LONDON W1

London Hilton on Park Lane
22 Park Avenue
Tel 071–493 8000

Traditional afternoon tea is served daily in the Café Brasserie, just off the lobby of this famous international hotel. Tables are laid with bone china and fine silver, and scones, French pastries and gâteaux – all made on the premises – are accompanied by a choice of tea blends. Pastries are available for takeaway at the chocolaterie counter.

Set tea £9.50
Open all year, every day, 3–6pm for afternoon tea
1️⃣ 2️⃣ 3️⃣ ♿

LONDON W1

Marriott Hotel, Regent Lounge
Grosvenor Square
Tel 071–493 1232

This charming hotel lounge overlooking Grosvenor Square is a relatively undiscovered oasis in the heart of Mayfair, and makes an ideal afternoon rendezvous. Full traditional afternoon teas, with sandwiches, scones and cake, or Devonshire cream teas are served in style, or if you prefer, you can have a selection of mouth-watering sandwiches or excellent pastries and gâteaux from the trolley. Specialities like Viennese Sacher Torte or New York cheesecake are hard to resist. Tea is freshly made and nicely served in china teapots by helpful waitresses. There is a choice of five different speciality teas and blends; ice cream and various coffees are also available.

Pot of tea £1.50, pastries and gâteaux £3.50, full afternoon tea £7.45
Open daily 3–5pm
1️⃣ 2️⃣ 3️⃣

Oak Room Lounge, Le Meridien
Piccadilly
Tel 071–734 8000

Owned by Air France, this de luxe, five-star hotel at the very centre of London has all the elegance associated with the interior décor of France, with chandeliers and mirrors everywhere, and spacious rooms with attractive, ornamental ceilings. The twenty four teas on offer include various blends of Indian and China tea, as well as Russian caravan, Kenyan and Ceylon orange pekoe. French pastries and gâteaux are the highlights of afternoon tea here, but there are also traditional English scones and sultana buns.

Pot of tea and one cake average £3.95, set tea £8.50
Open every day 3pm–6pm for afternoon tea
1 2 3 &

Park Lane Hotel
Piccadilly
Tel 071–499 6321

The Park Lane Hotel offers an excellent selection of herbal teas, China teas – gunpowder, China rose, passion fruit and jasmine – as well as the more usual Ceylon, Assam and Darjeeling. The setting is the Palm Court Lounge, a long-established, popular rendezvous with an elegant 1920s atmosphere, live piano music to entertain the clientèle, and pleasant service. You can have a full afternoon tea, or choose fresh or toasted sandwiches – perhaps a three-layered toasted sandwich of egg, bacon, chicken, tomato, or perhaps mayonnaise and coleslaw. The homemade cakes and pastries are excellent.

Pot of tea £1.75, set tea £7.25, pastries £2.20
Open daily for snacks 10am–11pm, set afternoon tea 3–6pm
1 2 3

Portman Intercontinental
22 Portman Square
Tel 071–486 5844

In the spacious foyer-lounge of this modern, international hotel, close to Oxford Street and Marble Arch, formal afternoon teas are served by polite waitresses. Guests enjoy excellent sandwiches, particularly good scones (served hot, with clotted cream), delicious pastries and a choice of tea blends that includes Earl Grey, China and Darjeeling.

Set tea around £8
Open all year, every day

LONDON W1

Richoux
172 Piccadilly
Tel 071–493 2204

A popular café-restaurant in the old English style with lovely decorated glass and fine floral prints. The alcoved banquette seating and rather close marble-topped tables, fresh flowers and waitresses in attractive Victorian dress make for a pleasant atmosphere in which to enjoy tea after a busy day's shopping. There is a display of homemade pâtisserie, a set English tea with hot baby scones, and a range of ice cream sundaes. A choice of Twinings teas is offered with herbal infusions, lemon tea and coffee in various forms, including iced tea and coffee.

Pot of tea and one cake average £3.75, set tea £5.75
Open daily 8.30am– 11.30pm

LONDON W1

Ritz Hotel
Piccadilly
Tel 071–493 8181

No other English hotel has such strong associations with afternoon tea as the Ritz, where the Palm Court Lounge is a byword for elegance and preserves an Edwardian atmosphere, with its pink-cupped chandeliers, rose-coloured Louis XVI chairs and marble tables. The Palm Court is very popular at tea time, so intending visitors are advised to book a table for either the first or second sitting. Service, under the supervision of an excellent maître d'hôtel, is very friendly, and the dainty sandwiches – cucumber, egg and cress, smoked salmon are traditional favourites – scones and delicious, light, creamy pastries and gâteaux are all freshly and expertly made every day. Tea at the Ritz is a unique experience.

Set tea £11.50
Open every day, first sitting 3pm; second sitting 4.30pm

LONDON W1

The Selfridge
Orchard Street
Tel 071–408 2080

The Selfridge Hotel simply could not be more conveniently placed to receive shoppers from the famous department store, being positioned just off Oxford Street and to the rear of the shop. Tea is served in the fine, panelled first-floor lounge which has comfortable seating around small tables. Service, by uniformed, tail-coated staff, is quiet and efficient. The set tea comprises sandwiches, scones, pastries and gâteaux. All are fresh and excellent, as is the choice of Earl Grey, Assam, Darjeeling and China teas on offer.

Pot of tea £1.75, set tea £9.25
Open all year, every day, 3–5pm

LONDON W1

Westbury Hotel
Conduit Street
Tel 071–629 7755

The Westbury Hotel is an attractive haven just off New Bond Street, at the centre of the West End shopping belt. Tea is served in a particularly pleasant, panelled lounge by staff who look after guests extremely well. Finger sandwiches, scones and pastries are accompanied by a choice of teas which includes Keemun, mint, Darjeeling, Indian and Earl Grey. The pretty, high-quality china adds to the enjoyment of the occasion.

Set tea £8.50
Open every day 3–6pm

LONDON W2

Royal Lancaster Hotel
Lancaster Terrace
Tel 071–262 6737

This is a large, modern hotel in Bayswater, with a cosmopolitan atmosphere and views over Hyde Park. There is a pleasant, first-floor lounge where afternoon tea is served by friendly and efficient staff who ensure that guests feel welcome. The set tea consists of finger sandwiches, scones and a selection of French pastries, accompanied by Indian, China and Earl Grey tea with milk or lemon served in a china teapot. To help you relax while you enjoy the refreshments a pianist entertains throughout the afternoon.

Pot of tea and one cake average £1.50, set tea £7.25–£10.50
Open every day, 3–6pm for afternoon tea

LONDON W8

Kensington Close Hotel
Wright's Lane
Tel 071–937 8170

This hotel stands close to Kensington High Street, just two minutes' walk from the tube station. Afternoon tea is served in a modern restaurant with a comfortable lounge area, the choice of Indian or China tea being accompanied by finger sandwiches, hot buttered scones with preserves and clotted cream, and a fresh strawberry tartlet.

Pot of tea 95p, set tea £3.95
Open all year, every day, 2.30–6pm

LONDON W8

Kensington Park Hotel
16–32 De Vere Gardens
Tel 071–937 8080

Recently opened, the Kensington Park Hotel stands in a quiet street not far from the Albert Hall. Elegant and comfortable surroundings make afternoon tea here a pleasant experience, and for a central London hotel the set tea is very good value. You can choose from several different blends of tea, and there are sandwiches, fruit loaf, freshly baked scones, and assorted pastries and gâteaux.

Pot of tea and one cake average £2.75, set afternoon tea £6.50
Open every day

LONDON WC1

Hotel Russell
Russell Square
Tel 071–837 6470

To enjoy afternoon tea in the majestic surroundings of the Hotel Russell Library is to sample the lifestyle of a bygone era's 'noble gentry' and to appreciate a little piece of English history. The meal comprises freshly-cut finger sandwiches, scones, delicious pastries and gâteaux and a selection of tea blends.

Pot of tea £1.60, set tea £8.25
Open all year, every day, 2.30–6pm

LONDON WC2

Savoy Hotel
Strand
Tel 071–836 4343

Afternoon tea at the Savoy, one of London's most famous hotels, could not be other than a memorable experience. The surroundings are sumptuous, and the ornate Thames Foyer, with its central gazebo is an evocative setting in which to enjoy this most traditional of English institutions. Service of the blend of tea of your choice, accompanied by excellent sandwiches, scones and pastries, is very much in the grand manner, with the tail-coated staff taking pride in making the occasion something special. If you have a taste for luxury, this is definitely the place to choose.

Set afternoon tea £10.50
Open daily, 3.30–5.30pm

LONDON WC2

Waldorf Hotel
The Aldwych
Tel 071–836 2400

On Friday, Saturday and Sunday 'You never know who you might meet at a Waldorf Afternoon Tea Dance', as the hotel's brochure invites you to discover. The Waldorf's delightful Palm Court is the setting for the revival of this fashionable pre-war entertainment, at which each course is served at a relaxed pace to allow plenty of intervals for dancing. On other days of the week a lavish afternoon tea is offered, without the dancing but with a pianist. Waldorf teas feature toasted English muffins, as well as sandwiches, bridge rolls, scones with clotted cream, fresh pastries or gâteaux, accompanied by a choice of blends of tea, all served with a courtesy that matches the surroundings and takes you back to an age of leisure.

Set afternoon tea £9.50–£15.25, afternoon tea dance £13.75
Open all year, every day, 3.30–6.30pm
Closed some Bank Holidays
1 2 3

LONGHORSLEY   Northumberland   Map 12 NZ19

Linden Hall Hotel
Tel (0670) 516611

This fine country mansion retains much of the grandeur of bygone days. Tea is served in the elegant, high-ceilinged drawing room which leads off an impressive galleried and domed hall. Amid the grandeur, service is friendly and in the traditional style, at tables covered with linen tablecloths, with cakes borne in on a tiered cake stand. The full afternoon tea consists of sandwiches (cucumber, smoked salmon, egg), scones with cream and jam, cakes and biscuits, all homemade and very enjoyable. Assam, Earl Grey, Ceylon, Darjeeling or peppermint infusion are the choice of teas.

Linden tea (scones, cakes, biscuits) £2.75, full afternoon tea £3.95
Open every day 4–5.30pm
1 2 3

LONG MELFORD   Suffolk   Map 05 TL84

The Gladstone Tearooms
4 Westgate Street
Tel (0787) 881544

This friendly teashop is situated in a small row of antique shops and houses just outside the town. Attractively decorated in floral prints, with clothed tables and fresh flowers, there is a display cabinet with a selection of appetising homebaked cakes. Darjeeling, Earl Grey and Assam teas are available. Smoking is not permitted.

Pot of tea 35p, set teas £1.95–£2.95
Open all year, Tue–Sun, 10am–6pm

LOUTH   Lincolnshire   Map 08 TF38

Crusty's
Pawn Shop Passage

A small modern café, Crusty's provides friendly table service. Toasted crumpets, muffins and teacakes are available with a range of homemade cakes. Full afternoon tea includes fresh sandwiches, and substantial hot meals are also served throughout the day. A choice of tea blends is offered. Smoking is not permitted.

Pot of tea 55p, full afternoon tea £2.30
Open all year, Tue, Wed, Fri, Sat, 10am–4pm
Hot snacks

LUDLOW   Shropshire   Map 07 SO57

Hardwicks
2 Quality Square
Tel (0584) 6470

In pleasant split-level ground floor premises, Hardwicks has white cottage style furniture, and is tucked away in a small cobbled square off the High street. As well as homemade scones and cakes, light cooked meals are served, including vegetarian dishes. Indian, China and herb teas are served in china teapots with matching crockery.

Pot of tea and one cake average £1.20
Open all year (except two weeks at Christmas), Mon–Sat, 10am–5pm

LULWORTH   Dorset   Map 03 SY88

Old Boathouse Café
Tel (092 941) 648

This small seafront café has been modernised with banquet seating, Formica tables and bright décor. The self-service counter displays a good range of homemade scones, cakes, pies and sandwiches. Hot snacks and dairy ice cream are available.

Cream tea £1.60
Open Easter–Oct, every day, 10am–6pm
Snack meals

LUNDIN LINKS   Fife   Map 12 NO40

The Cottage Tea Room
Largo Road
KY8 6DH
Tel (0333) 320648

On the eastern fringe of the village, beside the main street, sits a quaint cottage with a cosy front parlour-style tearoom and tiny adjoining gift shop. Here, light lunches and high teas are served as well as the sandwiches and homemade scones, cakes and traybakes of the popular afternoon tea menu. Earl Grey, Ceylon and Darjeeling tea are available.

Pot of tea and one cake average £1.20
Open Wed–Mon
Light lunches and high teas

LUSTLEIGH   Devon   Map 03 SX78

Primrose Cottage
Tel (06477) 365

This sunny yellow thatched cottage in the pretty moorland village of Lustleigh is well worth a visit and owners Miranda and Roger Olver ensure a warm welcome. The beamed interior is enhanced by carefully chosen antiques and objets d'art which are available for sale. A magnificent array of home baking is set out offering an impossible choice from freshly-baked warm scones (brown and white) with clotted cream and jam; cheese tea which includes scones, cheese and fruit, or salami platter. Cakes include strawberry pavlova, hazlenut and apricot meringue, poppy seed cake, apple strudel, raspberry and strawberry gâteau among others. Lunch is served between noon and 2pm, and on fine days seating is provided in the garden.

Pot of tea and one cake average £2.25, set teas from £1–£3
Open every day in summer
Lunches

LUTON   Bedfordshire   Map 04 TL02

Balzac's
Strathmore Thistle Hotel
Arndale Centre
Tel (0582) 34199

Balzac's is a clean and comfortable restaurant/café located within the Strathmore Thistle with access from both the hotel and the Arndale Centre. The Continental-style café serves freshly made European cuisine as well as afternoon teas. Cakes gâteaux, pastries, sandwiches and scones are available with a choice of tea blends.

Pot of tea and one cake average £1.40
Open every day
Lunches
1 2 3

LYME REGIS   Dorset   Map 03 SY39

Alexandra Hotel
Pound Street
Tel (02974) 2010

This hotel is splendidly situated high above the cob with fine views out to sea. Teas and a good range of food are served in the garden under umbrellas and in the cane-furnished sun-lounge or, during the colder months, in the cosy drawing room by the fire. Sandwiches, toast, toasted teacakes and gâteaux are available, or a Dorset cream tea, with a choice of tea blends.

Pot of tea and one cake average £2.05, cream tea £2.35
Open all year, every day except six weeks from 22 Dec
1 2 3

LYMINGTON   Hampshire   Map 04 SZ39

The Buttery
19 High Street
Tel (0590) 72870

A 15th-century teashop, the Buttery is simply appointed with counter service or waitress service sections. There is a good variety of home baking, including cheese scones, flapjacks and chocolate caramel shortbread. A range of tea blends is offered, served in china pots.

Pot of tea and one cake average £1.10, set teas £2.20–£2.45
Open all year Mon–Sat, 8.15am–5.15pm, Sun 10am–5.15pm self-service, 10am–4.45pm table service

LYMINGTON   Hampshire   Map 04 SZ39

Lentune Coffee House
4 Quay Street
Tel (0590) 72766

This charming beamed 16th-century cottage is set between the Quay and the High Street, with simple appointments and fresh flowers. Snack meals and a good selection of homemade cakes are offered, such as coffee gâteau, fruitcake, shortbread, almond slice and gingerbread. Earl Grey, lemon and herb tea are offered, as well as the popular blend.

Pot of tea 50p, cream tea £2, farmhouse tea £1.75
Open Mar–Nov, Wed–Mon, 10am–5pm

LYMINGTON   Hampshire   Map 04 SZ39

Passford House Hotel
Mount Pleasant Lane
Tel (0590) 682398

Relax in comfort with a choice of lounges, one with a log fire when it is chilly. Order Indian or China tea from the porter and help yourself to a selection from the trolley. A variety of sandwiches and scones with jam and cream are always available, with a choice of two other items such as homemade fruit or madeira cake, shortbread or fruit cream tartlet.

Sandwiches £1.50, cakes 50p–£1
Open all year, every day, 3.30pm–5.30pm
1 2 3 &

LYMINGTON   Hampshire   Map 04 SZ39

The Stanwell House Hotel
High Street
Tel (0590) 677123

A charming Georgian town house, just minutes from the busy marina and quay of this former maritime capital of the Solent, features a walled garden and patio. Here – or in the welcoming lounge or library in winter – guests can enjoy a traditional tea of sandwiches, scones with cream and jam, and fruitcake or cream cakes (all baked on the premises) accompanied by lapsang, Earl Grey or a standard tea blend.

Pot of tea and one cake average £1.75, set teas £1.95–£3.75
Open every day, 3.30–5.30pm
1 3

LYNDHURST   Hampshire   Map 04 SU30

Court House Tearooms
97 High Street
Tel (0703) 283871

These small, single-storey tearooms are on the Southampton side of Lyndhurst in a built-up area. There is a homely, relaxed atmosphere, with simple furnishings. Homemade white or wholemeal scones, rich fruit cake, date and walnut, apple and almond and chocolate cakes are served, with a choice of tea varieties. Sandwiches, filled rolls and jacket potatoes are also available.

Set teas £1.80–£1.90
Open all year Mon–Fri, 10.30am–5pm, Sat 10.30am–6.30pm, Sun 10.30am–7.30pm

LYNDHURST   Hampshire   Map 04 SU30

Crown Hotel
High Street
Tel (0703) 282922

Tea and country-style biscuits are available in the comfortable lounge, or outside on the terrace on a sunny day, at this elegant hotel. Earl Grey and English breakfast teas are served by uniformed staff.

Pot of tea and biscuits 80p
Open all year, every day, any time

The Honey Pot
Honeysuckle Cottage
Restaurant
Minstead
Tel (0703) 813122

The Honey Pot is a modern annexe building in the garden of the Honeysuckle Cottage Restaurant, an idyllic thatched New Forest Cottage. There are polished tables and Windsor chairs, and tables in the garden for sunny days. Home baking is served with a choice of Earl Grey, Darjeeling or standard blend teas in a china pot with hot water jug.

Queen Bee Tea £2.50, Beehive Tea £2.20, Drones Tea £1.60
Open Easter–Sep, every day, 10.30am–5.30pm (Oct–Easter weekends only)
1 3

The Pony Tearoom
21 High Street
Tel (042128) 2789

On a busy corner by the traffic lights, this is a simply-furnished teashop with wooden chairs and attractive tablecloths. Lemon meringue pie, rich chocolate gâteau, coffee and walnut cake and apricot and pineapple cheesecake are served.

Pot of tea 45p
Open all year, every day, 10.30am–5pm (3pm–5pm Sun)

Rock House Hotel
Tel (0598) 53508

During the summer months Devon cream teas are available all day in the tea garden of this delightful, personally owned and run little hotel which stands next to the Manor Gardens, in a unique position overlooking the picturesque harbour.

Pot of tea and one cake average £1.60, set tea £2.50
Open every day in summer only
  1 2 3

Combe Park Hotel
Hillsford Bridge
Tel (0598) 52356

This former hunting lodge – now a small, personally-run hotel – enjoys a unique setting at the heart of the National Trust's Watersmeet Estate. Set well back from the road in a quiet valley with the Hoar Oak Water flowing past its lawn, it offers a good range of cream teas with an abundance of home-cooked cakes and preserves.

Pot of tea and one cake average £1.60, set tea £2.20
Open all week in summer only

The Mews Tea Room
36 Clifton Street
Tel (0253) 730033

This small first-floor teashop, set at the rear of a passageway of shops, offers in its attractive beamed interior light snacks, freshly made sandwiches and home-baking ranging from scones and shortbread to chocolate or simnel cake. Fine china cups enhance the enjoyment of Earl Grey, lemon or standard tea blends.

Pot of tea and one cake average £1
Open Mon–Sat, 10am–5pm

LYTHAM ST ANNES   Lancashire   Map 07 SD32

Serendipity
Bedford Hotel
307–311 Clifton Drive
South
Tel (0253) 724636

A glass-fronted coffee and teashop at the front of the hotel, Serendipity has polished inlaid wood tables and very comfortable chairs – rather quaint in style. Light lunches are available and there is a good salad bar. Tea is served in an elegant silver pot with matching water jug, and homemade cakes are displayed on a three-tier stand. Smoking is not permitted.

Pot of tea and one cake average £1.00, set tea £3.25
Open all year, every day, 10am–5pm
Lunch
1   3

MACCLESFIELD   Cheshire   Map 07 SJ97

Dukes Coffee House
Dukes Court
Tel (0625) 511453

A café in a small new shopping centre comprises a series of brick-faced rooms with arched divisions, some of which are designated non-smoking. Friendly staff serve a variety of sandwiches, salads and snacks including lunch-time blackboard 'specials', while the daily selection of fresh cakes includes such favourites as éclairs, Danish pastries, walnut cake and chocolate fudge cake with hot fudge sauce.

Pot of tea 45p, cream tea £1.50
Open Mon, Tue, and Thu–Sat, 9.30am–4.30pm, Wed am only
Lunches and Snacks

MACCLESFIELD   Cheshire   Map 07 SJ97

Silks Buttrie
The Heritage Centre
Roe Street
Tel (0625) 613572

This bright café with whitewashed walls and a no-smoking area is located within the Heritage Centre – once a historic Sunday School, but now an award-winning museum devoted to the silk industry (with which the town has had links for over 400 years) and a conference/concert venue. Friendly staff serve such traditional teatime treats as toasted teacakes, homemade fruit scones or chocolate fudge cake.

Pot of tea and one cake average £1.05
Open Tue–Sat (also Sun pm)
Snacks

MACHYNLLETH   Powys   Map 06 SH70

Felin Crewi
Penegoes
Tel (0654) 703113

Part of the working watermill complex, which includes a craft sales area, this tearoom serves filled rolls, oaty biscuits, bara brith, granary-type cakes, scones and a good cup of tea in a choice of blends. There are ponies and goats outside, as well as ducks on the river.

Pot of tea and one cake average £1.15, set teas from £1.95
Open Easter to Sep, every day, 10.30am–5.45pm
♿

MACHYNLLETH   Powys   Map 06 SH70

National Milk Bar
17–19 Penrallt Street
Tel (0654) 70336

This purpose-built, modern milk bar situated near the famous town clock serves scones and pastries, along with a good cup of tea.

Pot of tea and one cake average £1.05
Open all year, daily (except Christmas and New Year) 9am–6pm, summer and holidays 9am–8pm
Snacks, hot meals

MALMESBURY   Wiltshire   Map   03 ST98

The Old Bell Hotel
Tel (0666) 822344

This delightful gabled hotel, next to the abbey, has a claim to be the country's oldest hotel, and retains many interesting features, including a 700-year-old fireplace. In the summer tea is served in the gardens, in the winter in the Garden Lounge or in the bar. The hotel's kitchen produces wonderful scones, cheese scones, cream cakes and gâteaux. The traditional afternoon tea starts with a round of sandwiches, then scones, cream and jam, followed by an éclair or slice of fruitcake, accompanied by Indian or China tea, Lapsang or Earl Grey.

Pot of tea and one cake
£1.75, set teas £1.95–£3.75
Open every day 3.30–5.30pm
1 3

MALVERN   Hereford & Worcester   Map 03 SO74

Café el Sol
Mount Pleasant Hotel
Belle Vue Terrace
Tel (0684) 561837

This elegant Victorian-style coffee lounge, adjoining the Mount Pleasant Hotel, serves a good selection of breads, cakes, pastries and gâteaux – some homemade – along with eight different blends of tea. Service is friendly and efficient

Pot of tea and one cake
£1.60–£2.35 for two
Open all year, daily (except Christmas Day and Boxing Day), 10am –6pm
Snacks
1 2 3

MALVERN   Hereford & Worcester Map 03 SO74

Royal Malvern Hotel
Graham Road
Tel (0684) 563411

Pleasant and efficient staff serve afternoon tea in the foyer-lounge of this town-centre hotel. A selection of sandwiches, scones and biscuits is available, along with a traditional pot of tea.

Pot of tea 75p
Open all year, daily (except Christmas Day), 3–6pm
1 2 3

MAN, ISLE OF   Ramsey   Map 06 SC49

Grand Island Hotel
Bride Road
Tel (0624) 812455

Afternoon tea is a relaxing occasion here at the island's only four star hotel, once a Georgian mansion, and commanding fine views over Ramsey Bay and the mountains. In a comfortable lounge overlooking the croquet lawns, guests can enjoy the set afternoon tea of sandwiches, scones and cakes, or just sample one of a selection of speciality tea blends which includes Lapsang Souchong, Assam, Darjeeling, Earl Grey, Piccadilly, rosehip and mixed fruit.

Pot of tea and one cake
average £1.85, set tea from £3.50
Open every day
1 2 3

MANCHESTER   Greater Manchester   Map 07 SJ89

Café Gallery
City Art Gallery
Princes Street
Tel 061–236 5244

A bright and stylishly modern café on the ground floor of the Manchester City Art Gallery offers a good range of homemade cakes (including such favourites as brownies, rum truffles, gingerbread and carrot cake), scones and pastries with a choice of tea blends. Although it is a self-service operation, smartly dressed, boater-hatted staff are on hand to lend assistance.

Pot of tea and one cake average £1.50
Open every day
☐1☐ ☐3☐

MANCHESTER   Greater Manchester   Map 07 SJ89

Holiday Inn Crown Plaza
Peter Street
Tel 061–236 3333

The elegant Terrace Lounge of this distinctive Edwardian hotel in the town centre offers an attractive setting for traditional afternoon tea. Home-baked cheesecakes, flans, cakes, pastries and sandwiches can be accompanied by one of the range of teas which includes China, Indian, flower and jasmin.

Pot of tea and one cake average £2.20, set teas £3.95 and £5.95, pot of tea £1.25
Open all year, daily for afternoon tea served 3–5pm
☐1☐ ☐2☐ ☐3☐

MANCHESTER   Greater Manchester   Map 07 SJ89

Hotel Piccadilly
Piccadilly Plaza
Tel 061–236 8414

Afternoon tea is served in the Garden Rooms lounge at this large town centre hotel. Cakes, gâteaux, fruit tarts, scones and Danish pastries are all home-baked and the tea is properly made.

Pot of tea £1, cakes from £1.60
Open all year, every day, all afternoon
☐1☐ ☐2☐ ☐&☐

MANCHESTER   Greater Manchester   Map 07 SJ89

Portland Thistle Hotel
Portland Street
Piccadilly Gardens
Tel 061–228 3400

Situated on Piccadilly Gardens in the city centre, this hotel serves afternoon teas in its compact, but comfortable lounges. Home-baked scones, gâteaux and pastries are accompanied by a fresh pot of tea.

Pot of tea and scone £2.25
Open all year, every day, 2.30–5.30pm
☐1☐ ☐2☐ ☐3☐

MANCHESTER   Greater Manchester   Map 07 SJ89

Ramada Renaissance Hotel
Blackfriars Street
Tel 061–835 3663/ 3671

Afternoon tea is served in the Fairbairns Lounge on the mezzanine floor of this large modern city-centre hotel. The home-baked selection includes scones, Danish pastries, fruitcake, tartlets and chocolate éclairs and the tea – there is a good choice of blends – is served in attractive china.

Set tea £4.25, pot of tea £1.75
Open all year, daily, 10.30am–11pm, afternoon tea 2.30–11pm
Morning coffee, snacks

MANSFIELD   Nottinghamshire   Map 08 SK56

Greenwood Craft Centre & Coffee Shop
A60, Nottingham Road
Tel (0623) 792141

In the heart of Sherwood Forest in the Portland Training College for the disabled, their volunteers have opened a craft centre and coffee shop by the entrance. The sandwiches, scones and cakes are all freshly prepared in the college kitchens and all proceeds go to the college. There is a children's adventure play area and a three-mile signed walk through the forest.

Pot of tea and one cake average 70p
Open every day 11am–4.30pm

MARKET HARBOROUGH   Leicestershire   Map 04 SP79

Aldwinckles
8c Church Street
Tel (0858) 431862

The entrance to Aldwinckles, between the hairdresser's and the flower shop, is easily missed but this 200-year-old shop provides a cosy retreat for tea, with a range of home-baked cakes, scones and gâteaux. The Dutch Beastie is an interesting choice – a light chocolate sponge with cherries and cream. Freshly-made sandwiches and a choice of Ceylon, Darjeeling and Earl Grey teas are available.

Pot of tea and one cake average £1.50
Open Mon–Sat

MARKET HARBOROUGH   Leicestershire   Map 04 SP79

Café Genevieve
53 High Street
Tel (0858) 410257

Tucked away behind the Genevieve dress shop, this pretty little café provides a choice of gâteaux, cakes, scones, teacakes and waffles and freshly made tea – a simple, shoppers' café with friendly staff.

Pot of tea from 55p
Open all year, Tue–Sat 10am–5pm, Sun 12 noon–5.30pm
Lunches, vegetarian dishes

MARKINCH   Fife   Map 12 NO20

Balbirnie House
Tel (0592) 610066

Afternoon tea at a superb 18th-century house set in 416 acres of parkland is an attractive proposition for walkers, golfers and horse-riders alike; in the tranquillity of its impressive drawing room or gallery-lounge, friendly but courteous young staff serve either set teas consisting of an interesting range of sandwiches with home-baked scones, cakes, pastries and gâteaux, or items from an à la carte selection: tea blends include Earl Grey, Darjeeling and Lapsang Souchong.

Pot of tea and one cake average £2.50, set teas from £5.75
Open all year, every day
⌈1⌉ ⌈2⌉ ⌈3⌉

MARKS TEY   Essex   Map 05 TL92

Poplar Pavilion
Coggeshall Road
Tel (0206) 210374

Part of a garden centre/retail nursery on the A120
three miles west of Coggeshall, this glasshouse
tearoom – fully carpeted, and furnished with white
wooden tables with wrought iron bases and matching
cushioned chairs – overlooks the display gardens. A
blackboard menu details sandwiches and light snacks,
while an attractive display of home-baked cakes
includes coffee and walnut, lemon sponge, sultana loaf
and carrot cake; Darjeeling, Assam, Earl Grey, lemon
and Indian tea blends are available. Fresh flower posies
and very pretty flowered crockery add a homely touch.

Pot of tea and one cake
average £1.10
Open all year, Thu–Mon

MARLBOROUGH   Wiltshire   Map 04 SU16

The Polly Tea Rooms
Tel (0672) 512146

The bow windows, low-beamed ceilings and flowered
tablecloths of the Polly Tea Rooms create the right
background for the stunning range of homemade
cakes, gâteaux and speciality ice creams, drawing in
crowds of people – especially pupils from
Marlborough College. Only set teas or ice creams are
served. The Polly Tea gives you plain or muesli scones
with cream, and a choice of preserves. The Special
Gâteau Tea allows you either one generous portion of
a luscious creamy gâteau (for example brandy butter,
berry yoghurt, Kiwi fruit) or three of the cakes from
the day's enormous selection. Delectable ice creams
include Dusty Road – coffee and chocolate ice cream
with butterscotch sauce, flaked chocolate and whipped
cream. There is a choice of blends of tea.

Set teas (or ice creams)
£2.50
Open every day (except
annual mop fair, first two
Fri and Sat in Oct), Mon–
Fri 8.30am–6pm, Sat 8am–
7pm, Sun 9am–7pm
Breakfast, opening time–
11.30am; Lunch 12–3pm
Credit cards accepted for
bills over £15

MARLBOROUGH   Wiltshire   Map 04 SU16

**The Tudor Tea
Rooms**
115 High Street
Tel (0672) 512853

These pretty tearooms are on two floors. Friendly
waitresses serve freshly-made tea (choice of Indian,
Earl Grey, Lapsang, Darjeeling or decaffeinated) in
attractive china teapots, with delicious homemade
scones or traditional home-baked cakes, such as
Victoria sandwich. Fresh cream cakes, or four different
sorts of shortcake, doughnuts, Danish pastries and ice-
cream dishes complete the extensive menu.

Pot of tea and one cake
average £1.50, cream tea
£2.80
Open daily, 9am–8pm
(except Christmas and
New Year)
All meals
1 2 3

MARLOW   Buckinghamshire   Map 04 SU88

Compleat Angler Hotel
Marlow Bridge
Tel (06284) 4444

An afternoon tea at this delightful Thames-side hotel, set on a picturesque curve of the river, gives you the additional pleasure of uninterrupted river views. The hotel takes its name from the famous book by Izaak Walton, written here in 1653. Nowadays, however, the scene is more of pleasure boats than solitary fishermen. On fine summer days you can enjoy the luxuriant, fragrant gardens all around the hotel as you sample the sandwiches, scones and pastries, beautifully served with the accompaniment of Indian, China, Earl Grey and Darjeeling teas.

Set teas from £8.50
Open every day, 3.30–5.30pm
1 2 3

MARWELL   Hampshire   Map 04 SU52

The Orchid House
Marwell Resort Hotel
Marwell Zoological Park
Colden Common
Tel (0962) 74681

Part of the Marwell Resort Hotel, this modern, pine-furnished coffee shop offers a snack lunch menu including toasted sandwiches, croissants and pizza, and afternoon tea comprising a round of sandwiches and a choice of gâteau or two scones with jam and cream or two pastries. Breakfast, Assam and Earl Grey teas are available.

Set tea £2.35
Open every day, lunch 12 noon–2pm, tea 2–5.30pm
Light lunches, licensed

MATLOCK BATH   Derbyshire   Map 08 SK25

Lea Gardens
Lea
Tel (0629) 534380

This small teashop at the entrance to the famous rhododendron gardens is proving to be a popular addition to the centre's amenities, offering sandwiches, salads, quiches and a range of cakes – including sponges, Dundees and ten varieties of small cake – baked by the proprietress. Family and friends help in the conservatory-style no-smoking tearoom that extends outside when weather permits.

Pot of tea and one cake average 90p
Open 20 Mar–31 Jul, every day, 10am–5.30pm

MATLOCK BATH   Derbyshire   Map 08 SK25

New Bath Hotel
New Bath Road
Tel (0629) 583275

In a lovely spot amid five acres of landscaped gardens overlooking the River Derwent, the comfortable lounge and bar of the New Bath Hotel offer a range of hot and cold snacks all day, with traditional choices for afternoon tea available between 3 and 5pm. Grosvenor, lemon or decaffeinated tea blends are served.

Pot of tea and one cake average £2
Open every day

MELMERBY   Cumbria   Map 12 NY63

The Village Bakery
(10 miles east of
Penrith on A686)
Tel (076881) 515

Converted farm buildings house this family-owned bakery and tearoom/restaurant. Flagstones, natural stonework and exposed beams preserve the rural character, and the emphasis is on organic produce and local stoneground flour. Baking is done on the premises, so everything is fresh. Typical of the mouthwatering specialities are scones with Cumberland rum butter, Parkin, Westmorland spice cake, Grasmere Gingerbread, Borrowdale tea bread and much, much more. The choice of tea blends includes Ceylon, Darjeeling, Earl Grey and Keemun, and there are also herbal and fruit-flavoured teas. In the upstairs gallery is displayed a selection of high-quality craftware, and there is also a conservatory.

Pot of tea and one cake average 70p, cream tea £3.60, cakes from about 45p
Open all year. Christmas–Easter, Mon–Sat, 8.30am–2.30pm. Easter–Christmas, every day (except Mon pm unless it's a bank holiday), Mon 8.30am–2.30pm, Tue–Sat 8.30am–5pm, Sun 9.30am–5pm
No smoking
Breakfast, lunch and snacks also served
1 3

MELVERLEY   Shropshire   Map 07 SJ31

The Old Rectory
Tel (069185) 455

This simple, yet clean and fresh teashop forms part of a pastoral craft centre which stands in meadows opposite the village inn and close to the timber-framed church of St Peter. A converted stable block displays unique examples of the work of some thirty local craftsmen, while the teashop offers hot buttered toast, teacakes, scones and homemade biscuits.

Pot of tea and one cake average 90p
Open in season only, Sun–Tue

MICKLETON   Gloucestershire   Map 04 SP14

Three ways Hotel
Tel (0386) 438429

Afternoon tea has been a popular feature of the Three Ways for some time. Guests can relax in the extensive lounges and there is plenty of outside seating. Home-baked scones, sponges and biscuits accompany a choice of teas and herbal infusions

Pot of tea and one cake average £1.25, cream tea £2.40
Open all year, daily, 7.30am (8am Sun)–9pm (9.30pm Fri and Sat)

MILFORD HAVEN   Dyfed   Map 02 SM91

Lawtons
11 Priory Street
Tel (0646) 690128

A mid-terrace property between Charles Street and the harbour houses a simply furnished restaurant offering a wide range of meals. Its teatime selection includes sandwiches, granary scones, teacakes and pastries, with a choice of Earl Grey, lemon or standard tea blends.

Pot of tea and one cake average 90p
Open all year, Mon–Sat

MILFORD HAVEN   Dyfed   Map 02 SM90

Rabaiotti's Café and Restaurant
31 Charles Street
Tel (06462) 2576

This large, self-service café offers a varied selection of home-baked cakes, pastries, sandwiches and hot snacks and a good pot of tea. The restaurant has waitress service.

Pot of tea and two Welsh cakes 98p
Open all year, Mon–Sat, 9am–6.30pm
Lunch and dinner in restaurant

MILTON ABBAS   Dorset   Map 03 ST80

Tea Clipper
The Street
Tel (0258) 880223

This tea shop, set near Milton Abbey in a grade two listed village of thatched cob cottages laid out to the design of Capability Brown, features oak dressers displaying home-baked cakes, pies and pastries. Its speciality is Hilda's Dorset Apple Cake, but everything is delicious, portions are generous and there is a choice of tea blends. Postcards and gifts are also available.

Pot of tea 60p, pot of tea and one cake average £1.50, cream tea £2.30
Open Mar–Oct, Tue–Sun, weekends in winter

MITTON   Staffordshire   Map 07 SJ81

Hillcrest Tea Rooms
Near Whalley
Tel (0254) 86573

A delightful little tearoom, with beams, stone walls and lace tablecloths, in beautiful surroundings close to a medieval church and the River Ribble, offering a very good selection of home baking, light meals and snacks. The set afternoon tea comprises a pot of tea, sandwich, scone with jam and cream and fruitcake or fruit pie. You will find Hillcrest two and a half miles from Whalley on the B6246, just over the bridge.

Pot of tea and one cake average £1.10, set tea £3
Open Sat–Thu
Light meals

MOFFAT   Dumfries & Galloway   Map 11 NT00

Fountain Coffee Shop
65–67 High Street
Tel (0683) 20938

An aroma of freshly-made coffee and home baking welcomes the visitor to this family-run teashop, decorated in traditional style with watercolour originals and a collection of china plates. As well as brown or white sandwiches, plain, fruit or cheese scones and a variety of cakes and pies, customers can enjoy homemade soup, salads and jacket potatoes, and a range of speciality teas is available.

Pot of tea and one cake average £1
Open all year, (except Jan and Feb, depending on weather), daily 9.30am–5.30pm and 6.30–10pm
1 2 3

MONIFIETH   Tayside   Map 12 NO53

Brookside Coffee House
12 Brook Street
Tel (0382) 535040

This quaint little family-run coffee room and ice cream parlour is tucked away in a quiet residential road behind the main shopping street. Most of the baking is homemade – cheesecake, banana loaf and hot cloutie dumpling with fresh cream – and the choice of tea ranges from 'everyday' to fruit and herbal blends.

Pot of tea and one cake average 75p
Open all year (except for variable annual holiday), Tue–Sat 10am–4.30pm
Morning coffee, snacks, ice cream specialities

MORECAMBE   Lancashire   Map   07 SD46

Tradewinds
Strathmore Hotel
East Promenade
Tel (0524) 421234

Traditional afternoon tea of home-baked scones, cream, preserve, cake, assorted sandwiches and a fresh pot of tea is served by friendly staff in the lounge of this seafront hotel.

Pot of tea and one cake average £2.65, set teas £2.65–£4.95
Open all day, tea served 2–6pm

MORETON-IN-MARSH   Gloucestershire   Map 04 SP23

Cotswold Restaurant, Coffeehouse and Patisserie
High Street
Tel (0608) 50365

This busy high street teashop and patisserie is wood-panelled with polished tables and chairs. Mr Kay and his staff provide attentive service along with homemade cakes, sandwiches and a traditional cup of tea. This is a 'no smoking' establishment.

Tea 60p, speciality tea 80p, set tea £2.35
Open Apr–Dec, Mon, Tue and Thur–Sat 9.30am–5pm, Sun, 10am–5pm (or later)
Lunch

MORETON-IN-MARSH   Gloucestershire   Map 04 SP23

Marshmallow Tearooms
High Street
Tel (0608) 51536

Old-fashioned cream teas, toasted tea cakes, strawberries, scones and cream are just a selection of the sweet things on offer at these tearooms. Recently reopened after extensive refurbishment, they provide a perfect, tranquil setting in which to relax and enjoy morning coffee, afternoon tea or a light lunch.

Pot of tea and one cake average £1.85, speciality tea 65p, set tea £1.95
Open all year, everyday, 9am–9pm
Light lunches

MORWENSTOW   Cornwall & Isles of Scilly   Map O2 SS21

Rectory Farm Tea Rooms
Tel (028883) 251

Close by a footpath down to the sea and the dramatic Cornish cliff-line, and opposite the church, the entrance is through a stone-flagged porch into a slate-floored low-ceilinged room with inglenook, circular tables and old wall settles. Service and food are good – sandwiches, rolls, jacket potatoes and a choice of four or five fresh cakes, scones and a selection of biscuits with a variety of tea blends.

Pot of tea and one cake average £1.30, Cornish cream teas £1.80
Open every day 10am–6pm
Hot and cold snacks

MOUSEHOLE   Cornwall & Isles of Scilly   Map 02 SW42

Annie's
2 Fore Street
Tel (0736) 731635

Near to the harbour, which can be viewed from the two window seats, this friendly tearoom offers an appealing selection of home-baked cakes and scones of excellent quality. Small tables are laid with cloths and good china, a choice of Assam or Earl Grey tea is offered, and a range of sandwiches is available.

Pot of tea and one cake average £1.30, Cornish cream tea £1.95
Open Easter–Oct & 3 weeks at Christmas, 10am–6pm

MUCH WENLOCK   Shropshire   Map 07 SO69

The Malthouse
44 High Street
Tel (0952) 727467

This delightful old Shropshire town with its lovely ruined Abbey attracts many visitors who find this coffee lounge and tea shop, with restaurant above, a welcome place for tea. Scones, teacakes and cakes are all home-made, and there is a choice of Indian, or Earl Grey tea and herbal infusions.

Pot of tea 55p, set teas £1.30–£2.95
Open all year, Tue–Sun, 3–5pm (6pm at weekends)
Light meals and dinners also served

1 3

MUDEFORD   Dorset   Map 04 SZ19

Waterford Lodge Hotel
87 Bure Lane
Friars Cliff
Tel (0425) 272948

Traditional afternoon tea is served by friendly and attentive staff in the lounge of this attractive hotel.

Set tea £1.50–£4.60
Open all year, every day, teas served 3–5pm

1 2 3

MULL, ISLE OF   Strathclyde   Map 13 NM45

Old Byre Tearooms
Dervaig
Tel (068 84) 229

Once a byre – and still retaining many original features – this tearoom incorporates craft and gift shops which are part of a Heritage Centre depicting life on Mull. Everything served here is home-baked, regional specialities like Cloutie Dumpling being offered as well as such traditional items as scones, shortbread and chocolate cake. Snacks, sandwiches and filled rolls are available, and standard, Earl Grey or herbal tea.

Pot of tea 40p
Open Palm Sunday–Oct daily 10.30am–6pm

MULL, ISLE OF   Strathclyde   Map 10 NM64

Balmeanach
Fishnish
Tel (0680) 300342

Cheery, informal service and a selection of mainly home-baked produce including chocolate cake, angel cakes, carrot cake, pancakes and shortbread are offered by a small tearoom and garden centre standing well back from the main road midway between Craignure and Salen; hot meals are available, and there is also a landscaped picnic park.

Pot of tea and one cake £1
Open every day

NAIRN   Highland   Map 14 NH85

Culloden Pottery Restaurant
The Old Smiddy
Gollanfield, Culloden
Tel (0667) 62749

On the first floor, above a gift shop and an established studio pottery, this restaurant specialises in freshly-prepared wholefood vegetarian cooking. There is a chair lift for the elderly and disabled. Homemade scones, cakes and biscuits are available, as well as a choice of tea blends. There are very pleasant views of the Moray Firth and the surrounding countryside.

Pot of tea and one cake average £1.25
Open Jun–Oct, every day (but closed between Christmas and New Year), 9.30am–6pm, Nov–May, 10am–5pm
Meals and snacks served

NAIRN Highland Map 14 NH85

The Tea Cosy
53 High Street
Tel (0667) 55527

This quiet, family-run tearoom, set at the heart of the shopping centre and popular with locals and visitors alike, enhances the old-world character created by its beamed walls and ceiling with an interesting display of bric-à-brac. The delicious range of home-baking produced daily on the premises includes scones, rock buns, truffles, coconut clusters, lemon Madeira cake and iced sponges, and these can be served with lemon or Earl Grey tea as an alternative to the standard tea blends. Filled rolls, soup, quiche, pies, jacket potatoes and an all-day breakfast are also available.

Pot of tea and one cake from 85p
Open all year, Mon–Sat

NANTWICH Cheshire Map 07 SJ65

Chatwin's Coffee Lounge
The Square
Tel (0270) 625127

This self-service first-floor coffee lounge is above a bakery/confectioners opposite the church in the pedestrianised centre of this historic and picturesque old town. There is a variety of freshly-made cakes and Continental patisserie, and a choice of Ceylon, Darjeeling or Earl Grey teas is available.

Tea about 45p, coffee 50p, cream cakes 65p
Open all year, Mon–Sat, 9.30am–4.30pm
Light meals available

NANTWICH Cheshire Map 07 SJ65

Piecemeal
7B Beam Street
Tel (0270) 624997

This canopied street-level restaurant in the town centre features cakes and cream teas, as well as light meals, a children's menu, and a Welsh rarebit special. All the food at Piecemeal is homemade.

Pot of tea 43p
Open all year, Mon–Sat, 9am–5pm
Light lunches served

NETHYBRIDGE Highland Map 14 NJ02

Pollyanna's
Tigh-na-Fraoch
Tel (047982) 342

This craft and teashop sells quality goods and gifts and local paintings, as well as speciality teas, herbal infusions and preserves. There is a good selection of cakes, including sultana scones, oat squares, florentines and 'millionaires shortbread', and a comprehensive choice of teas. Although small, this really is a delightful place – well worth a visit. No smoking is permitted.

Afternoon tea £1.65
Open mid Feb–mid Oct, Tue–Sun, 9.30am (10.30am Sun)–5pm (4pm Thu)

NEW ABBEY   Dumfries & Galloway   Map 11 NX96

Abbey Cottage
26 Main Street
Abbey Street
Tel (038782) 361

Visitors eating in the rear garden of this popular teashop look across to the historic abbey near which it and the adjacent quaint craft shop stand. A wide variety of home-baked cakes includes date slice, caramel shortbread and walnut cake, scones are served with homemade preserves and there is a choice of tea blends. Baked potatoes, ploughman's lunches and salads are also available.

Pot of tea and one cake average 98p
Open Easter–mid Oct every day
Snacks

NEWARK-ON-TRENT   Nottinghamshire   Map 08 SK75

Ponds
7/9 Millgate
Tel (0636) 74822

Set just off the main street, this old teashop, with its low-beamed ceiling and brick floors dates back to 1740. The décor is fresh and bright, with marble topped tables, fresh flowers and pot plants. Delicious homemade cakes, scones, crêpes and snacks are served, as well as a choice of very good-flavoured tea blends served in crockery pots. 'Excellent', according to our inspector.

Teas about £1
Open all year, Tue–Sun, 10.30am–5pm
Lunches served, dinners served Thu–Sat, 7–10.30pm

NEWBURY   Berkshire   Map 04 SU46

Le Café
22 The Mall
Tel (0635) 521122

Located in the central mall of Newbury's new covered Kennet shopping centre, this is a pleasant, bustling place for tea. A good variety of English and French pastries, breads and snacks are available, and a tasty cup of tea is served by friendly staff.

Tea about 42p
Open all year, Mon–Sat, 8am–5.30pm
Snacks available

NEWBURY   Berkshire   Map 04 SU46

Crafty Cat
5 Inch's Yard
Tel (0635) 35491

Pine tables and chairs and a fresh décor welcomes visitors to this well-run coffee house with gift and craft shop above. A nice choice of cake includes carrot cake, banana cake and caramel squares, and there is a selection of eighteen teas and herbal infusions. The staff provide efficient, friendly service.

Pot of tea 60p, cream tea £1.75
Open all year, Mon–Sat, 9.30am–5pm
Meals served

NEWBURY   Berkshire   Map 04 SU46

Penthouse Restaurant, Camp Hopson
Northbrook Street
Tel (0635) 523523

Located at the back of the first floor in this department store, this modern tearoom is simply furnished, with a tempting array of cakes and a sweet trolley. Scones, meringues and cheesecake are among the items available, as well as a choice of tea blends.

Pot of tea and one cake average £1.05, afternoon tea £2
Open all year, every day except bank holidays
9.30am–4.30pm

NEWCASTLE-UPON-TYNE   Tyne and Wear   Map 12 NZ26

Fenwick's Tearooms
Fenwick's Department Store
39 Northumberland Street
Tel 091–232 5100

This lively and popular department store has three café areas, some self-service, others with table service. All the food is made on the premises and there is a good choice of sandwiches, scones and pastries, and blends of tea. Staff are both friendly and efficient.

Pot of tea 40–45p, cakes from 58p, set tea £1.75–£3.25
Open all year except bank holidays, Mon–Sat 9am–5.30pm (Thu, 8pm)

NEWCASTLE-UPON-TYNE   Tyne and Wear   Map 12 NZ26

Next 'Brasserie'
15/19 Northumberland Street
Tel 091–232 0226 ext 134

This large popular in-store brasserie is styled on the theme of a 50s/60s milk bar. The self-service choices include a good range of baking, with the emphasis on wholefoods, vegetarian and healthy eating. There is a choice of tea blends, as well as a variety of other drinks – different coffees, hot chocolate and milkshakes.

Pot of tea 60p, afternoon tea £1.65
Open all year, Mon–Sat, 9.30am–5pm (5.30pm Sat)
Light snacks available

NEW GALLOWAY   Dumfries & Galloway   Map 11 NX67

The Smithy
High Street
Tel (06442) 269

This converted blacksmith's shop houses a craft and book shop and a tourist information centre, as well as a pleasant tearoom and restaurant. A range of homemade scones, shortbread, cakes and pies, as well as a menu of snacks and light meals, are available all day.

Pot of tea and one cake average 83p
Open Mar–Oct, every day, 10am–6pm (until 9pm Easter–Oct)
Lunches and snacks served

NEW MILTON   Hampshire   Map 04 SZ29

Chewton Glen Hotel
Tel (0425) 275341

Well-kept gardens surround this beautiful and luxurious New Forest hotel, a house associated with the Victorian author Captain Marryat, who wrote *Children of the New Forest*, his much-loved children's story, here. Afternoon tea is an elegant occasion consisting of delicate sandwiches, homemade scones with clotted cream and preserves, and a selection of tempting homemade pastries. The choice of speciality teas includes Keemun, China Oolong, Rośe Pouchong, jasmine, gunpowder, Darjeeling, Earl Grey, Lapsang Souchong, traditional English, or herbal infusions.

Pot of tea and one cake average £3.50, traditional afternoon tea £8, with strawberries and cream (in season) £10
Open all year, every day, 3.30pm–6pm

NEWTONMORE Highland Map 14 NN79

The Tea Cosy
Main Street
Tel (05403) 315

This small teashop is part of a book and craft shop. It only seats 15 people, but it is well worth waiting for a table, browsing among the books and crafts while you do so, because Anne Bertram's country baking is a treat it would be a pity to miss. Shortbreads, scones, ginger biscuits, sponge and fruitcakes, coffee and walnut cake, lemon cake, banana bread and homemade jams present a stunning choice. The good range of teas includes Blue Lady and several fruit-flavoured teas (mango and strawberry, lemon, passion fruit). Smoking is not permitted inside, but weather permitting, there is one table out-of-doors.

Afternoon tea £3.25, pot of tea (for one) 42p–50p, scone and jam 50p
Open Easter–Oct 10am–5pm

NEWTON STEWART Dumfries & Galloway Map 10 NX46

The Chatterbox
73 Victoria Street
Tel (0671) 3967

This small high-street tea and coffee shop has a fresh décor, with pretty tablecloths and upholstered chairs. Friendly and efficient staff offer a good selection of homemade scones, tea breads, cakes and biscuits, as well as a choice of several tea blends – all well-flavoured and freshly made. Lunchtime is always busy.

Pot of tea 50p
Open all year, Mon–Sat, 10am–5pm (Jul and Aug 9.30am–6pm)

NEWTOWN Powys Map 06 SO19

Bank Cottage Tea Rooms
The Bank
Tel (0686) 625771

A listed 17th-century black and white timbered building a short walk from the town's main post office, with a beamed ceiling, tiled floor, cottage furniture and willow pattern china. Full lunches, snack lunches, sandwiches and sweets are available, and two set afternoon teas, or a choice of homemade scones, fruitcake and Welsh cakes, among others. A selection of tea blends is offered.

Pot of tea and one cake average £1, set teas £1.45–£1.90
Open Mon–Sat
Lunches and snacks

NORMANTON Nottinghamshire Map 08 SK75

Reg Taylor's Garden Centre
Tel (0636) 813184

A teashop within the garden centre serving hot snacks at lunch time and homemade cakes and pastries. In fine weather garden chairs are provided on the patio amid the plants.

Pot of tea and one cake average 90p
Open every day 10am–5pm
Light lunches

NORTHALLERTON　　North Yorkshire　　Map 08 SE39

Betty's Café Tea Rooms
188 High Street
Tel (0609) 775154

This café is part of a small group of establishments based in Harrogate (see entries under Harrogate, Ilkley, York). The quality of food is very high, and all made by Betty's own bakery in Harrogate. The uniformed waitresses give efficient and friendly service, and the café is very popular and busy. Several excellent tea blends are available.

Pot of tea and one cake average £2.75, cream tea £3.48
Open all year, every day (except some bank holidays), 9am (10am on Sun)–5.30pm

☐1☐ ☐3☐

NORTHWICH　　Cheshire　　Map 07 SJ67

Bratts Coffee Shop
2–6 Witton Street
Tel (0606) 43344

Situated on the second floor of this town-centre department store, Bratts offers various homemade biscuits, flapjacks and cakes, locally-made cream cakes, as well as speciality homemade scones. A choice of quality tea blends is available.

Pot of tea 44p
Open all year, Mon–Sat, 9.30am–5.30pm
Lunches available

NORWICH　　Norfolk　　Map 05 TG20

Friendly Lodge Hotel
2 Barnard Road
Bowthorpe
Tel (0603) 741161

A recently-opened brick-built hotel, ideally situated on the A47 to the west of the city and offering both plentiful car parking and level access for the disabled, serves afternoon tea in a lounge that has sofas and armchairs grouped around a fountain. A range of freshly prepared sandwiches, savouries, cakes and pastries is accompanied by a choice of tea blends which includes English Breakfast, China and Earl Grey.

Pot of tea and one cake average £2
Open all year, every day
Breakfast and lounge menu available to non-residents 7am–midnight

☐1☐ ☐2☐ ☐3☐

NORWICH　　Norfolk　　Map 05 TG20

Hotel Nelson
Prince of Wales Road
Tel (0603) 760260

Its position across the river from the station making it an ideal meeting/waiting place, this hotel offers afternoon tea in a comfortable lounge where uniformed waiters serve freshly made sandwiches, cakes and pastries to informally seated groups of guests. Tea blends include Ceylon, lapsang souchong and Earl Grey, while juices, wines and spirits are also available.

Pot of tea and one cake average £1.95
Open all year, every day

☐1☐ ☐2☐ ☐3☐

NOTTINGHAM　　Nottinghamshire　　Map 08 SK54

Jessops and Sons
Victoria Centre
Tel (0602) 418282

This comfortable restaurant, situated on the second floor of a good department store, is a well-known and popular meeting place throughout the day, its efficient waitresses serving coffee, lunch, high teas and afternoon teas which include fresh cream cakes and homemade scones with Cornish cream, together with a choice of tea blends.

Pot of tea and scone £1.40
Open all year except bank holidays, Tue–Sat, 9am–5pm (late night shopping Wed)

NOTTINGHAM Nottinghamshire Map 08 SK54

Nottingham Moat House
Mansfield Road
Tel (0602) 602621

This four-star hotel is on the A60, only ¾ mile from the city centre and has good parking facilities. Afternoon tea is served in a comfortable lounge, and consists of fresh sandwiches, scones and tea.

Pot of tea and one cake average £1.65
Open every day, serving tea 3–5.30pm

NOTTINGHAM Nottinghamshire Map 08 SK54

Raffles Tea Rooms
Angel Row
Tel (0602) 474344

These excellent Victorian-style tearooms are very nicely furnished, with carpeted floors, pictures of old Nottingham on the walls, and pretty lace cloths on the tables. Visitors are personally greeted at the door, and very pleasant and efficient staff are dressed in Victorian/Edwardian black and white uniforms. A bonus are the piano concerts at certain times of the day. A choice of excellent quality tea blends is available, served in Royal Worcester tea service. There is a most attractive display of delicious home-baked gâteaux and cakes.

Pot of tea 75p–95p, pot of tea and one cake average £1.45, high tea £5.25
Open all year, Mon–Sat, 9.30am–6pm
Breakfast and lunch available

OAKHAM Leicestershire Map 04 SK80

Barnsdale Lodge Hotel
The Avenue
Rutland Water
Tel (0572) 724678

This country farmhouse hotel, set on the A606 about three miles east of Oakham and furnished in Edwardian style, offers traditional cream teas and high teas where cucumber sandwiches, scones, curd tarts and cakes are accompanied by a range of speciality tea blends. Home baking provides a different choice of items each day, and preserves are also homemade.

Pot of tea and one cake average 75p, set teas £2.50–£4.50
Open all year, every day, 3–6pm for afternoon tea

OAKHAM Leicestershire Map 04 SK80

The Coffee Pot
13–15 Market Place
Tel (0572) 723130

Pleasant ground-floor cottage-style premises, set at the rear of an art gallery with lots of country bric-à-brac on display. Homemade cakes, scones and teacakes are served, with some light meals and a choice of tea blends. Tea is properly presented with good china.

Pot of tea 50p, set teas £1.50–£4.50
Open all year, every day 9.30am–4.30pm
Light meals

OAKHAM   Leicestershire   Map 04 SK80

Muffins
9 Mill Street
Tel (0572) 72350

This family-run tearoom, brightly decorated in cottage style and providing a no-smoking area, serves light meals as well as sandwiches and a range of home-baked scones, cakes, muffins, teacakes and gâteaux. Various tea blends are available, with filter, espresso and capuccino coffee; coach parties can be accommodated by appointment, and there is a takeaway service.

Pot of tea 70p, cream tea £2.50
Open all year, Mon–Sat 10am–5pm (Sun Mar–Oct only 2.30pm–5.30pm)

OAKHAM   Leicestershire   Map 04 SK80

Normanton Park Hotel
Tel Stamford (0780) 720315

This former 18th-century coach house is all that is left of Normanton Hall. Situated in beautiful countryside on the south shore of Rutland Water, it has been transformed into a very pleasant hotel, including a popular coffee lounge with seating on the ground floor and two gallery levels. Homemade cakes and scones are served and a range of toasted sandwiches and ice creams.

Pot of tea 85p, set teas £1.60–£3.80
Open all year, every day, 9am–6.30pm

$\boxed{1}$ $\boxed{2}$ $\boxed{3}$ $\boxed{\&}$

OAKHAM   Leicestershire   Map 04 SK80

Orchard Cuisine
The Maltings
Mill Street
Tel (0572) 723435

These simple but pleasant ground floor premises adjoin a bread and cake shop, close to the town centre. Leaf tea is served from attractive crockery, and a choice of blends is available. Cakes, scones and teacakes, some homemade, are offered, as well as light snacks.

Pot of tea 50p, pot of tea and one cake £1.15
Open all year, every day (except Christmas Day)
Mon–Sat, 8.45am–5pm, Sun 11am–5pm
Light meals

OBAN   Strathclyde   Map 10 NM83

Argyll Tea Room
Argyll Street

Timber-lined walls and a simple beamed ceiling give a homely aspect to this small, family-run tearoom tucked away in a side street just off the waterfront. Popular with both local residents and visitors for the excellence of its home baking, it offers a range of snacks – including homemade soups, sausage rolls and pies – as well as sandwiches, filled rolls, scones, pancakes, shortbread and a variety of cakes. Other items, such as their own date and fruit bread, apple pies and macaroon tarts, are also available to take away.

Pot of tea and one cake 80p
Open all year, Mon–Sat

OLDHAM   Greater Manchester   Map 07 SD90

**King John Café
Restaurant**
Kings Hall
King Street
Tel 061–633 7088

A spacious café restaurant above a shoe market in the centre of town, café-style tables and hanging plants. A good range of hot and cold dishes is served, and there is a colourful ice cream bar selling homemade ice cream. Cakes, scones, gâteaux, sausage rolls and meat pies are available, with a choice of tea blends.

Pot of tea and one cake average 95p
Open all year, Mon–Sat, 9am–5.30pm
Lunch

ONIBURY   Shropshire   Map 07 SO47

Park Farm
A49 between Onibury
& Craven Arms
Tel (058477) 368

This pretty, white-painted hillside farmhouse which looks toward the Shropshire hills from its setting of parkland offers morning coffee and afternoon tea in both dining room and garden during the warmer months. As well as home-baked cakes and scones with cream, there is a range of speciality ice creams made from Jersey milk.

Pot of tea and one cake average £1.25, family menu set tea (2 adults, 2 children) £7.50
Open all year, every day

OTLEY   West Yorkshire   Map 08 SE24

Chatters Tea Shoppe
3 Bay Horse Court
Tel (0943) 466691

This lovely little teashop, set in a charming courtyard with access through a stone alleyway, stands at the centre of the historic market town. In a characterful interior with old beams, a spiral iron staircase, lace tablecloths and good crockery, waitresses in Victorian-style dresses serve a good range of home-baked specialities – including delicious, piping hot Eccles cakes – with a choice of tea blends.

Pot of tea and one cake average £1.50
Open Mon–Sat 9.30am–5pm, summer Sun 11am–4pm
Light meals

OTLEY   West Yorkshire   Map 08 SE24

**Cobblestones Tea
Room**
3 Bondgate
Tel (0943) 467874

Small, cosy and bow-fronted, this homely teashop stands on the main Leeds road, near the church. Tables with lace cloths and attractive china are set against stone walls hung with pictures (for sale), and the hospitable owner provides friendly service. Hot snacks, salads and sandwiches are available throughout the day, and teatime customers can choose either a set menu or a selection from the range of homemade scones, cakes and pastries, served with a choice of tea blends.

Pot of tea and one cake £1.50, set teas £1.30–£2.20
Open all year Thu–Tue, 9.30am–5pm

OXFORD   Oxfordshire   Map 04 SP50

Randolph Hotel
Beaumont Street
Tel (0865) 247481

Public rooms have been magnificently refurbished to provide two comfortable lounges at this large and Gothic-style city-centre hotel dating from the Victorian period, and teas are served in these as well as in the café. Sandwiches, scones, muffins and pastries are available with a choice of tea blends.

Cream tea £5.00, full afternoon tea £6.50
Open all year, every day, 3pm–5.30pm
[1] [2] [3]

PAMPHILL   Dorset   Map 03 ST90

Pamphill Parlour
Near Wimborne
Tel (0202) 880618

Housed in a high-ceilinged barn, together with a farm produce shop, this pleasantly informal teashop displays a tempting range of scones, flapjacks and cakes; Old England and Earl Grey teas are available as alternatives to the standard blend.

Pot of tea 45p, pot of tea and one cake average 95p, set teas £1.65–£2
Open every day
Lunches and snacks

PATELEY BRIDGE   North Yorkshire   Map 07 SE16

Apothecary's House Tea Rooms
37 High Street
Tel (0423) 711767

Claiming to be the oldest house in Pateley Bridge, this stone-fronted building certainly looks the part, the interior exudes warmth with its panelled walls, dark wooden tables and large open fire. Very spick and span, this is an excellent place to enjoy some good homemade fare selected from a display of at least a dozen types of cakes, sponges, flapjacks and shortbreads. Two set teas and a variety of tea blends are available and well dressed waitresses provide prompt and friendly service.

Pot of tea and one cake average £1.50, set teas £2.05–£3.75
Open every day

PEEBLES   Borders   Map 11 NT24

Kailzie Gardens Restaurant
Kailzie
Tel (0721) 22807

Kailzie Gardens, Art Gallery and Waterfowl Pond, now open to the public, are situated within a private estate in a beautiful position on the River Tweed. The licensed restaurant, in the former stables, offers morning coffee, lunch and afternoon tea in congenial surroundings. The homemade scones, gâteaux and meringues should not be missed.

Pot of tea and one cake average £1.75, set tea £2.75
Open Mar–Oct, every day, 11am–5.30pm
Lunch

PEEBLES   Borders   Map 11 NT24

Sunflower
4 The Bridgegate
Tel (0721) 22420

This small licensed restaurant and craft shop just off the High Street has lots of bric-à-brac and paintings for sale. Excellent light meals, vegetarian dishes, morning coffee and afternoon tea are served in each of four small dining rooms. Homemade scones, bread, cakes and gâteaux are available, with a choice of speciality teas.

Pot of tea 40p–55p
Open all year, Mon–Sat,
9.30am–5.30pm
Light meals

PEMBROKE   Dyfed   Map SM90

Richmond Coffee House
Castle Terrace
Tel (0646) 685460

An attractive coffee shop/restaurant very close to the castle, furnished in rustic style with round polished tables and wooden chairs, it features a display of watercolour paintings. Here you can relax with a pot of Earl Grey, Darjeeling, Assam, Lapsang Souchong, Ceylon or herbal tea and your choice from a mainly home-baked range of items including scones, Welsh cakes, bara brith, jam tarts and Danish pastries

Pot of tea and one cake average £1.05
Open Mon–Sat 9am–5pm (and evenings for evening meal)

PENARTH   South Glamorgan   Map 03 ST17

Windsor Tea Gardens
Ludlow Lane

This is a pretty establishment with a pink theme – carpet, wall panels, drapes and table linen, with modern cane furniture. Snacks and some light meals such as salads and jacket potatoes are served. For afternoon tea there are Welsh cakes, walnut slices, pastries, scones and teacakes.

Pot of tea 40p
Open all year, Mon–Sat,
9.30am–5pm
Light meals

PENMAENMAWR   Gwynedd   Map 06 SH77

Y Bedol Bach Tea Room
Capelulo
Tel (0492) 623670

At the foot of the Sychnant Pass, this attractive black-and-white building houses the village shop and post office, and also offers a range of hot snacks and homemade cakes and scones, and, of course, bara brith. Cosy and bright, with fresh flowers and pot plants, the welcome here is warm and genuine.

Pot of tea 50p, cream tea £2.10
Open all year, every day, 8.30am–7pm (Closed Tue pm and all day Wed in winter)

PENRITH   Cumbria   Map 11 NY53

Bobbins Tea Shop
Angel Lane
Great Dockray
Tel (0768) 67999

The exposed stone walls of this charming little teashop are decked with old pictures, plates and bric-à-brac, while a low beamed ceiling, polished wooden floorboards, tables which once held Singer sewing machines, and an abundance of pot plants complete the attractive setting. In the friendly atmosphere you can enjoy a good range of cakes with a choice of tea blends. Smoking is not permitted.

Pot of tea and one cake average £1.75
Open Mon–Sat 9am–5pm, Sun 10am–5pm
Hot and cold snacks

PENSHURST   Kent   Map 05 TQ54

Fir Tree House Tea Rooms
Tel (0892) 870551

The delicious aroma of excellent home-baked scones, cakes and teabreads draws one into these Tudor tearooms. A range of set teas can include dainty sandwiches and a choice of fine teas with such delights as cream sponge, iced cakes and walnut and cinnamon buttered teabread. The exposed beams, wooden tables, pew seating and polished floorboards enhance the charm of this well run establishment.

Pot of tea and one cake average £1, set teas £2–£3.25
Open Apr–Oct Tue–Sun 3–6pm, weekends Jan–Easter

PERSHORE   Hereford & Worcester   Map 03 SO94

Sugar 'n' Spice
20 High Street
Tel (0386) 553654

A teashop at the rear of a glassware and china shop serves a wide range of snacks, sandwiches, scones and cakes, with Indian or Earl Grey tea, in a friendly, informal atmosphere.

Pot of tea and one cake average £1
Open all year, Mon–Sat 9am–5pm

PERSHORE   Hereford & Worcester   Map 03 SO94

Terrace Bistro
Unit 9 Royal Arcade
Broad Street
Tel (0386) 552778

A light airy bistro in the centre of Pershore with outside seating on the terrace. A wide variety of cakes, gâteaux, scones and sandwiches are available in addition to the blackboard menu of hot meals and snacks. Darjeeling, Assam, Earl Grey and herbal teas are offered.

Pot of tea and one cake average £1.50
Open every day 10am–10pm (5.30pm Sun)
Light meals & snacks
1 3

PERTH   Tayside   Map 11 NO12

Goodfellow and Steven, Strawberry Tea Room
50 High Street
Tel (0738) 30327

Conveniently situated beside the pedestrianised area in the High Street, this smart little tearoom, above a baker's shop is reached by means of a spiral staircase. Clean, bright and decorated with strawberry-patterned wallpaper, it displays a blackboard menu of daily 'specials' as well as a selection of hot and cold snacks, sandwiches and a good range of cakes and pastries produced by a local bakery with a sound reputation – the Strawberry Cream Tea (scones with cream and strawberry jam) being particularly popular. The company is especially noted for the quality of its chocolate violets, which are available in the shop below.

Pot of tea and one cake £1.02
Open Mon–Sat
Smoking not permitted

PERTH   Tayside   Map 11 NO12

The Kilnhouse Tearoom
Lower City Mills
West Mill Street
(0738) 30572

This tearoom forms part of a complex which is a unique example of a Victorian watermill, restored to full operation after 35 years of disuse. Said to be the largest working waterwheel in Scotland, it processes local organically-grown grain into the stoneground oatmeal and wholewheat flours which form the basis of much of the home-baked produce available here and which is also available for purchase. The tearoom, reflecting the original character of the mill in its partly panelled natural stone walls and beamed ceiling, is popular with locals and visitors alike, light meals being served all day, while a good range of speciality tea blends is offered. Entrance to the mill costs £1, but admission to the tearoom is free.

Pot of tea and one cake average £1.55
Open every day

PETERBOROUGH   Cambridgeshire   Map 04 TL19

Maxines
Queens Gate Shopping Centre
Tel (0733) 48620

At this popular, Continental-style café in a busy shopping centre, polite, uniformed staff serve the tables inside and out in the shopping mall. Morning coffee, snacks, light lunches and afternoon tea are served. A good selection of scones, pastries, cakes and pancakes is available.

Pot of tea and one cake average £1.10, set tea £1.75
Open all year, every day (except Christmas Day), 8am–6pm (teas not served 11.30am–2pm)

PITLOCHRY   Tayside   Map 14 NN95

The Old Smithy
154 Atholl Road
Tel (0796) 2356

This family-run business includes a tearoom and restaurant combined with a shop selling quality fashions, crafts and gifts. The cottage-style tearoom is pleasantly decorated and the walls are hung with prints, many of which are for sale. Open sandwiches are a speciality, with homebaked scones, carrot cake and apple pie. A choice of tea blends is offered.

Pot of tea 50p
Open Feb–Dec, winter Mon–Wed, Fri, Sat, 10am–5pm, summer Mon–Sat, 10am–8pm, Sun, 11am–5pm
1 2 3 &

PLUNGAR   Leicestershire   Map 08 SK73

Our Little Farm
Lodge Farm
Harby Lane
Tel (0949) 60349

The tea/gift shop in this fascinating farm park is housed in a converted cow shed, with large windows overlooking the fields and the stalls still evident. All the cakes and pastries are homemade and displayed in a chilled cabinet. Ploughmans, filled rolls, and home cured ham salads are also available, and Tisson, Earl Grey and various herbal teas are offered, in addition to the standard blends. It is possible to have a picnic hamper made up to take on explorations of the nature trail and if the weather turns wet, the Old Hay Loft can be used as a picnic room. No dogs except guide dogs.

Pot of tea and one cake average 90p, no set teas
Open Apr–Nov, Tues–Sun and BH 10.30am–5.30pm
There is an entrance charge to the Farm and Nature trail
&

POOLE   Dorset   Map 04 SZ09

Hospitality Inn
The Quay
Tel (0202) 666800

This modern commercial hotel on the quayside has good views over Poole Harbour. Refreshments are served in the first floor lounge. There is a tray service for tea, with a choice of Earl Grey or China tea, as well as the standard blend. Homemade cakes, scones and sandwiches are served.

Pot of tea £1, set teas £3.00–£7.00
Open all year, every day, 3pm–5pm for tea

POOLE   Dorset   04 SZ09

Salterns
38 Salterns Way
Lilliput
Tel (0202) 707321

This modernised hotel overlooks the marina with comfortable, tastefully appointed public rooms. There is also a patio with fine views of the harbour. Homemade cakes and scones are served, with a choice of tea blends.

Afternoon tea £3.50
Open all year, every day, 3pm–5pm for tea
1 2 3

POOLE   Dorset   04 SZ09

Towngate Café
Dolphin Hotel
High Street
Tel (0202) 673612

Part of the Dolphin Hotel and situated in the main shopping precinct, this is a modern conservatory-style coffee shop with hanging baskets and cane furniture. Light meals, sandwiches, scones, cakes and pastries are available on a self-service basis.

Pot of tea and one cake average £1.05, afternoon tea £2.60
Open all year, every day, 8am–5.30pm
Light meals

POOLEY BRIDGE   Cumbria   Map 12 NY42

Heughscar
Tel (08536) 453

This corner bed-and-breakfast establishment has the dining room properly set up for tea, and offers fresh sandwiches, various types of scone, biscuits and cakes. There is a good choice of speciality teas.

Pot of tea 45p, afternoon tea £2.20
Open all year, every day Apr–Oct, Sun only Nov–Mar, 10am–5.30pm

POOLEY BRIDGE   Cumbria   Map 12 NY42

Sharrow Bay Hotel
Tel (08536) 301 478

This unique hotel enjoys a superb position on the shores of Lake Ullswater, with wonderful views over the lake and surrounding fells. For the past forty-two years and more the hotel's owners, Francis Coulson and Brian Sack have provided their unique blend of hospitality and excellent cooking to an ever-growing and appreciative clientèle. Afternoon tea is served either in the lounge or in the conservatory, and only a small number of non-resident guests can be accommodated. Pastries, scones and cakes are so light that they melt in the mouth, and the service and the china are both equally fine.

Full afternoon tea from £7.50
Open Mar–Nov, every day, 4–4.45pm

PORTESHAM   Dorset   Map 03 SY68

Millmead Country Hotel
Tel (0305) 871432

A pleasant country hotel in this quiet little village. The dining room for non-residents is a light, airy conservatory with garden-style furniture and many attractive plants. Cakes and scones are served with a choice of tea blends. Smoking is not permitted.

Pot of tea and one cake from £1.20, afternoon tea about £1.65
Open all year (except Christmas) every day

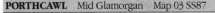

PORTHCAWL   Mid Glamorgan   Map 03 SS87

Sea Bank Hotel
The Promenade
Tel (065671) 2261

The comfortable lounge and lounge-bar of a three-star hotel on the promenade provide a convenient and civilised setting in which to enjoy afternoon tea with a choice of scones, pastries, cakes and gâteaux.

Pot of tea and one cake average £2.40
Open every day

PORTHCAWL   Mid Glamorgan   Map 03 SS87

See Green
James Street
Tel (065671) 5185

The menu of this small Friends of the Earth coffee shop, with polished floorboards, oilskin-covered tables and rustic chairs, includes a limited selection of snacks, filled pitta breads and sandwiches, wholefood scones, cakes and tarts, and a good choice of speciality teas. Environmentally friendly products are also offered for sale.

Pot of tea and one cake average 85p
Open Mon–Sat, 9am–5pm

PORTLOE   Cornwall & Isles of Scilly   Map 02 SW93

Tregaine Tea Room
The Post Office
Tel (0872) 501252

This tearoom – run in conjunction with the community sub post office and shop – occupies premises that were originally three tiny Cornish stone cottages said to be the oldest in the village. In the cosy, low-beamed interior, or on the terrace in front, a choice of Earl Grey or Indian tea accompanies either a set cream tea or a selection from the wide range of cakes, locally-made bread and pastries, shortbread and meringues; light lunches are available, while a bistro-style menu is served in the evenings.

Pot of tea and one cake average £1.20, cream tea £2.25
Open Mar–Oct every day
Light lunches and evening meals

PORT TALBOT   West Glamorgan   Map 03 SS79

Gossip
1 Riverside Shops
Aberavon Shopping
Centre
Tel (0639) 890622

This small café is on two floors in a busy town shopping centre. Light meals are available with some homemade gâteaux, cheesecakes and teacakes.

Tea and cake around 95p
Open all year, Mon–Sat, 9am–5pm
Lunch

POYNTON   Cheshire   Map 07 SJ98

Romany's Restaurant and Coffee Shop
Brookside Garden Centre
Macclesfield Road
Tel (0625) 877178

This garden centre, now becoming a tourist attraction, features a fully equipped scenic route railway – six magnificent engines, both steam and diesel, providing pulling power for rides of up to twenty passengers at a time – which appeals to adults and children alike. Romany's (so called because of the caravan on the lawn) is also very popular, tea-time visitors choosing from a mouthwatering chilled-cabinet display of homemade scones, strawberry shortcake, gâteaux, pastries, trifle and other sweets, and from a range of tea blends.

Pot of tea and one cake average £1.75
Open Tue–Sun and Bank Holiday Mon, 9am–5pm
Breakfasts, snacks, lunches (booking essential for Sunday lunch)

PREES GREEN   Shropshire   Map 07 SJ53

Cruckmoor Farm
Tel (0948) 840217

During the tourist season an old farmhouse just off the A49 Whitchurch–Shrewsbury road offers cream teas in a sympathetically converted cowshed in its yard. Luxury ice cream in a variety of flavours, produced from their own cows' milk, is a speciality, and cream teas are available.

Set teas £1.50–£1.60
Open tourist season only, every day 10am–6pm

PRESTATYN   Clwyd   Map 06 SJ08

Bryn Gwalia Inn
Gronant Road
Tel (07456) 2442

This busy inn is open all day and extremely popular at lunchtime with local customers. The interior is pretty and homely, with sofas and easy chairs, and a large array of bric-à-brac. Cream teas are served and homemade biscuits and sponge cake are also available.

Pot of tea 45p, cream tea £1.85
Open 2.30pm–6pm for afternoon tea
Lunch, dinner
♿

PRESTEIGNE   Powys   Map 03 SO36

Radnorshire Arms Hotel
High Street
Tel (0544) 267406

Attractively positioned amid lawns and gardens, this half-timbered inn has public rooms of great character. Lounge service is available for afternoon tea.

Cream tea £2.50
Open all year, every day
[1] [2] [3]

PUDSEY   West Yorkshire   Map 08 SE23

Coffee house
Booths Yard

A charming little tea/coffee shop, formerly a weaver's cottage dating back to the 1720s, situated in a narrow cobbled street at the centre of the town. It has a low-beamed ceiling, wheelback chairs, lace clothed tables with fine bone china cups and decorative bric-à-brac. A good selection of tea blends (including herbals) accompanies a range of home-baked scones and cakes – fresh cream trifle also being available.

Pot of tea and one cake average £1.50
Open Mon, Tue and Thu–Sat 10am–4pm, Wed 10am–3pm

PULBOROUGH   West Sussex   Map 04 TQ01

Arun Cosmopolitan Hotel
Lower Street
Tel (07982) 2162

This delightful, well-furnished and capably managed small hotel offers afternoon tea beside a log-burning fire in the lounge, or in the rear garden on sunny days. Freshly-made sandwiches and home-baked biscuits and cakes supplement the traditional cream tea, and a good selection of speciality tea blends is available.

Pot of tea and one cake average £1.65, set teas £2.10–£2.85
Open every day
1 2 3

RANGEMORE   Staffordshire   Map 07 SK12

Byrkley Park Centre
(5 miles west of Burton-on-Trent, off A38 beyond Tatenhill)
Tel (0283) 716467

Tearooms and a carvery are set in a landscaped area within the walled garden of the estate belonging to the Bass family of brewing fame. Staff are friendly, home-baking is of an excellent standard, and full meals are also available.

Set teas at various prices
Open every day, Apr–Aug 9am–6pm (9pm, Thu, Fri, Sat), Sep–Mar, 9am–5pm
1 3 &

RAVENSHEAD   Nottinghamshire   Map 08 SK55

Longdale Rural Craft Centre
Longdale Lane
Tel (0623) 794858

At the side of this rural craft centre – which is the headquarters of the Nottinghamshire Craftmen's Guild and undertakes commissions of all types – stands a restaurant which can satisfy the hungriest of visitors, serving not only Longdale cream teas and high teas with home-baked scones and cakes accompanied by a choice of Earl Grey, herbal or standard tea blends, but also a range of main courses and snacks that is available right through the evening. Smoking is discouraged.

Pot of tea and one cake average £1.20, set teas £2.15–£2.50
Open all year, every day

REDDITCH   Hereford & Worcester   Map 07 SP06

Druckers
New Walk
Kingfisher Centre
Tel (0527) 67512

A modestly decorated and furnished self-service establishment within the Kingfisher Shopping Centre offers sandwiches, croissants and quiches as well as the pastries, cakes and gâteaux made at the company's central pâtisserie.

Pot of tea and one cake average £1.50
Open Mon–Sat 10am–5pm

REDLYNCH   Wiltshire   Map 04 SU22

Mop's Cream Teas
Forest Road
Tel (0725) 21593/21516

Attractive cottage-style tearooms just inside the New Forest, refreshingly decorated with lace-covered emerald green tablecloths, with additional seating outdoors on the terrace. The cream tea comprises two large scones, clotted cream and strawberry jam, and homemade cakes include chocolate gâteau, date and walnut loaf and butterfly cakes. Sandwiches are also available, and a selection of tea blends

Pot of tea and one cake 80p–£1.70, cream tea £2.50
Open Mon–Wed & Sat 2–6pm, Sun 11am–6pm

RETFORD   Nottinghamshire   Map 08 SK78

John Sinclair's Coffee Shop
22 The Square
Tel (0777) 709670

A charming coffee shop furnished with antiques occupies the first floor of a china shop, its window tables overlooking the town square. A choice of sandwiches supplements the trolley display of home-baked cakes and pastries ranging from scones to Pavlova – meringues being the establishment's forte – while Earl Grey, Darjeeling and Assam tea blends are available.

Pot of tea and one cake average £1.45
Open all year, Mon–Sat 9.30am–4pm
1 3

RHAYADER   Powys   Map 06 SN96

The Strand Restaurant & Cake Shop
East Street
Tel (0597) 810564

Part of a small bread and cake shop set on the crossroad of this mid-Wales town, the restaurant offers a wide range of snacks in addition to such traditional teatime items as sandwiches, toasted teacakes, scones and cakes.

Pot of tea and one cake average 76p
Open all year, Mon–Sat

RHOS-ON-SEA   Clwyd   Map 06 SH88

Penrhos Restaurant
53 Llandudno Road
Tel Colwyn Bay (0492) 49547

A small restaurant with pretty lace cloths, exposed beams bedecked with a jug collection and a loud chiming clock. There is also a small patio outside. Popular with both locals and tourists, light snacks and meals are served throughout the day. Pies, pastries and scones are homemade while cakes and gâteaux are from a local bakery.

Pot of tea 45p
Open all year, Mon–Fri 9am–5.30pm, Sat 9am–2pm

RHOS-ON-SEA   Clwyd   Map 06 SH88

Summers Restaurant & Tearoom
Rhos Road
Tel Colwyn Bay (0492) 44790

A bright, cheerful restaurant close to the promenade, with pretty floral wallpaper, beamed ceiling and lace tablecloths. Light savoury snacks, scones and cakes are served with a selection of gâteaux and pastries from the trolley. A choice of tea blends is available.

Pot of tea 45p, cake 80p–£1.10
Open all year, Tue–Sun (Mon–Sun high season). 10am–5pm winter, 10am–8pm summer

RICHMOND   North Yorkshire   Map 07 N210

Mary's
5–6 Trinity Church Square
Tel (0748) 4052

Mary's is situated in the main square over a very good delicatessen which supplies the tea and coffee blends and cooked meats. Hot dishes are served as well as homemade cakes, scones, sandwiches and teacakes. Seven blends of leaf tea are available.

Pot of tea and one cake average £1.80, full tea £2.60
Open all year, every day, summer, 9.30–5.30pm, winter, 10am–5pm

RINGFORD   Dumfries & Galloway   Map 11 NX65

Old School Tearoom
Tel (055722) 250

An old, three-roomed school beside the A75 six miles west of Castle Douglas has been converted to create this tearoom with a craftshop behind it and ample parking to the side. Lofty, spacious rooms with polished wooden floors remain pleasantly reminiscent of schooldays, but the refreshments offered are a far cry from school dinners, including toasted, open and traditional sandwiches whose fillings range from home-cooked ham to a mixture of cheese, sultanas and celery, home-baked scones, pies and cakes, and a selection of tea blends.

Pot of tea and one cake average £1, set teas £1.30–£1.50
Open every day

RINGWOOD   Hampshire   Map 04 SU10

Daisy Darling
35 High Street
Tel (0425) 474563

A single-fronted restaurant in the centre of Ringwood with a cottagey atmosphere, padded Windsor chairs and Indian tree pattern china. A comprehensive menu of hot meals, snacks and speciality ice creams is offered. Commercially produced cakes, scones and pastries are available for afternoon tea.

Pot of tea and one cake average £1.00, set teas £2.00–£2.15
Open all year, Mon–Fri, 9am–5pm, Sat 9am–9pm
Lunch, dinner

ROCHESTER   Kent   Map 05 TQ76

Bridgewood Manor Hotel
Bridgewood
Roundabout
Maidstone Road
Tel (0634) 201333

This modern, Gothic-style hotel at the junction of the A2 and A229 serves afternoon tea in extensive lounge areas divided into attractive drawing rooms where antiques complement the comfortable modern sofas and armchairs grouped round large open fireplaces. A set traditional afternoon tea is available, as well as an à la carte menu of snacks, savouries, cakes and pastries with traditional, Earl Grey or lapsang souchong tea.

Pot of tea and one cake average £2.25, set tea £4.95
Open every day

ROCKCLIFFE   Dumfries & Galloway   Map 11 NX85

The Garden Room
Rockcliffe
Dalbeattie
Tel (055663) 402

A delightful, flag-floored tearoom featuring local crafts offers additional seating in its attractive gardens. Service is friendly and cheerful, but an array of home baking that encompasses scones, carrot cake, banoffee pie, and butterscotch and walnut gâteau does not make choice easy! Savoury items include the popular Frenchman's sandwich – a croissant filled with salad and turkey, ham, chicken or cheese.

Pot of tea and one cake average £1
Open Easter–Nov every day
Light lunches

ROMSEY   Hampshire   Map 04 SU32

Cobweb Tearooms
49 The Hundred
Tel (0794) 516434

Attractive, beamed tearooms with green-clothed tables and captain's chairs. The table is laden with homemade cakes and cream teas, and a sweet trolley displays dishes such as hazelnut torte, pavlova and cheesecake. Lunches are also served.

Pot of tea and one cake average £1.00, set teas from £1.70
Open all year, (except 2 weeks Sep/Oct and 1 week Christmas), Tue–Sat, 10am–5.30pm
Lunches

ROSS-ON-WYE   Hereford & Worcestor   Map 03 SO62

Copperfields
29 Gloucester Road
Tel (0989) 67734

Pleasant, bright ground floor teashop, part of a delicatessen and pâtisserie, popular with shoppers and tourists alike. Scones, teacakes, cream cakes and gâteaux, many of which are baked on the premises, are served. There is also a good range of hot and cold snacks and a choice of tea blends is offered. Smoking is not permitted.

Tea 59p
Open Jan–Dec, Mon–Sat, 9am–5pm
Hot and cold snacks

ROSS-ON-WYE   Hereford and Worcester   Map 03 SO26

Pengethley Manor
Tel (0989) 87211

A lovely Georgian manor house, now a country-house hotel, situated in 15 acres of grounds and gardens with splendid views of the surrounding countryside, four miles north-west of the town on the A49. Home baking, sandwiches and strawberry teas in season are served with a choice of tea blends, presented in silver teapots with Wedgwood china.

Pot of tea £1, set teas from £3.75
Open all year, every day, 3pm–6pm

ROSS-ON-WYE   Hereford & Worcester   Map 03 SO62

The Royal Hotel
Palace Pound
Tel (0989) 768058

A hotel set high in the town, with good views over the horseshoe bend of the River Wye, serves afternoon tea either in its comfortable lounge or, weather permitting, in the gardens. Service is both professional and friendly, and the limited menu offers two set teas and individual items such as teacakes and gateaux; speciality tea blends include lapsang souchong and Earl Grey.

Pot of tea and one cake average £1.50, set teas £2.95–£3.95
Open all year, every day
1 2 3

ROTHERHAM   South Yorkshire   Map 08 SK49

Consort Hotel
Brampton Road
Thurcroft
Tel (0709) 530022

Conveniently set at the M18/M1 intersection and having ample car parking space, this privately-owned, modern, two-storey hotel serves tea in the attractive surroundings of a spacious lounge where comfortable armchairs and sofas are grouped around coffee tables. An à la carte menu offers freshly made sandwiches and scones, pastries and cakes baked on the premises.

Pot of tea and one cake average £1.50, set teas £2.50–£4.75
Open all year, every day
1 2 3

RUTHIN   Clwyd   06 SJ15

Bay Tree
Ruthin Craft Centre
Tel (08242) 2121

A modern café with waitress service in the middle of the large Craft Centre, the Bay Tree has a modern décor, with a quarry-tiled floor, pine furniture and a small outside patio area. Teas, light snacks and quite substantial lunches are served. Sandwiches, scones and bara brith are available with a selection of gâteaux and Danish pastries.

Pot of tea and one cake average £1, set teas £1.80–£2.20
Open all year, every day, 10.30am–5pm (12 noon–5pm Sun)
Lunches

RUTHIN   Clwyd   Map 06 SJ15

Ruthin Castle Hotel
Tel (08242) 2664

This cottage-style tearoom offering sandwiches, bara brith, cakes and cream teas is set in the wing of an authentic castle – now an hotel – which stands in thirty acres of grounds and gardens a few minutes' walk from the town centre.

Pot of tea and one cake average £1.30, cream tea £2.65
Open every day

RYE   East Sussex   Map 05 TQ92

Cobbles Tea Room
1 Hylands Yard
Tel (0797) 225962

A small, quaint tearoom, tucked away up a cobbled path and providing an ideal escape from the town's busy main street, serves traditional cream teas, full English teas or a selection of homemade scones, cakes and cookies, all offered with a range of specialist tea blends. If something more substantial is required, Welsh Rarebit or toasted sandwiches are available. There is limited outside seating.

Pot of tea and one cake average £1.50, set teas £1.75–£3

RYE   East Sussex   Map 05 TQ92

Mermaid Inn
Mermaid Street
Tel (0797) 223065

Afternoon tea is served in the Tudor Room of this welcoming medieval inn which dates from 1157, and has wonderful beamed and oak-panelled public rooms. Soup and sandwiches are available for light meals, and for tea homebaked scones are served with a choice of good professionally made pâtisserie.

Pot of tea and biscuits £1.50, cream tea £3.50
Open Easter–Sep, every day, noon–5pm
Lunches
[1] [2] [3]

RYE   East Sussex   Map 05 TQ92

The Playden Oasts Hotel
Playden
Tel (0797) 223502

Snacks, a range of homemade puddings, teacakes, scones, croissants and gateaux – as well as traditional cream teas – are served all day in the character bar, small restaurant or attractive rear garden of this hotel on the edge of the historic town by the A268. The building, dating from about 1800, was once used for drying the hops grown in nearby fields which were then used to flavour local beer.

Pot of tea and one cake average £1.60, set teas £2.25
Open all year, every day
[1] [2] [3]

ST AGNES   Cornwall & Isles of Scilly   Map 02 SW75

Sunholme Hotel
Tel (087255) 2318

A teapot sign at the end of the drive points the way to a well-presented and friendly small hotel on St Agnes Beacon. Here you can enjoy superb views of countryside and coast as you sample home-made scones and a freshly made pot of Earl Grey or Indian tea.

Cream tea £2.50
Open Apr–Oct, every day, 3–5pm
Bar snacks

ST ALBANS   Hertfordshire   Map 04 TL10

Dahlia Coffee Shop
Aylett Nurseries Ltd
The North Orbital
Road (A414)
London Colney
Tel (0727) 22255

This attractive, conservatory-style tea/coffee shop, with its pleasantly airy atmosphere and abundance of plants, offers Earl Grey and camomile teas as alternatives to the more traditional blends, whilst friendly, attentive staff serve a good range of homemade scones and cakes as well as quiches, rolls and sandwiches.

Tea 45p–55p per person
Open all year, every day, except Christmas Day and Boxing Day, 9.30am–5pm

ST ALBANS   Hertfordshire   Map 04 TL10

Noke Thistle Hotel
Watford Road
Tel (0727) 54252

An attractive hotel, retaining much of its Victorian charm and cosy atmosphere, offering refreshments in both comfortable lounge and bar. Tea is properly made and well presented, with a choice of China, Earl Grey, Assam and Darjeeling blends. A range of croissants, sandwiches, pastries, gâteaux and home-baked cookies is available – or you can indulge in a cream tea.

Pot of tea and one cake average £3
Cream tea £3.50
Open all year, every day (all day)

ST ALBANS   Hertfordshire   Map 04 TL10

Waffle House
39 St Giles Street
Kingsbury Watermill
St Michael's Street
Tel (0727) 53502

A characterful tearoom with open fires and exposed beams is set in an Elizabethan house adjoining a working watermill which has been converted into a museum; guests can also browse in the art gallery and gift shop. Predictably, the establishment specialises in a wide variety of waffles – both sweet and savoury – and if offers a good choice of speciality teas.

Pot of tea 70p, pot of tea and one plain waffle £1.50
Open all year (except between Christmas and New Year) Wed–Sun, 11.00am (12.00 Sundays and bank holidays) – 5.00pm (6.00pm Summer)

ST ANDREWS   Fife   Map 12 NO51

MacGregor's Coffee Shop
71 Market Street
Tel (0334) 77106

In a quaint cobbled street in the centre of town, this is a well established coffee and gift shop. The coffee lounge is on an open mezzanine above the gift area and a vast selection of hot and cold dishes is served all day, but most popular seems to be the home baking: scones, carrot cake, passion cake, Danish pastries, shortbread and chocolate traybakes. A choice of tea blends is offered and a good range of sandwiches.

Pot of tea and one cake average £1.05
Open every day
Light lunches
[1] [2] [3]

ST ANDREWS   Fife   Map 12 NO51

The Merchant's House
49 South Street
Tel (0334) 72595

Dating back to the 17th century, this fine town house has been beautifully restored and retains old painted ceilings and the original vaults, now glass roofed to give a bright, airy atmosphere. The range of home-baking is excellent and there is a wide choice of China, Indian and herbal teas. Service is good and the surroundings full of interest. Other meals are also served.

Pot of tea and one cake average £1.10
Open every day (except 2 weeks over Christmas and New Year) Apr–Oct, Mon–Sat, 10am–10pm, Sun 10am–9pm, Nov–Mar, Wed–Sat 10am–10pm, Sun–Tue 10am–5.30pm

ST ANDREWS   Fife   Map 12 NO51

Mill Ring Restaurant
Clayton Caravan Park
(between Dairsie and Guardbridge, 5 miles west of St Andrews)
Tel (0334) 870630

The restaurant is as popular with passing customers as with caravanners in the park, and has the added attraction of a children's play area outside. 'Worth a visit for Patsy's scones alone,' says our Inspector, but there is a wide range of other good home-baking, all very good value.

Pot of tea and one cake average 90p
Open Easter–Nov, every day, 8.30am–6.30pm
Light refreshments also served
[1] [3]

ST ANDREWS   Fife   Map 12 NO51

Old Course Hotel
Old Station Road
Tel (0334) 74371

Afternoon tea is served in the Conservatory with its splendid view across the Old Golf Course to the sea beyond. Staff are courteous, attentive and professional, and there is a wide choice both of good baking and blends of tea, properly made and correctly served.

Pot of tea and one cake average £3, afternoon teas £3.00–£7.50
Open all year, every day, 7am–6.30pm
Light refreshments also served

ST CLEARS Dyfed Map 02 SN21

County Tea Rooms
Pentre Road
Tel (0994) 231061

In a small room furnished with polished tables and cottage-style chairs you can enjoy a good, traditional cup of tea accompanied by a scone, custard slice or Danish pastry – or perhaps by sandwiches or a hot snack if you require something more substantial. Staff are particularly friendly here.

Cup of tea and Danish Pastry 95p
Open all year, Mon–Sat
Hot meals available all day

ST CLEARS Dyfed Map 02 SN21

Forge Hotel and Restaurant
Tel (0994) 230300

This pleasant, small, and personally-run motel is set conveniently back from the A40 and is a most welcome stopping place. Meals, including cream teas are served in the comfortable bar, and they make a very good cup of tea.

Cream tea £1.40
Open every day, teas served in the afternoons
Other meals also served
[1] [3]

ST CLEARS Dyfed Map 02 SN21

Savoy Country Inn
Tenby Road
Tel (0994) 230664

A modern lounge-bar and restaurant complex, comfortably appointed and offering plush seating, stands beside the A477 just to the Tenby side of St Clears. Lunches, dinners, bar meals and snacks are available, as well as afternoon teas.

Pot of tea and one cake average 86p, set tea £1.25
Open all year, every day
[1] [3]

ST COLUMB MAJOR Cornwall & Isles of Scilly Map 02 SW96

Meadowside Farm
Winnards Perch
Tel (0637) 880544

A modern sectional cedarwood building on a small farm beside the A39 between St Columb Major and Wadebridge. The farm has three coarse fishing lakes stocked with mixed fish, including some carp up to 14lbs. There are facilities for the disabled, and a license for five caravans. Cold snacks and sandwiches, cream teas and homemade fruitcake are served.

Pot of tea and one cake average 90p, cream tea £1.70
Open every day
Snacks

ST FAGANS South Glamorgan Map 03 ST17

Welsh Craft Shop and Post Office
Tel (0222) 561240

A Welsh craft shop that doubles as the village post office stands near the church and not too far from the Folk Museum; the small area set aside for the serving of tea and coffee also offers a limited range of eatables which includes Welsh cakes, pasties and custard slices.

Pot of tea 55p
Open Mon–Sat (closed Wed and Sat pm in winter)
[1] [3]

ST GERRANS   Cornwall & Isles of Scilly   Map 02 SW93

Turnpike Cottage Antiques and Tearooms
The Square
Tel (087258) 853

Beyond the stable door of this pretty white cottage is a delightful small tearoom – just the place for a delicious Cornish cream tea after an afternoon on the nearby beaches around Portscatho. Cakes are served in the traditional way on porcelain cake stands, while the other pieces of porcelain and small antiques which decorate the room are all for sale.

Pot of tea 55p, set tea £2
Open all year, Easter–end Oct, Tue–Sun (rest of year weekends only) 3–6pm for tea
Morning coffee, light lunches and Cornish suppers also available

ST IVES   Cornwall & Isles of Scilly   Map 02 SW54

Bumbles Tea Shop
Digby Square
Tel (0736) 797977

The Georgian frontage of this pretty, cottage-style tearoom is complemented by the quality of its interior, and there are pleasant views from all windows. Guests not tempted by the cream tea can choose from a range of sandwiches, scones, cakes and pastries, many home-made, complemented by a large range of tea blends, including Earl Grey, Darjeeling, Ceylon, and Lapsang, as well as fruit and herbal infusions.

Pot of tea 45p, Cornish cream tea £1.95
Open all year, 10am–5pm
Light snacks also available

ST IVES   Cornwall & Isles of Scilly   Map 02 SW54

Coasters Tea Shop
15 St Andrews Street
Tel (0736) 794184

This compact, granite-walled shop near the harbour wall, its exposed beams complemented by polished tables, benches and wheelback chairs, offers a selection of fresh scones, date and walnut bread, peanut, rich chocolate and yogurt cakes accompanied by a range of teas which includes Darjeeling, Earl Grey and some herbal blends, all served with a choice of milk or lemon.

Pot of tea and one cake average £1.60, Cornish cream tea £2.25
Open Easter–end Oct every day, 10am–5.30pm (7am–9.30pm in main season)

ST IVES   Cornwall & Isles of Scilly   Map 02 SW54

Cobblestones Coffee House
5 St Andrews Street
Tel (0736) 797613

A cottage-style teashop with exposed beams, polished wood tables and wheelback chairs, commanding views along the coast from its picture window. Cobblestones serves an enjoyable cream tea with homemade scones and a good pot of tea. Freshly prepared vegetarian and wholefood dishes are also available.

Pot of tea 45p, cream tea £1.95
Open all year, every day, summer 9am–10pm, winter 9am–5pm

ST IVES   Cornwall & Isles of Scilly   Map 02 SW54

Dolphin Hotel
Bridge Foot
London Road
Tel (0480) 66966

Modern and purpose built, a three-star hotel overlooking open countryside and only a minute's walk from the town centre offers teas both in its comfortable bar area and on a large riverside terrace. Friendly and efficient uniformed staff serve a range of good quality, freshly prepared and attractively presented items that include sandwiches, teacakes, scones, doughnuts and pastries; the menu is shortly to be extended to introduce a range of set teas to supplement the cream tea already available.

Set teas £1.60–£1.75
Open every day
1 2 3

ST MAWES   Cornwall & Isles of Scilly   Map 02 SW83

Broomers
14 Marine Parade
Tel (0326) 270440

A small, cottage-styled restaurant just up from the Harbour Master's office, overlooking both harbour and the sea beyond, offers cream teas from three o'clock, together with a range of freshly-made sandwiches (plain or toasted), teacakes, scones, clotted cream cakes and chocolate fudge cake; a choice of Earl Grey or house tea is served in large, sensible cups.

Pot of tea and one cake average £1.85, cream tea £2
Open every day
Breakfast, morning coffee, snacks and light lunches.

ST MAWES   Cornwall & Isles of Scilly   Map 02 SW83

Idle Rocks Hotel
Tel (0326) 270771

The lounge and sun terrace of this hotel provide a splendid vantage point from which to enjoy uninterrupted sea views or watch the ever-changing harbour scene. A cream tea, scones or biscuits are accompanied by a choice of Assam, Darjeeling or Earl Grey tea, professionally served in Wedgwood bone china, while morning coffee and light lunches are also available.

Pot of tea and one cake average £1.95, set teas from £1.95
Open every day
1 2 3

SALCOMBE   Devon   Map 03 SX73

Bolt Head Hotel
Tel (054884) 3751

In the comfortable lounges of this friendly hotel, with its fine views across the estuary, you can enjoy a typical Devon cream tea in which appetising sandwiches are succeeded by homemade scones and pastries, courteous staff offering a choice of traditional, Darjeeling or Earl Grey tea.

Cream tea £2.95
Open mid May–end Oct, every day, 11am–6pm

SALCOMBE   Devon   Map 03 SX73

The Austro Pâtisserie
61 Fore Street
Tel (054884) 2511

A little teashop area at the back of the Austro Pâtisserie, in the main street of the village, has been tastefully decorated and comfortably furnished; pleasant staff create a friendly, relaxed atmosphere in which to enjoy the range of English and Austrian cakes made on the premises by the proprietor – an Austrian Pâtissier. Earl Grey tea provides an alternative to Indian, and an Expresso machine produces good coffee.

Pot of tea and one cake average £1.25, cream tea £2.20
Open Mon–Sat in season, otherwise Mon–Fri

SALCOMBE   Devon   Map 03 SX73

Marine Hotel
Tel (054884) 2251

A large, traditionally-styled hotel with unrestricted views across the estuary offers quality afternoon teas in its spaciously comfortable public rooms. Guests can opt for the cream tea or take their pick from a wide selection of homemade scones, pastries and cakes accompanied by a well-flavoured, correctly-brewed pot of tea, whether it be Lapsang, Darjeeling, Earl Grey or a more traditional blend.

Pot of tea £1.20, set tea £3.95
Open all year, every day, 3 – 5.30pm
1 2 3

SALCOMBE   Devon   Map 03 SX73

The Ward Room
Salcombe Chandlers Ltd
19 Fore Street
Tel (054884) 2620

Occupying a beautiful position beside the estuary at the centre of the village, behind the chandler's store, this teashop has adopted a bright, nautical theme. Patio doors lead onto a little paved terrace with white iron tables and chairs. Fresh Devon clotted cream accompanies the varied selection of homemade cakes and scones available at a self-service counter which also offers salads, quiche and soups.

Pot of tea and one cake average £1.95, cream tea £2.50
Open every day 10am–5.30pm

SALISBURY   Wiltshire   Map 04 SU12

Michael Snell Tea Rooms
8 Saint Thomas's Square
Tel (0722) 336037

Homemade gâteaux, cream cakes and pastries are the speciality of tearooms which take in the old town-miller's house to the front and a former church school at the rear. Earl Grey, Darjeeling, Lapsang and Assam teas are available, all carefully brewed and attractively served by helpful staff.

Pot of tea from 63p, cream tea £2.35
Open all year, Mon–Sat, 9am–5pm

SALISBURY   Wiltshire   Map 04 SU12

Reeve the Baker
Butcher Row
Tel (0722) 20367

This two-storey corner shop overlooking the market place is supplied by its own bakery and offers a selection of set teas served by friendly young staff: Earl Grey and Old England teas offer alternatives to the more traditional Indian blend.

Set teas £2–£3
Open all year, Mon–Sat, 9am–5.30pm

SALISBURY   Wiltshire   Map 04 SU12

White Hart
St John Street
Tel (0722) 27476

In the pleasant, open-plan lounge of this city-centre hotel you can enjoy a set tea which complements homemade scones and cakes with a good cup of Earl Grey, Grosvenor or Indian tea, properly brewed and served in a china pot.

Set teas from £1.95–£2.75 and £3.75
Open all year, every day, 3pm–5.30pm

SANDBACH   Cheshire   Map 07 SJ76

The Old Hall Hotel
Newcastle Road
Tel (0270) 761221

A beautifully preserved, timber-framed hall dating back to 1656, its interior displaying a wealth of oak panelling and attractive fireplaces, offers set teas where freshly-made sandwiches and scones and cakes baked on the premises are accompanied by a choice of Earl Grey, Darjeeling or lapsang tea. Coffee, decaffeinated coffee, hot chocolate and milk shakes are also available on request.

Set teas £2.75–£3.95
Open every day

SAUNDERSFOOT   Dyfed   Map 02 SN10

Cavalier Restaurant
High Street
Tel (0834) 812806

Set in a slightly elevated situation just off the harbour front, a restaurant with good quality polished tables and wheelback chairs, its walls displaying a selection of pictures offered for sale by local artists, serves cream teas or a choice of sandwiches, scones and teacakes with Darjeeling or Earl Grey tea. A full range of meals is available throughout the day.

Pot of tea and one cake 80–90p, set teas from £1.35
Open Easter–Oct, every day 9am–9pm
[1] [3]

SCARBOROUGH   North Yorkshire   Map 08 TA08

Le Café Jardin
25, Huntriss Row
Tel (0723) 354572

Light, modern styling brings a conservatory/patio effect to the ground floor of these attractive tearooms while cane/rattan furniture and floral décor make for relaxed surroundings upstairs. Waitresses are prettily dressed in peach-coloured uniforms, and the blackboard menu of daily specials, hot snacks and sandwiches supplement a counter display of homemade cakes ranging from Yorkshire curd tart to cream gâteaux. A choice of tea blends and a children's menu are available.

Pot of tea and one cake average £1.35
Open every day (except Sun Oct–Mar), 8am–5.30pm
Light meals and snacks

SEAHOUSES   Northumberland   Map 12 NU23

Koffee and Kreme
15 Main Street
Tel (0665) 720278

The owner of this neat, homely, little tearoom personally supervises the ministrations of its friendly staff and also the production of such homemade delicacies as scones, shortbread, lemon meringue pie, sponges and gâteaux; hot snacks are also available. Tea is properly made and accompanied by hot water for 'topping up', Earl Grey being offered as an alternative to the standard blend.

Open all year, every day, 9am–4.30pm (winter) or up to 8pm (summer)
Hot dishes served all day

SEAHOUSES   Northumberland   Map 12 NU23

Seafarers
Main Street
Tel (0665) 720931

Neat, spacious and conveniently situated in the centre of the town, this family-run tearoom accompanies a good, traditional pot of tea with a range of scones, cakes, teabreads and preserves that are all homemade on the premises. Spotless surroundings, attractive tablecloths and friendly service combine to create a homely atmosphere.

Tea 45p
Open Easter–Oct, every day, 10am–6pm (Sundays 11am–6pm) (also open 8–10am for breakfasts during holiday period)
Coffee and light lunches

SEATON   Devon   Map 03 SY29

The Kettle
15 Fore Street
Tel (0297) 20428

A 400-year-old, town-centre, terraced house retains much of its original character, complementing the old oak beams with comfortable pine furniture. Darjeeling, Ceylon, Earl Grey and Indian teas – correctly brewed in china pots – are available, and guests are offered a choice of Cottage Tea or Cream Tea, with home-baked scones and cakes.

Pot of tea and one cake average 90p, set teas £1.10–£1.95
Open all year (except annual holiday in June), Thur–Tue 10am–4pm and (in summer) 7pm–9pm
Coffee

SELWORTHY GREEN   Somerset   Map 03 SS94

Periwinkle Cottage
(near Porlock)
Tel (0643) 862769

This pretty little thatched cottage is everyone's dream of a traditional teashop, with roses and periwinkles in the garden, looking out on the village green and across to Exmoor. Winner of the National Tea Council Award in 1988, it naturally serves a good pot of tea, and several blends are available, including some fruit-flavoured and herb teas. Scones and cakes are freshly baked on the premises, and the scones, served with the local clotted cream, even more irresistible than the delicious cakes. This is fine walking country so you can either enjoy a walk to work up an appetite for your tea, or to disperse the calories afterwards. No smoking in the tearoom.

Pot of tea 50p, cream tea £1.95, cakes from 75p
Open mid Mar–Oct, Tue–Sun (and also bank holiday Mons) 10am–5pm
Morning coffee and lunch also served

SETTLE   North Yorkshire   Map 07 SD86

Liverpool House
8 Chapel Square
Tel (07292) 2247

Both a set tea and a choice of wholemeal sandwiches with a good range of home-baked scones and cakes (including seed cake, Yorkshire Courting Cake, gingerbread and fruit loaf served with Wensleydale cheese) are served in the downstairs dining room of this centrally but quietly sited licensed guest house whose building dates back to the 18th century. Earl Grey, Assam, Darjeeling, Kenyan, Yorkshire Gold and fruit teas provide an alternative to the standard blend. Morning coffee and light lunches are also available at appropriate hours.

Pot of tea and one cake average £1.50, set tea £2.95
Open Feb–Dec (closed Christmas), Mon, Tue, Fri, Sat 10.30am–5pm, Sun 2–5pm

SHAFTESBURY   Dorset   Map 03 ST82

Milestones
Compton Abbas
Tel (0747) 811360

Painted stone walls, rafters and polished antique furniture make this attractive 17th-century cottage, set in a colourful garden beside the A350, a pleasant place in which to relax and enjoy sandwiches with homemade scones and cakes and either Indian or China tea. Four set teas are available including a cream tea and the Farmhouse Tea with boiled eggs.

Pot of tea 60p, set teas £2.20–£3.20
Open Easter–Nov, Sat–Wed

SHAWBURY   Shropshire   Map 07 SJ52

Ladybird Nurseries
Edgebolton
Tel (0939) 250367

A newly-built tearoom in the Ladybird Garden complex on the A53 Stoke to Shrewsbury road, where the aroma of cakes actually being baked tempts one to make a choice from the display counter from among chocolate, coffee and walnut, and sticky date cakes. By 1991 there will also be a patio area for further seating.

Pot of tea and one cake average 80p, cream tea 90p
Open every day

SHEFFIELD   South Yorkshire   08 SK38

Henry's Café Bar
28 Cambridge Street
Tel (0742) 752342

This is the original Henry's Café Bar, now a small chain across the country, open all day Continental-style. Not a traditional teashop, but a popular rendezvous for the young and shoppers alike who favour items such as passion cake, Washington walnut and the filling club sandwich. Toasted teacakes. gâteaux, fresh pastries, toasted sandwiches and filled baguettes are available with a choice of tea blends including fruit varieties.

Pot of tea and one cake average £1.75
Open Mon–Sat 8am–11pm, Sun 7–10.30pm
Hot & cold snacks

1 2 3

SHERBORNE   Dorset   Map 03 ST61

The Eastbury Hotel
Long Street
Tel (0935) 813131

This delightful Georgian town house at the heart of Thomas Hardy country features a lovely English walled garden with listed walnut trees – a perfect setting in which to enjoy one of the hotel's traditional afternoon teas of sandwiches, home-baked scones with cream and jam, and an eclair or fruitcake, served with Indian, China, Earl Grey or decaffeinated tea.

Pot of tea and one cake average £1.75, set teas £1.95–£3.75
Open every day

1 3

SHERINGHAM   Norfolk   Map 09 TG14

Pretty Corner
Tel (0263) 822358

Tea and coffee rooms with a Dutch/Indonesian flavour in a restaurant surrounded by beautiful gardens and occupying a lovely setting beside the A148 on the south east side of the town. The Old English Cream tea is completely traditional, however, comprising hot buttered toast, homemade scones with jam and cream, cakes and a choice of English and Dutch tea blends. Freshly prepared, well presented snacks, savouries and lunches are also available. The building is on more than one level, but rampways make all areas accessible to the disabled.

Pot of tea and one cake average £1.10, set teas £2–£2.50
Open every day, 10am–5.30pm

1 3

SHIPDHAM   Norfolk   Map 05 TF90

Shipdham Place
Church Close
Tel (0362) 820303

Tltis country-house hotel, dating from the 17th century, was formerly the village rectory. Afternoon tea is served in either the drawing room or the parlour – both tastefully decorated rooms with comfortable chesterfields, chairs and sofas, giving a tranquil setting in which to enjoy the tempting homemade biscuits, cakes and scones.

Pot of tea and one cake average £2.50, set tea £2.50–£4
Open all year, every day, 2–6pm
1 3

SHREWSBURY   Shropshire   Map 07 SJ41

Casa Fina
St Austins Street
Tel (0743) 232388

The proprietor of a rather chic establishment specialising in imported furniture, ceramics and objects d'art has utilised the floor above to create a teashop which is conveniently close to town centre and bus station. Here, guests enjoy a good cup of tea, either Indian, Earl Grey, Darjeeling or China, accompanied by sandwiches and a selection of homemade scones, cakes and gâteaux.

Tea 65p, set tea £2.40
Open all year, Mon–Sat, 9am–5pm
Light cooked meals

SHREWSBURY   Shropshire   Map 07 SJ41

Emstrey Coffee Shop
Emstrey Garden Centre
A5
Tel (0743) 56012

Part of a garden centre complex, this bright little café furnished with white plastic tables and chairs – and with additional wooden seating provided outside in a small lawned area during the summer – serves sandwiches, teacakes and a range of homemade cakes with a standard tea blend; light lunches are also available.

Pot of tea and one cake 80–90p
Open every day in summer, closed Mon winter

SHREWSBURY   Shropshire   Map 07 SJ41

Intermission Restaurant and Café
Pride Hill Shopping Centre
Tel (0743) 25393

This very pleasant, smart establishment – part of larger premises which include a self-service restaurant, but operated separately – stands in a new, modern shopping centre at the heart of the city. Savouries, scones and a wide variety of cakes and pastries are available, with a choice of Indian, Darjeeling, Assam and Earl Grey tea.

Tea 57p
Cream tea £1.55
Open all year, Mon–Sat, 8.30am–5.30pm
Grills, brunch, omelettes, pasta, salads

SHREWSBURY   Shropshire   Map 07 SJ41

Music Hall
The Square
Tel (0743) 58057

Pleasant, ground-floor premises in a town-centre theatre house a tearoom where friendly waitresses serve a well-made, traditional cup of tea with a range of sandwiches, scones, cakes and pastries; a good selection of light, cooked meals is also available. Coach parties and functions can be catered for by arrangement.

Tea 40p
Open all year, every day (except Sun, Nov–Easter), 10am–5pm (3.30pm Sun)

SHREWSBURY   Shropshire   Map 07 SJ41

Poppy's and the Stables
19 Princess Street
Tel (0743) 232307

A simple but charming little town-centre teashop is housed in premises where the fire-engine horses were stabled in the 18th century, and a pleasant courtyard area and stable annexe are brought into use in summer. Freshly brewed Earl Grey, Darjeeling, Assam and caffeine-free teas are available as well as the more traditional Indian blend, with scones, teacakes, flapjacks and pastries.

Pot of tea and one cake average £1.25, set tea £2.20–£2.60
Open all year, Mon–Sat, Summer 9.45am–6.30pm, Winter 9.45am–4.30pm

SHREWSBURY   Shropshire   Map 07 SJ41

Tiffin Coffee House
30 The Parade
St Mary's Place
Tel (0743) 247350

In part of what was once a hospital but is now a pleasant indoor shopping centre, with an attractive terrace overlooking the River Severn, friendly waitresses serve sandwiches (including the toasted variety), salads and snacks; tea, whether Indian, Earl Grey or China, is properly brewed in crockery pots.

Pot of tea from 50p, pot of tea and one cake average £1.10
Open all year, Mon–Sat, summer 9.30am–5pm, winter 9.30am–4pm
Coffee, snacks

SHREWSBURY   Shropshire   Map 07 SJ41

Traitors Gate Restaurant
St Mary's
Water Lane (off Castle Street)
Tel (0743) 249152

These fascinating basement premises dating back to the 12th century and retaining their original arched-brick, cellar ceilings are actually part of the castle walls – the café name commemorating the admittance of the Parliamentarians through a river gate during the Civil War.

Pot of tea and one cake average £2.50, set teas
Open all year, every day 11am–3pm (Also Thur–Sat, dinners 7–11pm)

SIDBURY   Devon   Map 03 SY19

The Old Bakery
(Three miles from Sidmouth)
Tel (03957) 319

This attractive tearoom, housed in a 400-year-old building, stands in the village centre and is well placed for visitors to Sidmouth and other coastal resorts, as well as to the nearby Donkey Sanctuary. There are comfortable sitting rooms as well as the formal tearoom, and a garden for the fine weather. Cakes, scones and shortbreads are all delicious, but the speciality is meringues with clotted cream – impossible to resist, so forget your diet. There are three different set teas as well as the daily selection of cakes and to drink, a choice of the house tea, Earl Grey, or China with lemon.

Pot of tea and one cake average £1.10, set teas £1.20–£1.95
Open Apr–Sep, every day except Wed and Sun, 10am–12.30pm, 2–6pm
No smoking in the tearoom

SIDMOUTH   Devon   Map 03 SY19

The Chattery
67 High Street
Tel (0395) 515853

The double-fronted shop stands in the town centre, close to the Post Office, its interior made homely by hanging plants, pictures and ornaments. Both the Plain Tea and the Devon Cream Tea include a good selection of homemade scones and cakes, served with a choice of Indian or Earl Grey tea.

Plain Tea £1.50 Devon Cream Tea £1.75
Open all year, Mon–Sat (Sun in summer), 10am (11am on Sun)–5pm
Lunchtime dishes

SIDMOUTH   Devon   Map 03 SY19

Hotel Riviera
The Esplanade
Tel (0395) 515201

A bow-fronted Regency hotel on the sea front offers tea in either its well-presented lounge or, during the summer, on a paved patio where white tables and chairs are shaded by blue and white umbrellas. Three set teas are available, but guests can also choose from a range of items including finger sandwiches, homemade scones with clotted cream and jam and toasted fruit buns. Earl Grey, Darjeeling, China, lemon or traditional English tea blends are available.

Pot of tea and one cake average £3.50, set teas £3.50–£5
Open every day

SIDMOUTH   Devon   Map 03 SY19

Victoria Hotel
The Esplanade
Tel (0395) 512651

In the spacious, comfortable lounge areas of this fine Victorian hotel – which overlooks the sea from a convenient location only a short, level walk from the town centre – you can choose from a range of set afternoon teas with homebaked cakes and a selection of blends which includes China, Darjeeling and Earl Grey.

Pot of tea £1 per person, set teas from £1.75
Open every day, 24 hours
Lunches and dinners

SILLOTH   Cumbria   Map 11 NY15

Susanna's Pantry
16 Eden Street
Tel (06973) 32244

A small teashop in the town centre – plain and simply decorated, but having a pleasant, friendly atmosphere – offers either the set afternoon tea or a choice of sandwiches (plain or toasted), rolls and homemade cakes with Earl Grey, Darjeeling, lemon or a standard tea blend. Smoking is not permitted.

Pot of tea and one cake average £1, set tea £2.59
Open Wed–Mon 9am–7pm, Tue 9am–5pm

SIMONSBATH   Somerset   Map 03 SS73

Boeveys
Simonsbath House
Hotel
Tel (064383) 259

This tearoom and restaurant, created from a 200-year-old barn at the heart of the Forest of Exmoor, is appropriately furnished with oak settles and old farmhouse tables. The tea served here provides a refreshing break for the hikers and tourists who throng the area.

Pot of tea and one cake average £1.10, set teas £2–£2.60
Open Feb–Nov, every day 9.30am–9pm (3–5.30pm for tea)
Morning coffee, light lunches, dinners
[1] [3]

SIMPSON CROSS   Dyfed   Map 02 SM81

Cream Teas
Near Haverfordwest
Tel (0437) 710465

A Victorian-style conservatory restaurant with an abundance of indoor plants and flowers, and modern white metal furniture with cushioned seats. Snacks, coffee, a choice of tea blends and cream teas are served all day with a range of home-baked cakes.

Pot of tea and one cake average 70p, cream tea £1.95
Open Mar–Oct every day
[3]

SIX ASHES   Shropshire   Map 07 SO78

Six Ashes Tea Room
(between Bridgnorth and Stourbridge on A458)
Tel (038488) 216

This neat, small tearoom is behind a craft shop which sells a wide range of giftware and is a handy stopover on a journey. Scones, cakes, gâteaux and pies are homemade and very acceptable. Cream teas are popular.

Pot of tea and one cake average £1.40, set teas from £1.95
Open all year (except 2 weeks annual holiday), Tue–Sat, 10am–5pm

SKYE, ISLE OF   Highland Map 13 NG60

The Stables Restaurant
Clan Donald Centre
Armadale
Tel (04714) 305

This spotlessly clean, attractively light and airy restaurant forms part of the award-winning Clan Donald Centre which occupies ten acres at the south end of the island, convenient to the Armadale-Mallaig ferry. Amid its clan shields and tartans visitors can sample an enjoyable range of homemade scones, cakes and shortbread, with friendly staff always at hand to help, though the operation is self-service.

Pot of tea and one cake average £1.20
Open Mar–Oct, every day 10–11.45am and 3–5pm

SKYE, ISLE OF   Highland   Map 13 NG35

The Three Rowans
Kildonan
Tel (047082) 286

A converted croft with exposed stone walls, woodburning stove and pine furniture – well signposted from the Portree-Dunvegan road – enjoys fine views over Loch Greshornish from its elevated position. Homemade scones, pancakes, pies, tarts, shortbread and cakes are accompanied by a choice of tea blends.

Pot of tea and one cake average £1.20
Open Mon–Sat

Pipers Moon
Luib
Tel (04712) 594

This neat and simple little tearoom is run by a very charming and friendly owner who makes extremely good scones and delicious fresh salmon sandwiches. There is a range of craft and knitware for sale.

Pot of tea and one cake average £1.35
Open Mar–end Oct, every day, 9am–6pm

The Green House
Struan
Tel (047072) 293

The name of this establishment not only reflects the colour of the paintwork but the commitment to organic and natural ingredients. A wide variety of food is available for morning coffee, lunch, tea and dinner, and a good choice of tea blends. Everything is prepared on the premises from the bread and jam to the apple, cinnamon and whisky pudding or Ecclefechan tart. The first floor level restaurant, with large picture windows, offers fine views down Loch Harport to the Cuillin Hills.

Pot of tea and one cake average £1.50
Open Easter–Oct Sun–Fri 11am–9pm
Lunch and dinner

The Clootie Dumpling Tearoom
Speyside Heather Centre and Scottish Heather Heritage Centre
Dulnain Bridge
Tel (047985) 359

The tearoom takes its name from a traditional Scots delicacy that it actually serves – a fruit dumpling, usually eaten as a pudding, but also suitable for teatime when sliced cold. This homely establishment, with its pine furniture, chequered tablecloths and wood-burning stove, also serves home-baked cakes and various scones and jams, with a choice of Earl Grey, Assam, Darjeeling or herbal tea by the cup, mug or pot.

Tea from 50p
Open Nov–Feb, Thu–Sat, 9am–5pm, Mar–Oct, every day, 9am–6pm

SLEAFORD   Lincolnshire   Map 08 TF04

Blanchard's Coffee Shop
24 Southgate
Tel (0529) 302146

Established as a grocery shop in 1922 and now extensively modernised, this coffee shop stands in a passage flanked by Blanchard's delicatessen and wine shop. Furnished with cottage refectory-type tables and chairs, it has a red telephone box at one end, and French windows opening onto a patio with additional seating. Speciality or standard tea blends accompany a good range of sandwiches (including club and open sandwiches), filled mini French rolls and baguettes – bread being baked freshly each day – and there is a wide selection of cakes, gâteaux, pies and pastries as well as the set afternoon tea. A full à la carte menu also offers substantial meals and savouries.

Pot of tea and one cake average £1.15, set tea £3.25
Open Mon–Sat

SOUTH MOLTON   Devon   Map 03 SS72

The Corn Dolly
115A East Street

The tearoom adjoins a craft shop in a traditional, old, terraced building with exposed beams and stonework and rush matting on the floor. The set teas are delicious, all cakes being made on the premises, and include both savoury and sweet dishes. For the former, try Kings Ransom, a large toasted teacake with grilled Stilton cheese, or a Seafarers Tea, a hot fillet of smoked mackerel served with buttered toast and gooseberry sauce. There are also three special children's teas, with favourites like toast and marmite, jelly and ice-cream. The selection of fresh teas includes Darjeeling, Earl Grey, Lapsang Souchong, Assam, or the house blend of Ceylon. The complete menu is served all day.

Pot of tea and one cake average £1.95, cream tea £1.95
Open all year, Tue–Fri 9.30am–5.30pm; Sat 10am–5.30pm

SOUTH MOLTON   Devon   Map 03 SS72

The Parlour Tea Room
East Street
Tel (07695) 4144

Housed in an attractive Georgian building on the outskirts of the town, the tearooms are charmingly decorated with Laura Ashley fabrics and antique furniture. The owners, Mr and Mrs Koch, make their visitors extremely welcome, serving homemade scones, sponges, fruit cakes and pastries, with a good choice of blends of tea, properly made and served. This is an excellent place to stop for tea, and the town is a convenient centre for exploring the many attractions of North Devon. There is limited parking in the street outside the tearooms.

Pot of tea for two 90p
Open all year, Mon–Sat
8.30am–6pm

SOUTH QUEENSFERRY   Lothian   Map 11 NT17

The Potting Shed
Dougal Philip's Walled Garden Centre
Hopetoun Gardens
Tel 031–319 1122

A cottage-style tearoom with a raftered roof and natural stonework, on the site of the original garden shed. French windows open onto an attractive patio where tea can be taken in the walled garden. Most items from the tea trolley are home baked, daily papers are provided, and paintings are hung for sale. Although within the grounds of Hopetoun House, admission to the centre is free.

Pot of tea and one cake average £1.80, cream tea £1.95
Open Mon–Fri 10am–4pm, weekends 10am–5pm
Light meals

SOUTHPORT   Merseyside   Map 07 SD31

Nostalgia
Lord Street
Tel (0704) 501294

An elegantly furnished first-floor tearoom overlooking fashionable Lord Street offers a wide range of home baking and set teas, including the Nostalgia Special with smoked salmon and cucumber sandwiches, in addition to a selection of cakes. Freshly cut sandwiches, toasted snacks, homemade soup, baked potatoes and salads are served along with an array of cakes, biscuits, 'spectacular sweets', gâteaux and ices. Service is provided by friendly waitresses in traditional dress, and a choice of tea blends is available.

Pot of tea and one cake average £1.90, set teas £1.10–£4.70
Open Mon–Sat 9.30am–5pm, Sun 12 noon–5pm
Light meals

SOUTHPORT   Merseyside   Map 07 SD31

Nostalgia
8 Liverpool Road
Birkdale
Tel (0704) 66517

In a parade of shops beside the railway station in Birkdale village, this pleasant tearoom is under the same ownership as the establishment in Lord Street, and offers a similar range of tasty homemade cakes and teas. A selection of hand-made crafts is also for sale.

Pot of tea and one cake average £1.90, set teas £1.10–£4.70
Open Mon–Sat 9.30am–5pm, Sun 12 noon–5pm

SOUTHWELL   Nottinghamshire   Map 08 SK75

Gossips
King Street
Tel (0636) 815214

This two-storey tearoom in the main street – a bustling, popular meeting place – is also a baker's shop selling locally made cakes. Old oak beams are complemented by plain walls displaying pictures for sale, and by old church pew seating on the ground floor. Waitresses in black and white with coloured berets serve good, flavoursome Indian and Earl Grey tea.

Tea 50p–55p, cream tea £1.95
Open all year, Mon–Sat (Sun in summer), 9am–5pm
Coffee, salads and hot dishes

SOUTHWOLD   Suffolk   Map 05 TM57

Swan Hotel
Market Place
Tel (0502) 722186

Southwold must rank as the most attractive seaside town in Suffolk, and the Swan Hotel stands right at the centre. Afternoon teas are served in the comfortable lounge and although the winter menu is limited to scones and shortbread, there is more choice in summer. Darjeeling, Ceylon, Lapsang, Earl Grey, Breakfast Tea Blend and herbal infusions are available.

Set teas £5.50–£7.50
Open all year, every day, 3–5pm
[1] [2] [3] [&]

SPETISBURY   Dorset   Map 03 ST90

Marigold Cottage
High Street
Near Blandford
Tel (0258) 452468

A pretty thatched cottage with seating in the flower garden among honeysuckle, roses and an aviary. There is an extensive range of lunch-time dishes from beans on toast to a choice of roasts. Delicious homemade cakes include Dorset apple cake and New Zealand carrot cake; sandwiches are available and a selection of tea blends.

Pot of tea and one cake average £1.35, Dorset clotted cream tea £2.15
Open Tue–Sun
Lunches; evening meals Fri & Sat
[1] [3]

SPILSBY   Lincolnshire   Map 09 TF46

Buttercross Restaurant
18 Lower Market
Tel (0790) 53147

A pleasant restaurant, housed in a Grade-two, listed Georgian building overlooking the market place, it serves lunches only from noon–2pm, but lighter snacks at other times. Friendly staff will serve you with either the set afternoon tea or a selection of scones and cakes and tea is freshly made and well presented, with Passion Fruit as well as more traditional blends.

Pot of tea and one cake average £1.55, set tea £2.30
Open all year (except 2 weeks Christmas, 1 week end May, 1 week end Oct), Mon & Wed–Sat 10am–4/4.30pm, Fri & Sat evenings from 7.30pm

STAFFORD   Staffordshire   Map 07 SJ92

Stephanie's
St Mary's Place
Tel (0785) 212034

Bright, stylish décor has transformed this Victorian schoolhouse beside St Mary's Church into a quality Continental café with outdoor seating for finer days. The cabinet display of pastries and gâteaux and a range of ice creams and sorbets are particularly tempting – everything being homemade – and a range of speciality tea blends is offered. Savoury snacks and main courses are served.

Pot of tea 50p
Open Mon–Sat 8am–6pm

STAMFORD   Lincolnshire   Map 04 TF01

George Hotel
St Martins
Tel (0780) 55171

In a beautiful 16th-century inn retaining much of its historic charm and atmosphere, you can enjoy a good cup of freshly brewed tea – Indian, Assam, Darjeeling, Earl Grey or Camomile – in any of the pleasant public rooms or in a courtyard with hanging baskets and flower tubs. Friendly and courteous staff serve a good range of sandwiches, scones, tarts and cream cakes.

Pot of tea and one cake average £2.95, tea and scone £3.25
Open all year, every day, 3.30–6pm for tea
☐1 ☐2 ☐3

STAMFORD   Lincolnshire   Map 04 TF01

Lady Anne's Hotel
37–38 High Street
St Martins
Tel (0780) 53175

Tea is served in the large, lovely lounge with comfortable armchairs and sofas overlooking well-tended gardens. Additional linen-clothed tables are set out in the conservatory. Friendly staff provide professional service with an à la carte menu of meals, snacks, savouries and a dessert trolley with up to 18 homemade cakes, pastries and gâteaux. There is a choice of Indian or China tea.

Pot of tea and one cake average £1.35, set tea £2
Open every day
Meals
☐1 ☐2 ☐3

STAMFORD BRIDGE   Humberside   Map 08 SE75

Waterside Tea Rooms
6–8 The Square
Tel (0759) 71115

Popular tearooms in a building dating back to 1760 in the centre of the village with a small garden to the rear overlooking the River Derwent. Service is both friendly and informal with a range of fresh cakes, gâteau and speciality ice creams, and a choice of tea blends.

Pot of tea and one cake average £1.10, cream tea £1.90
Open every day 9.30am–6pm (closed Mon in winter)

STANBURY   West Yorkshire   Map 07 SE03

Ponden Mill
Colne Road
Tel (0535) 43500

This converted mill at the heart of Brontë Country is now a retail outlet selling interesting textiles, traditional clothing, crafts and gifts. Its buttery serves a range of eatables from light snacks to full meals, including a set afternoon tea and the Brontë Cream Tea, together with a small selection of scones, cakes and gateaux.

Pot of tea and one cake average £1, set teas £1.95–£2.95
Open every Tue–Sat 9am–5.30pm, Sun 10am–5.30pm, Mon 9.30am–5.30pm

STIRLING   Central   Map 11 NS79

Old Town Coffee House
28 Spittal Street
Tel (0786) 63231

In the street leading up to the castle this family-run tearoom, with a fine Victorian fireplace and range, is well worth the short climb up the hill. Everything is home-baked on the premises and most of the popular cakes, traybakes and sponges are available, but it was the range of delicious tarts, available with cream or ice cream, which appealed to our inspector. A selection of tea blends, including herbal, is offered.

Pot of tea and one cake average £1
Open 10am–5pm (Sun 11.30am–4pm) in summer, 10am–4pm (closed Sun) in winter. One ½ day in 1991
Light lunches and snacks, licensed

STOCKPORT   Greater Manchester   Map 07 SJ88

Tiviots Restaurant and Tea Room
Vernon Street
Tel 061–447 20434

Set in a conservation area close to the town's historic market, yet adjoining the main shopping area, the tearoom boasts an exceptionally comprehensive list of teas, including examples from China, India, Ceylon and Africa as well as herbal infusions and such exotic fruit blends as Bitter Almond, all well-made and correctly served. Homemade delicacies include scones and fruit, carrot and orange cake.

Pot of tea 40–45p
Open all year, Mon 9am–5pm, Tue–Sat 9am–late pm, Sun 11am–4pm
Speciality coffee, snacks, special 4 course dinners

STOKE-ON-TRENT   Staffordshire   Map 07 SJ84

The Frit Kiln Restaurant
Heron Cross Pottery Visitor Centre
Chilton Street
Fenton
Tel (0782) 334659

On the signposted Heritage Trail, Heron Cross Pottery is a Grade 11 Listed Building with a shop, craft centre, small museum and first-floor restaurant. Lunches are served, and local dishes are featured: Trentham tart, an almond-flavoured dessert; 'lobby', a filling soup, and Staffordshire oatcakes, a pancake-like snack, all made on the premises along with various gâteaux and fresh cream scones served with a choice of tea blends.

Pot of tea and one cake average £1.15
Open every day
Lunches

STONE   Staffordshire   Map 07 SJ93

Astaires
7A Radford Street
Tel (0785) 815252

Whilst only a modest range of scones, teacakes and gâteaux – some items homebaked and some bought in – is offered here, the restaurant's clean, bright décor and the friendly helpfulness of the waitresses make it a pleasant place in which to enjoy a cup of their speciality tea. Snacks are served throughout the day, with an à la carte menu available in the evening.

Pot of tea 50p (80p for 2), speciality tea 30p per cup
Open all year, Tue–Sat 9.30am–3pm (may soon be later)
Connoisseur Coffee, Sunday lunch, snacks, à la carte evening meals

STON EASTON   Avon   03 ST65

Ston Easton Park
Nr. Bath
Tel Chewton Mendip
(076121) 631

The hotel is a gracious Palladian mansion of real architectural distinction set in beautiful landscaped grounds not far from Bath. The Saloon has been described as 'the finest room in Somerset' and the tea laid out on side tables here echoes this description. Scones, clotted cream, strawberry jam, chocolate éclairs, strawberry tarts and Eccles cakes are amongst the wide selection to which you help yourself, and you are invited to take as much as you can eat for a set price. Tea (there is a choice of ten herbal infusions, as well as Earl Grey, Assam and Darjeeling) is served in silver pots from butlers' trays, and the cups are of fine china. Given suitable advance notice, the hotel will make up sumptuous picnic hampers with wine for you to take into the gardens.

Afternoon tea £6.50
Open all year, every day,
3.30–6pm

1 2 3

STONEHENGE   Wiltshire   Map 04 SU14

Underground Tea Rooms
Amesbury
Tel (0980) 622136

Not truly underground, but using the contours of the land to avoid obtruding on the skyline of Stonehenge, a purpose-built, single-storey café serves such typically British fare as rock cakes and bread pudding; counter service only is offered, but staff are polite and attentive, whilst tea is well-flavoured though served in paper cups.

Tea 40p
Open all year, every day,
9.30am–6.30pm (4pm in winter)

STONEHOUSE   Gloucestershire   Map 04 SO80

Stonehouse Court Hotel
Bristol Road
Tel (0453) 825155

A 17th-century manor house set in six acres of secluded gardens complete with gazebo. Afternoon teas are served overlooking the peaceful Gloucestershire countryside or, in winter, by the firesides of the mellow panelled lounges. The hotel kitchens produce wonderful plain and cheese scones, cream cakes and gâteaux. The traditional tea comprises a round of cucumber or ham sandwiches, scones with cream and jam, an éclair or fruitcake accompanied by a choice of tea blend.

Pot of tea and one cake average £1.75, set tea £1.95–£3.75
Open every day 3.30–5.30pm

 1 3

STOURPORT-ON-SEVERN   Hereford & Worcester   Map 07 SO87

Tudor Tea Room
Bridge Street
Tel (02993) 2446

The café is at the back of the cake shop, and serves a selection of scones, cakes and fresh cream gâteaux. It is conveniently close to the riverside area with its many amusements.

Pot of tea 55p, cream tea
£2.50
Open all year, Mon–Sat
(Suns from Mar–Oct)
9am–5pm

STOWE-BY-CHARTLEY   Staffordshire   Map 07 SK02

Amerton Farm
Tel Weston (0889)
270294

A working farm on the Stafford/Uttoxeter road has opened its doors to the public, converting outbuildings into craft, bakery and produce shops, developing a garden centre and encouraging visitors to view the milking parlour or follow a farm trail. A large tearoom serves its own ice cream and a wide range of home-baked pies, tarts and cakes.

Pot of tea and one cake
average £1.20, cream tea
£2.60, farmhouse tea
£3.20
Open all year, every day,
9am–5pm (6pm Apr–
Sep)

STOW-ON-THE-WOLD   Gloucestershire   Map 04 SP12

Ann Willow Tea Room
The Square
Tel (0451) 30000

Traditional Cotswold teas are served with quiet efficiency by the owner of this bow-fronted cottage café, set beside the picturesque town square, the plain wooden furniture of its attractive interior setting off the aptly-chosen Willow Pattern crockery. Teatime treats include gâteaux, passion cake and brandy snaps as well as sandwiches, teacakes and homebaked scones.

Pot of tea 75p, set tea
£2.25
Open all year, every day,
9.30am–5.30pm
(summer), 10am–5pm
(winter)

STOW-ON-THE-WOLD   Gloucestershire   Map 04 SP12

The Royalist Hotel
Digbeth Street
Tel (0451) 30670

Listed in The Guinness Book of Records as the oldest inn in England, and with beams that carbon dating has proved to be more than 1000 years old, the hotel provides both plain and cream teas, homemade fare including scones, flapjacks, shortbread, chocolate slabs and cherry butter fingers; tea is correctly made and well presented, with a limited choice of blends.

Set teas £2.20 and £2.50
Open all year, every day,
3–5.30pm
Bar snacks and Brasserie

STOW-ON-THE WOLD   Gloucestershire   Map 04 SP12

Shepherd of the Hills
Sheep Street
Tel (0451) 31526

Set in one of the main thoroughfares of this attractive Cotswold town, and flanked by interesting shops, this popular, efficiently-run tearoom offers a good range of teas, snacks and light lunches, having the added advantage of being licensed. A wide variety of tea blends (including some herbal) accompanies the set cream tea or guests' choice from a selection of homemade scones, pies and cakes.

Cream tea £1.90
Open all year, every day,
10am–9pm
Snacks and light lunches

STOW-ON-THE-WOLD Gloucestershire Map 04 SP12

Simpson's
Digbeth Street
Tel (0451) 30151

This traditional-style teashop stands in a terraced row of cottages stretching from the Square towards the Lower Town car park. Windsor chairs and lace-clothed tables are set against walls displaying works offered for sale by local artists. You can take either the Cotswold Cream Tea or your choice of homemade cakes, with Earl Grey or Darjeeling tea.

Pot of tea 60p–80p, set Cotswold Cream Tea £2.35
Open all year, Mon–Sat 10am (12am Mon)–5pm
Coffee and light lunches
Licensed

STOW-ON-THE-WOLD Gloucestershire Map 04 SP12

Teapots
10 Talbot Court
Tel (0451) 32242

Housed in a listed building that once provided stabling for brewery horses, Teapots offers light lunches and afternoon teas – the Vicarage Tea being particularly popular – with homemade cakes and pastries. Pots of well-made tea are always available, even at lunch time, the choice including Earl Grey, camomile and herbal blends.

Pot of tea 65p–75p, cream teas £2.25
Open all year, every day 10am–6pm (or later)
Coffee, light lunches

STRATFORD-UPON-AVON Warwickshire Map 04 SP25

Mistress Quickly
59–60 Henley Street
Tel (0789) 295261

Close to Shakespeare's birthplace, this is a very attractive and popular eating place which serves meals until late evening. Teacakes, scones, Danish pastries and gâteaux are all made on the premises and served by friendly staff. Cream teas are popular, especially with foreign visitors.

Pot of tea 65–75p, cream tea £2.50
Open all year, every day, 9am–late evening
[1] [2] [3]

STRATFORD-UPON-AVON Warwickshire Map 04 SP25

Richoux of London
Old Red Lion Court
Bridge Street
Tel (0789) 415377

Richoux has built its reputation on the wide range of pastries and gâteaux it offers. This Stratford branch is tucked away in a courtyard off the main street and is busy all day, serving a range of light meals and snacks. There is a choice of tea blends and service is prompt and efficient.

Pot of tea from £1.10, afternoon tea £3.60
[1] [3]

STRATFORD-UPON-AVON Warwickshire Map 04 SP25

Shakespeare Hotel
Chapel Street
Tel (0789) 294771

The hotel, set only a short stroll from Stratford's shops and theatre, offers a formal afternoon tea of finger sandwiches, scones, toasted teacakes and fresh cream cakes, with a choice of well-made Indian, China or Earl Grey tea. A wider range of snacks and light meals is also available.

Set teas £3.75 and £5.25
Open all year, every day for teas, 3–5.30pm
Range of meals

STRATHPEFFER   Highland   Map 14 NH45

The Old Mill
Millnain
Tel (0997) 21623

An old mill house situated on the roadside between Strathpeffer and Dingwall has been converted into a charming craft shop and small tearoom, where the retention of the main mill machinery helps to preserve the original atmosphere. Here visitors can sample a small but tasty range of sandwiches followed by homemade scones, shortbread and cakes. Only one variety of tea is available, but it is attractively served.

Pot of tea and one cake average £1.40
Open Easter–Oct, every day 12 noon–5pm

STRATHYRE   Central   Map 11 NN51

An Carraig Tea Room
Main Street
Tel (08774) 281

Once a stable building – the hatch to the hay loft still visible above its entrance – this cosy, homely little tearoom stands beside the main road at the northern end of the village. Home-baked scones, fruit loaves, cakes and traybakes are accompanied by a choice of tea blends, both leaf and sachet, served in bone china. Snacks are also available, and a selection of Aran knitwear is displayed for sale.

Pot of tea and one cake average 90p
Open Thu–Tue, 11am–5pm (until 5.30pm, Sat and 6pm, Sun in season)

SUTTON COLDFIELD   West Midlands   Map 07 SP19

Druckers
The Parade
Tel 021–350 2496

This modest self-service establishment in the town centre, simply furnished and decorated, offers sandwiches, filled croissants, pancakes and quiches in addition to the extensive range of tarts, pastries and gâteaux produced at the company's central pâtisserie.

Pot of tea and one cake average £1.50
Open Mon–Sat 10am–5pm

SWANAGE   Dorset   Map 04 SZ07

Grand Hotel
Burlington Road
Tel (0929) 423353

A family resort hotel in an excellent cliff-top position offers scones, cakes and pastries as accompaniment to the well-made pots of Indian, Earl Grey or jasmine tea which are pleasantly served in its comfortable lounge and sun-lounge.

Set teas £3.50
Open all year, every day for teas, 3–5.30pm

SWANSEA   West Glamorgan   Map 03 SS69

Chattery Restaurant and Coffee Shop
57 Uplands Crescent
Tel (0792) 473276

An authentic Welsh dresser and wooden farmhouse tables and chairs set the tone of this small, shopping-centre coffee shop. Here you can enjoy a cup of Assam, Darjeeling, Earl Grey or lemon tea, served with scones, teacakes and pastries; snacks and hot meals, including a vegetarian menu, are also available.

Pot of tea and one cake from 80p
Open all year Mon–Sat, 11am–5.30pm (8.30pm Thur–Sat)
Snacks, hot meals

SWANSEA   West Glamorgan   Map 03 SS69

Children's World Ltd
Parc Tawe
North Dock
Quay Parade
Tel (0792) 475020

Located in a children's store at the heart of a large shopping complex near the city centre, this completely new cafeteria is light, brightly decorated and equipped with modern tubular steel and plastic furniture. Youngsters will appreciate the range of established children's favourites included among the snacks, whilst adults may enjoy a good, refreshing cup of tea with a sandwich, scone or cake.

Pot of tea with scones
£1.40
Open all year, Mon–Fri
10am–8pm, Sat 9am–
6pm, bank holidays 10am–
6pm

SWANSEA   West Glamorgan   Map 03 SS69

Littlewoods
St Mary's Square
Tel (0792) 469200

This self-service area, part of the main store's first floor, offsets modern furnishings with an array of potted plants. A range of meals is available, but customers requiring only a light snack may well opt for scones, gâteaux or pastries complemented by a good cup of tea – properly made and offering Earl Grey, Assam, Ceylon and Darjeeling as alternatives to the more traditional blends.

Pot of tea 49p
Open all year, Mon–Sat,
9am–5.30pm
Coffee, lunches

SWANSEA   West Glamorgan   Map 03 SS69

Windsor Café
3 Craddock Street
Tel (0792) 652748

Clean and bright, furnished with wooden chairs, Formica-topped tables and a separate take-away area, the café serves toasted teacakes, pastries and gâteaux with a good, traditional cup of tea; ice cream and hot meals (including fish and chips) are also available.

Pot of tea and one cake
average 90p, set tea £2
Open all year, Mon–Sat,
8.30am–6.20pm
Hot meals (lunch, high tea,
fish and chips)

TALSARNAU   Gwynedd   Map 06 SH63

**Maes-y-Neuadd
Hotel**
Nr Harlech
(unclassified road off
B4573)
Tel (0766) 780200

This old house dates back to the 14th century and enjoys a beautiful setting in the Welsh hills, looking out to the sea. Afternoon tea is served in the attractive, comfortable lounge, and an excellent array of homemade scones, cakes and biscuits, is laid out on the sideboard for you to help yourself. Tea, in a choice of several blends, is served in china pots by the young and friendly staff.

Pot of tea and one cake
average £1.50
Open all year (except 9–
20 Dec), every day, 3.30–
5.30pm
1 2 3

TAL-Y-CAFN   Gwynedd   Map 06 SH77

**Bodnant Garden
Pavilion**
Tel (0492) 650460

Bodnant Garden, a National Trust property, is a popular tourist attraction on the A470 eight miles south of Llandudno. The timber-built, mountain chalet-style refreshment pavilion was opened in 1989 with simple bench seating for 140 people. A wide range of fresh locally-made scones and cakes, plus sandwiches and a selection of simple hot dishes is served, with Earl Grey or the standard tea blend.

Pot of tea and one cake £1
Open mid Mar–Sep, every
day 11am–5.30pm
Light lunches and snacks

TATTENHALL   Cheshire   Map 07 SJ45

Cheshire Farm
Drumlan Hall
Newton Lane
Tel (0829) 70995

A well-signposted fully-operational dairy farm with a tea and dairy shop in a converted barn. The teashop, a no-smoking area, is furnished with pine tables and chairs; orders are taken in the kitchen for a choice of 30 flavours of ice cream made at the farm, tea, coffee or a cream tea (scone, jam and cream).

Cream tea £1.40
Open every day

TAUNTON   Somerset   Map 03 ST22

Coffee & Cream
6–8 Crown Walk
Tel (0823) 283764

A modern, glass-fronted building with a quarry-tiled and carpeted floor, fixed tables and benches or chairs, floral drapes, dried flowers and a long buffet-style service counter. Home-baked scones, cakes, and gâteaux are available with bought-in Danish pastries.

Cup of tea 48p
Open all year, Mon–Sat,
8.30am–5pm

TAUNTON   Somerset   Map 03 ST22

Riverside Restaurant
Riverside Place
St James Street
Tel (0823) 251761

Set in a small courtyard beside the River Tone, the restaurant has a modern décor with festoon blinds, formica-topped tables and aluminium framed chairs. There is an extensive buffet counter serving cream teas, sandwiches, salads, soup and homemade cakes, gâteaux, pastries and biscuits.

Cup of tea 45p, cream tea
£1.75
Open all year, Mon–Sat,
9am–5.30pm
3 hot dishes served
11.45am–2.30pm
Coaches welcome

TAUNTON   Somerset   Map 03 ST22

Victorian Rooms
County Hotel
East Street
Tel (0823) 337651

An attractive split-level room with a bow window facing the main shopping street and many pictures and plants. There are wooden topped tables and wicker-backed chairs. Crumpets, sweet biscuits, teacakes, scones and Danish pastries from the local baker are served with a choice of tea blends. Good china pots are used with a pleasing mixture of crockery.

Cup of tea 90p, cream tea
£2.80
Open all year, Mon–Sat,
9.30am–5pm
1 2 3

TAVERNSPITE   Dyfed   Map 02 SN11

Tavernspite Garden Centre
Near Whitland
Tel (083483) 671

A large, converted timber building within a garden centre in the middle of this small village, furnished in bright, modern style and offering a wide range of snacks, sandwiches, scones and cakes as well as its set afternoon teas.

Pot of tea and one cake
average 70p, set teas
£1.50–£3
Open every day
1 3

TAVISTOCK   Devon   Map 02 SX47

The Coffee Mill
44 Brook Street
Tel (0822) 612092

You will easily find this Georgian-fronted shop in the town's main street. Inside, the wood-panelled walls, plants, pictures and brown earthenware crockery create a pleasant atmosphere, and Mr Martindale and his staff will make you very welcome. There are usually at least 30 different cakes to tempt you, virtually all of them homemade, and the excellent cheesecakes are renowned in the locality. Blackcurrant and almond slice, marmalade cake and pear and ginger cake are just some of the other goodies on offer. The choice of freshly made teas is also excellent.

Pot of tea 55p, cream tea £2
Open all year, Mon–Sat 9.30am–5pm, Sun 12 noon–5pm (in summer open until 8pm)
Snacks and light meals also served

TAYNUILT   Strathclyde   Map 10 NN03

Riverside Tearoom and Restaurant
Crunachy
Tel (08662) 310

A modest little restaurant with adjacent filling station and shop, set beside the main road 2 ½ miles east of the town at the foot of Ben Cruachan, offers an ideal break on a journey. Home baking of an excellent standard produces generously sized scones, chocolate cake, cheesecake, apple and lemon meringue pies and regional dishes like Argyll tart and Islay loaf; full meals and snacks are also served.

Pot of tea and one cake average £1
Open every day, 10am–7pm in season

TAYNUILT   Strathclyde   Map 10 NN03

Shore Cottage Tearoom
Tel (08662) 654

Shore Cottage stands beside Loch Etive, in the shadow of Ben Cruachan. The countryside round about is superb and a paradise for walkers. Lilly NcNaught, the owner, draws customers from far and wide to sample her excellent baking, which she does every day, so the selection of tempting sponges, cakes and pastries is constantly varied. Scones, with her homemade rhubarb and orange jam, are always popular and the fruit slice is especially to be recommended. The tea, served in bone-china cups, is also delicious and there is a choice of blends. Craftware and paintings are on sale in the tearooms. No smoking is permitted.

Pot of tea from 40p, cakes from 40p
Open Easter–mid Oct, every day except Wed, 10am–6pm

TEIGNMOUTH   Devon   Map 03 SX97

Beachcomber
The Promenade
Tel (0626) 778909

This coastal tearoom, in a central position on the promenade, has a modernised interior with good pine tables and chairs; tables are also available outside during the summer months, weather permitting. A choice of teas is available and a range of homemade cakes, scones, biscuits and desserts is served by uniformed staff.

Pot of tea and one cake from 80p, Devon cream tea £2
Open all year (except Christmas Day and Boxing Day), every day, 10am–8pm (6pm in winter)
Lunches

TEIGNMOUTH   Devon   Map 03 SX97

Bow Window and Secret Garden Café
The Royal Dairy
Teign Street
Tel (0626) 774142

A teashop adjacent to the Dairy Delicatessen, through which it may be entered, stands in an old cow passage with cob walls and cobbled floors; this leads into a secluded walled garden where tables and chairs are shaded by sun umbrellas. Inside, 18 cinema seats are set at cloth-clad tables with fresh flowers, the room's pleasant atmosphere further enhanced by pictures and pot plants. As well as the set cream teas there is a wide choice of scones, sponge cakes, pastries and gâteaux, some baked on the premises and others produced locally – Grandma's Rock Cakes and doughnuts being the work of the proprietor's mother in Teignmouth.

Pot of tea and one cake average 95p, set teas £1.75
Open all year, Mon–Sat, 10am–5pm

TENBY   Dyfed   Map 02 SN10

Charny's Licensed Restaurant
High Street

A friendly restaurant in the centre of this most attractive seaside resort, it is easy to find, being situated almost opposite the church. A full range of hot meals is served and teacakes, cream teas and doughnuts are also available in the afternoons to accompany a good pot of tea.

Tea 45p, cream teas £1.25, set teas £1–£1.25
Open Apr–end Oct, every day, 10am–10pm (6pm until Whit)
Hot meals

TENTERDEN   Kent   Map 05 TQ83

Peggoty's Tea Shoppe
122 High Street
Tel (05806) 4393

Set back from the road with its own ornamental pavement seating, this attractive shiplap and beamed terraced cottage offers both a cream tea with freshly-baked scones and an assortment of homemade cakes with a choice of herbal and fine tea blends. Morning coffee and savoury lunch-time specials are also available.

Pot of tea and one cake average £1.75, set tea £2.30
Open Thu–Tue (Sun am only)

TETBURY Gloucestershire Map 03 ST89

The Close Hotel
Tel (0666) 52272

The Close Hotel dates back 400 years and is built on the site of a ruined monastery. Although right in the centre of this charming old Cotswold town, it has all the tranquillity and atmosphere of a country-house hotel. The traditional afternoon tea is a substantial feast of dainties, all homemade in the hotel and you can enjoy your cream tea, your chocolate and banana cake with vanilla ice-cream or your apple and poppy seed cake in the lounge, under the elegant domed ceiling of the withdrawing room, or in the hotel gardens.

Pot of tea and one cake average £1.70, set tea £1.70–£3.10
Open all year (except first 2 weeks in Jan), every day 3–5.30pm
1 3

TETBURY Gloucestershire Map 03 ST89

Two Toads
19 Church Street
Tel (0666) 50696

This family-run, town-centre restaurant has a tongue twister of a name, but thankfully only the first two words form the shop title: 'Two toads totally tired tried to trot to Tetbury'. There is a wide-ranging snack and lunch menu, and for tea, homemade cakes, scones, teacakes and doughnuts. A choice of tea blends is offered, including herbal. During fine weather tea can be enjoyed in the garden.

Pot of tea from 45p, cream tea £1.75
Open all year, Tue–Sun, 9am–5.30pm, teas served 2–5.30pm
Lunches

TEWKESBURY Gloucestershire Map 03 SO83

Abbey Tearooms
59 Church Street
Tel (0684) 292215

About 450 years old, these tearooms are full of olde worlde charm with exposed beams, an open fireplace and polished wood tables and chairs. Light lunches are available, but it is the range of homemade cakes and puddings, traditional cream teas and gâteaux that have made the tearooms popular. A choice of teas is offered. Smoking is not permitted.

Pot of tea 50–55p
Open early Mar–mid Nov, Wed–Mon, 10.30am–5.30pm
Lunches

THATCHAM   Berkshire   Map 04 SU56

Garlands
Shop 3
16 High Street
Tel (0635) 61017

This coffee shop takes its name from the garlands of dried flowers which adorn the walls, where plain dark wooden tables and chairs are arranged to one side of a healthfood shop. A range of delicious homemade cakes is displayed, such as Earl Grey cake, chocolate-topped oatcakes, Manchester tart and meringues, and the friendly proprietor takes orders at the table. A choice of tea blends is available, along with about 20 herbal varieties, served in attractive white pots with extra water. There is a blackboard menu for hot snacks, and facilities for children including a high chair, feeder cups and special cutlery. Smoking is not permitted.

Pot of tea and one cake average £1.20
Open Mon–Sat, closed 25, 26 Dec & 1 Jan
Light meals

THORNHAM MAGNA   Suffolk   Map 05 TM17

Red House Forge Tearooms
Redhouse Yard
Tel Mellis (037 983) 794

In a really lovely setting, the teashop is found in the old forge, up a few steps, where there are pretty clothed tables, brightly coloured chairs, bare floorboards and wicker mats. There is also a pottery and a silk-screen printers in the yard, and a park with Ramblers walks. There are assorted wholesome homemade cakes and a range of tea blends. Smoking is not permitted.

Pot of tea 45p
Open Mar–Dec, every day,
10.30am–5.30pm

TICKNALL   Derbyshire   Map 08 SK32

Daisy's Tearoom
The Old Coach House
Hayes Farm
Tel (0332) 862696

A delightful tearoom behind Sam Savage's antique shop, decorated with dried flowers, silk cushions and hand-embroidered baby gifts which are for sale. Daisy's offers good home baking with some more unusual items such as chocolate courgette cake. There are six set teas: Daisy Jones Cream Tea, Cricketer's, Summer Garden, Old Fashioned, Nursery and Fireside, with a good choice of tea blends.

Pot of tea and one cake average £1.45, set teas £2.45–£3.75
Open Tue 10.30am–5pm (5.30pm in summer)

TINTERN   Gwent   Map 03 SO50

Royal George
Tel (0291) 689205

Cream teas or Welsh teas with toast, teacakes, pastries, scones and Welsh cakes are served in the comfortable lounge or the very pretty garden where there are pleasant lawns and a small trout stream. A choice of tea blends is offered.

Pot of tea and one cake average £1.95, set tea £1.95
Open every day
Full restaurant facilities

TIVERTON   Devon   Map 03 SS91

Carwardine's
1 Phoenix Lane
Tel (0884) 254687

A town-centre coffee/tea house and restaurant with comfortable booth seating. Meals and snacks are served all day from breakfast to afternoon tea. A good range of homemade pastries and desserts is available with various blends of good, large-leaf teas and freshly roasted coffees. There is also a selection of ice creams. A retail section sells speciality teas, coffee freshly roasted on the premises, and gifts.

Pot of tea and one cake average £1.50
Open all year, Mon–Fri 9am–5.30pm, Sat 8.30am–5.30pm, Sun and bank holidays 10am–5pm (9pm Tue–Sat in summer
Breakfast, lunch

 3

TORPOINT   Cornwall & Isles of Scilly   Map 02 SX45

The Orangery Restaurant
Mount Edgcumbe Country Park
Tel (0752) 822236

A light, airily spacious restaurant within the beautiful grounds of Mount Edgcumbe Country Park is furnished with bamboo tables and chairs and an abundance of potted plants; additional seating is provided outside. Guests can choose between the set Cornish cream tea and an assortment of sandwiches and homemade cakes accompanied by Earl Grey, herbal or standard blend tea.

Pot of tea and one cake average £1.30, set tea £1.90
Open every day, 11am–5.30pm
Light meals

TOTNES   Devon   Map 03 SX86

Anne of Cleves
56 Fore Street
Tel (0803) 863186

The main street of this picturesque old town climbs steeply uphill, and this tearoom is a very popular resting place. Making the range of about 50 assorted cakes, pastries, scones and other temptations keeps two chefs on the go all day. As everywhere in this part of the country, cream teas are favourites, but there are also excellent teacakes, crumpets and muffins to precede your plate of gâteau. The tea blends are also very good and there is a choice of well-made Indian, lemon, Earl Grey or herbal infusions.

Pot of tea and one cake average £1.00, Devonshire cream tea £2.25, gâteaux from £1
Open all year, every day (except Christmas Day), 9am–5.30pm
Hot snacks from £1.50

TOTNES   Devon   Map 03 SX86

The Old Forge
Seymour's Place
Tel (0803) 862174

A restored 600-year-old building of historic interest with a fully operational smithy workshop and guest house accommodation. Teas are available in the dining room or garden, where wrought ironwork from the forge is used to good effect. Snack meals, sandwiches, cakes (including banana bread and carrot cake), gâteaux and the Old Forge speciality, waffles with maple syrup and cream, are served in a warm, welcoming atmosphere. Smoking is permitted in the garden only.

Pot of tea and one cake average £1.30, Devon cream tea £2.25
Open every day
Snacks

TREFRIW   Gwynedd   Map 06 SH76

Trefriw Wells Spa Teahouse
(on B5106 at entrance of Roman Spa Cave of Wells)
Tel (0492) 640057

In Victorian times this attractive tea rooms was the Pump Room Bathhouse, and you can still buy bottles of the chalybeate spa water in the adjoining shop. A selection of homemade scones, teacakes and cakes is on offer and there is a choice of blends of tea on request. Guided tours also available.

Pot of tea and one cake average £1.20
Open all year (except 2 weeks at Christmas), Easter–end Oct, 10am–5.30pm, Nov–Easter, 10am–5pm (from 12 noon on Sun)
Light lunches and snacks

TREGONY   Cornwall & Isles of Scilly   Map 02 SW94

Kea House
Near Truro
Tel (087253) 642

A cottage-style licensed restaurant serving morning coffee, light lunches and à la carte dinners (with locally-caught sea food as a speciality) also offers Cornish cream teas and a selection of homemade scones and cakes supplemented by sandwiches, teacakes and crumpets.

Pot of tea and one cake average £1.75, set tea £1.95
Open every day
1 3

Chocolate Centre
70 Camden Road
Tel (0892) 31683

As might be expected from the name, this delightful shop, with a restaurant at the rear, makes and sells the most delicious chocolates. Its restaurant is very attractive and displays its appealing, homemade cakes and gâteaux, on a trolley, so that you can inspect the day's range of delicacies with ease. Among the specialities which may tempt you are Normandy apple tart, gypsy tart, butter creams and Wellington squares. There is a choice of blends of tea or herbal infusions and everything is nicely served. No smoking is permitted.

Pot of tea and one cake average £1.55, cream tea £2.00
Open all year, every day, 9am–5.30pm

Importers Tea and Coffee House
22 Monson Road
Tel (0892) 27567

An attractive establishment, with plain wooden tables and chairs, to the rear of a shop selling speciality teas and freshly roasted coffees. The cake trolley is tempting, displaying homebaked scones and apple pies as well as gâteaux and cheesecakes. A choice of teas is offered.

Pot of tea and one cake average £1.65, set tea £3.50
Open all year (except bank holidays), Mon–Sat, 9am–5pm
1 3

Rupert's
High Street
Tel (0892) 511045

An attractive multi-purpose bar-café, light and airy with plants and a walled garden. Sandwiches, filled rolls, scones, gâteaux and Danish pastries are served, and a range of Indian and China tea blends.

Pot of tea 90p, Kentish cream tea £2.35
Open all year, Mon–Sat, 10am–4.30pm
1 2 3

Spa Hotel
Mount Ephraim
Tel (0892) 20331

In the elegant, comfortable lounge of this Georgian manor house, an afternoon tea comprising freshly-made sandwiches and scones, pastries, cakes and gâteaux prepared on the premises is formally served at linen-clothed tables by friendly staff; an à la carte menu of snacks and savouries is also available. Earl Grey and China tea are offered as an alternative to Indian.

Pot of tea 75p, afternoon tea £5
Open every day, 3.30–5pm for tea
Snacks
1 2 3

TURNBERRY   Strathclyde   Map 10 NS20

The Turnberry Hotel
Tel (0655) 31000

This high-quality hotel overlooking the Firth of Clyde and the massive rock of Ailsa Craig is famed for its championship golf courses and for its traditional Scottish hospitality. Afternoon tea is served in the comfortable Ailsa Lounge in an atmosphere of elegance and refinement reminiscent of days gone by. There is an excellent selection of sandwiches, scones, pancakes, crumpets, cakes and pastries, all freshly made. The fine bone china is in keeping with the surroundings and there is a choice of three China teas, as well as Indian, Ceylon, and Earl Grey.

Full afternoon tea £6.25, pot of tea £1.65, cakes £1.65
Open all year, every day, 2.30–5pm
1 2 3

TUTBURY   Staffordshire   Map 08 SK22

Mulberry House
High Street
Tel (0283) 815170

A cottage-style restaurant at the end of the village High Street comprises not only a quality dining room serving lunch and dinner but also an attractive teashop offering sandwiches, homemade scones, teacakes, sponges and desserts together with a choice of tea blends.

Pot of tea 55p–75p
Open Tue–Sun
1 2 3

TWIGWORTH   Gloucestershire   Map 03 SO82

Wooden Spoon
Wallsworth Hall
Tel (0452) 731422

Wallsworth Hall is the international centre for wildlife art. The Wooden Spoon is also open to non-visitors and snacks and meals are available throughout the day. There is a wide range of homebaking on offer, including wholefood items. Good tea nicely served and a choice of blends is available. Smoking is not permitted.

Tea £1.80
Open all year, Tue–Sun, 10am–5pm
Lunches

TY NANT   Clwyd   Map 06 SH94

Bronant Teashop
Corwen
Tel (049 081) 344

A quaint white-painted gift and teashop on the busy A45. Home-cooked cakes and pastries, savoury snacks and breakfasts are available in the high season. A variety of tea blends is offered, and a choice of whole or skimmed milk for the health-conscious.

Pot of tea 55p–75p, set teas £1.80–£3.30
Open Mar–mid Nov, every day (except Wed, Mar and Oct), 9am–7pm (8am–9pm high season)
1 3

TYWYN　Gwynedd　Map 06 SH50

The Proper Gander Tearooms and Gift Shop
High Street
Tel (0654) 711270

Recently opened, this lovely little first-floor tearoom stands above a craft shop in the popular resort's High Street. Furnished in cottage style and spotlessly clean, it serves hot meals at lunch time and all-day snacks which include sandwiches (plain and toasted) with homemade scones, cakes and sweets as well as its aptly-named Gosling, Goose, Gander and Proper Gander Special set teas.

Pot of tea and one cake average £1.20, set teas £1.15–£2.50
Open all week (except Tue pm)

ULLAPOOL　Highland　Map 14 NH19

Ceilidh Place Hotel
West Argyle Street
Tel (0854) 2103

A popular, comfortable tourist hotel. The self-service coffee shop has an informal atmosphere and is full of character with rough cast and timber walls, a stone floor with bright rugs and a log burner when required. Some of the seating is made from old church pews. Bread, scones and cakes are all homebaked and there is a wide selection of speciality leaf teas.

Pot of tea and one cake average 90p
Open mid Jan–Dec, every day 10am–6pm winter, 10am–10pm summer

1 2 3

ULVERSTON　Cumbria　Map 07 SD38

The Peppermill
64 Market Street
Tel (0229) 57564

This small, popular restaurant has a cottage feel to it, with exposed beams, white walls, red-clothed tables and flower paintings. The attractive garden is also used in summer. As well as light meals, a selection of scones, teabreads, meringues and lovely sweets like banana toffee pie are served in the afternoons. A choice of tea blends is offered.

Pot of tea and one cake average £1
Open all year, Mon–Sat, 9.15am–5.15pm
Lunch

1 3

ULVERSTON　Cumbria　Map 07 SD38

Renaissance Coffee Shop
Fountain Street
Tel (0229) 53974

A low, beamed ceiling, flagstone floor and stone walls give character to this charming little coffee/teashop, which is the centre for the Renaissance Theatre Trust Old chairs and polished wooden tables are in keeping with the character of the room, and in its pleasant atmosphere customers can relax and enjoy a selection of homemade cakes and scones accompanied by a choice of tea blends.

Pot of tea 55p
Open Mon–Sat, 10am–4.30pm

UPPER DEAL　Kent　Map 05 TR35

The Tea Gardens
224 London Road
Tel (0304) 375270

An attractive tearoom, fully carpeted with polished cottage tables, wooden chairs and pot plants. There is a small terrace outside with tables and umbrellas. The menu offers a selection of snacks, light refreshments and substantial roasts. A choice of tea blends is offered, and cakes, fruit pies and teabreads are available.

Pot of tea and one cake average £1.59
Open all year, Wed–Sun, 11.30am–6.30pm
Lunches

UPPINGHAM   Leicestershire   Map 04 SP89

Baines Tea Room
High Street West
Tel (0572) 823317

Part of a butcher's and baker's business, housed in
17th-century premises in the centre of this historic
Rutland town, the tearoom has quaint cottage-style
furniture with lace table cloths, napkins and good
china. A wide range of delectable homemade cakes,
teabreads and sandwiches are offered as well as light
meals. A selection of tea blends, including herbal, is
available. Smoking is not permitted.

Pot of tea 45p, cream tea
£1.25
Open all year, Mon–Sat
(ex Mon and Thu pm in
winter), 9am–5pm
Lunches

UPTON ST LEONARDS   Gloucestershire   Map 03 SO81

Hatton Court Hotel
Upton Hill
Tel (0452) 617412

Set in lovely countryside just outside Gloucester, 600
feet above sea level with panoramic views over the
Severn Valley, Hatton Court is surrounded by parkland
and gardens. Afternoon tea is served in the
comfortable lounge or on the garden terraces, and all
the produce is freshly baked by the hotel. There is a
choice of blends of tea.

Pot of tea and biscuits
£1.25, set teas £1.50–
£5.50
Open all year, every day,
3–5.30pm
1 2 3

UWCHMYNYDD   Gwynedd   Map 06 SH12

Pen Bryn Bach
Aberdaron
Tel (075 886) 216

A pleasant little café-tearoom situated near the end of
the Lleyn Peninsula in a lovely rural setting. Split-level,
with pretty green checked cloths on its tables and
good crockery, the room is decorated with pictures
and dried flowers, and there is piped music. A good
selection of homemade cakes is offered and full meals
are also available.

Pot of tea 65p
Open Easter–Sep, every
day, 10am–10pm
Lunch and evening meals

WALSALL   West Midlands   Map 07 SP09

Druckers
Saddlers Centre
Tel (0922) 646870

A modest, friendly self-service pâtisserie in a modern
shopping precinct in the centre of Walsall, displaying a
range of cakes, gâteaux and pastries made at the
company's central pâtisserie.

Pot of tea and one cake
average £1.50
Open Mon–Sat 10am–
5pm

WALTHAM ABBEY   Essex   Map 05 TL30

**Beeches Coffee
Shop**
Swallow Hotel
Old Shire Lane
Tel (0992) 717170

The coffee shop forms part of a stylish hotel with
ample parking space at junction 20 of the M25. Set on
the balcony of the main lobby, it is furnished
completely in art deco style with modern sofas and
stools. A full range of sandwiches, scones, cakes and
pastries is available, with a choice of tea blends.

Pot of tea and one cake
average £3
Open every day 10am–
7pm

WARE   Hertfordshire   Map 05 TL31

Van Hage's Coffee Shop
Van Hage's Garden Centre
Amwell Hill
Great Amwell
Tel (0920) 870811

Located within the garden centre, the self-service coffee shop is a wooden building with red and white furnishings giving a bright and cheerful effect. A good selection of homemade cakes, scones, shortbread, sponges and flapjacks are offered with a choice of tea blends. Smoking is not permitted.

Tea 40p
Open all year, (except Christmas week), every day, 10am–5pm

WAREHAM   Dorset   Map 03 SY98

Priory Hotel
Church Green
Tel (0929) 551666

In a tranquil setting next to the church, with four acres of garden running down to the river, the converted 16th-centruy priory offers gracious, comfortably appointed lounges where tea is served. Scones, cakes, gâteaux, sandwiches and cream teas are available with a choice of good leaf-tea blends and herbal infusions. There is a minimum charge of £3.00 per head for non-residents.

Pot of tea 85p–£1.50, set teas £2.50–£5.50
Open all year, every day, tea served 3pm–5pm

1 2 3

WARRINGTON   Cheshire   Map 07 SJ68

IKEA
910 Europe Boulevard
Westbrook
Tel (0925) 445670

A café with a difference is housed in a large out-of-town store on an industrial estate reached via junction nine of the M62. The store specialises in Scandinavian products, and this influence extends to the café, where customers can enjoy open sandwiches, meat balls or Danish pastries while the Swedish Shop allows them to take home the real flavour of the country.

Pot of tea and one cake average 85p
Open Mon–Sat

1 3

WARWICK   Warwickshire   Map 04 SP26

Brethren's Kitchen
Lord Leycester Hospital
Tel (0926) 491580

Tearooms with quarry floors and exposed beams – part of the medieval Lord Leycester Hospital, founded by the Earl in 1571 for his aged relatives – interspersed antiques with Windsor chairs, gingham-clothed tables and blue-and-white china. Hot snacks are available, as well as freshly prepared sandwiches, the scones, cakes and traybakes cooked in the owner's home, and a choice of tea blends.

Pot of tea and one cake average £1.10, set teas £1.80
Open Mon–Sat 10am–5pm
Hot Snacks

WARWICK   Warwickshire   Map 04 SP26

Charlotte's Tea Rooms
6 Jury Street
Tel (0926) 498930

A Georgian terraced house furnished with polished tables and bentwood chairs with food available all day from 'elevenses' through to an imaginative dinner menu. Tea items include a good range of tea blends, homemade scones and cakes, Yorkshire Dales ice cream and a selection of sandwiches which can be served toasted.

Pot of tea and one cake average £1.20
Open every day
Lunches, snacks, dinner

1 3

WATERMILLOCK   Cumbria   Map 12 NY42

Leeming House
Ullswater
Tel (08536) 622

A country house hotel set in twenty acres of landscaped garden and natural woodland on the shores of Lake Ullswater offers tea in the peaceful and elegant surroundings of sitting rooms where log fires burn in cooler weather. Guests can choose between tea and biscuits and the full tea comprising sandwiches, scones, cakes and biscuits: a selection of tea blends is available, served in Wedgwood china.

Tea and biscuits £1.65, full tea £6.50
Open all year, every day, morning coffee 10.30am–noon, afternoon tea 3–5pm

WELLS   Somerset   Map 03 ST54

The Cloister Restaurant
Wells Cathedral
Tel (0749) 76543

Situated in the west cloister of this magnificent Cathedral, the Cloister Restaurant is an unusual setting for afternoon tea. Several tea varieties, including herbal, are offered and the food is all homemade with some wholefood items. There are 'healthy' cakes, cream cakes and sponges. Morning coffee and lunches are also served. Smoking is not permitted.

Pot of tea 40p, cakes 25p–65p
Open all year (except Christmas), Mon–Sat, 10am–5pm, Sun 2–5pm
Lunches

WELLS   Somerset   Map 03 ST54

The Good Earth
4 Priory Road
Tel (0749) 78600

This is a licensed vegetarian restaurant and wholefood store. The restaurant comprises several pine-floored rooms plus the garden courtyard. Everything is homemade with natural, unrefined ingredients. Moist cakes include carrot cake and traditional Somerset dappy. A selection of teas is available including herb teas. A blackboard menu offers a range of lunch-time dishes.

Pot of tea 50p, cakes 50p
Open all year, Mon–Sat, 9.30am–5.30pm
Lunches (dish of the day £1.65)

WELLS-NEXT-THE-SEA   Norfolk   Map 09 TF94

Corner House Restaurant and Tearoom
Staithe Street
Tel Fakenham (0328) 711317

A fully restored tearoom and restaurant away from the busy sea front but close to the shops. It has a cottage-style interior with pretty embroidered tablecloths, lace curtains and quality china. A warm, cheery welcome, a good cup of tea and a range of scones, pastries and fruit pies are offered. A choice of tea blends, including fruit teas, is available.

Pot of tea 50p–75p
Open all year (except for annual holidays), every day, in summer, Fri–Sun winter, 10.30am–4pm approx
1

WELSHPOOL   Powys   Map 07 SJ20

The Inglenook Teashop
Union Street
Tel (0938) 5188

A cottage-style teashop with wooden tables and farmhouse chairs. A small range of Welsh crafts is on display and for sale. Pastries, scones and pies, all homemade, are available with some hot snacks as well. A choice of tea blends is offered.

Tea 50p, cream tea £1.25
Open all year, Mon, Fri and Sat 9am–5pm; Tue, Wed and Thu 9.30–5pm

WELSHPOOL   Powys   Map 07 SJ20

National Milk Bar
21 Church Street
Tel (0938) 2470

A popular rendezvous for local youngsters, this is a café-style operation in the centre of town, with formica tables and plastic seating. Some hot snacks are served and cream cakes and scones.

Tea and scones £1.40
Open all year, every day,
8am–8pm

WESTBURY-ON-SEVERN   Gloucestershire   Map 03 SO71

Craft Kitchen
The Lecture Hall House
Tel (045276) 698

Originally the village lecture hall, just off the High Street, Craft Kitchen serves a range of very good home baking: fruit scones, carrot cake, chocolate cake and sponges along with sandwiches and hot snacks. An array of crafts and foodstuffs is displayed for sale.

Pot of tea and one cake
average £1.20
Open Wed–Mon (Tue am)
Snacks

WEST DOWN   Devon   Map 02 SS54

The Long House
West Down
Ilfracombe
Tel (0271) 863242

The old post office at the centre of the village has been tastefully converted to provide a teashop whose exposed stone walls, whitewashed ceilings, and homely pictures and china combine to create a welcoming, cheerful setting in which to enjoy a selection of speciality teas with sandwiches and delicious homemade cakes and scones.

Pot of tea and one cake
average £1.70, cream tea
£1.95
Open Easter–Oct every
day

WESTON-SUPER-MARE   Avon Map   03 ST36

Grand Atlantic Hotel
Beach Road
Tel (0934) 626543

An imposing Victorian Gothic hotel overlooking the seafront. Traditional tea-time fare such as crumpets, scones, teacakes and muffins along with fruitcake and pastries are served in the spacious open-plan lounge with its comfortable seating and lace-clothed tables. A choice of tea blends is available.

Pot of tea and one cake
average £1.45
Open morning coffee
10am–12.30pm, tea 3–
5.30pm
[1] [2] [3]

WETHERBY   West Yorkshire   Map 08 SE44

Le Bon Appetit
12 Bank Street
Tel (0937) 580027

The proprietors of this small, quaint teashop take great pride in their menu which boasts all homemade food for morning coffee, light lunch and afternoon tea. Homemade croissant, cakes and delicious gâteaux are served, with a choice of tea blends, by courteous staff.

Teas £1.50–£2
Open all year, Mon–Sat,
9.30am–4.30pm
(occasionally 8pm)

WETHERBY   West Yorkshire   Map 08 SE44

Open Faces
9 The Shambles
Tel (0937) 66031

In the town centre, on the first floor above the shopping area, this is an attractive and inviting little restaurant with its white and blue colour scheme, the décor being based on pottery masks. There is a mouthwatering array of pastries and unusual cakes and gâteaux as well as superb open sandwiches with the most interesting fillings. A choice of teas is served in china teapots.

Pot of tea and one cake average £1.85
Open all year (except 25 Dec–2 Jan), Mon–Sat, 9.30am–4pm

WHITBY   North Yorkshire   Map 08 NZ81

Magpie Café
14 Pier Road
Tel (0947) 602058

This popular café – an attractive black and white building overlooking the bustling town's busy harbour – provides a wide range of salads (including crab and other seafood) and light snacks, together with a selection of homemade puddings and cakes that includes such delights as sticky toffee pudding and marzipan and cherry cake. Herbal and fruit teas are served, as well as a choice of tea blends.

Pot of tea and one cake average £2
Open one week before Easter–Nov, every day, 11.30am–6.30pm
Lunches

WHITEHOUSE   Strathclyde   Map 10 NR86

Old School Tearoom
Tel (088073) 215

A homely village tearoom with timber-clad walls and varnished wood floor. A coal fire burns on cooler days and there are outside tables for the better weather. Savoury items feature local produce such as venison, salmon and crab and the cake trolley is laden with tempting homemade cakes and pastries. Our inspector particularly recommends the deep rum and choc cheesecake. A choice of tea blends is available.

Pot of tea 45p–55p
Open Easter–Oct, Wed–Mon, 10.30am–6m

WHITMORE   Staffordshire   Map 07 SK84

Whitmore Gallery and Tea Rooms
Keele Road
Tel (0782) 680879

Originally built as a public house, this 17th-century cottage was a saddlery until its recent transformation. Knitwear, pottery and paintings are on sale while speciality teas are served with good homemade cakes. Lunches are served, and vegetarians well catered for. The menu offers two local dishes: oatcakes, and lobby, a filling soup.

Scone, jam and cream from 60p
Open all year, every day, 10am–6pm
Lunches
1 3

WHITTINGTON   Shropshire   Map 07 SJ33

Whittington Castle Tea Rooms
Tel (0691) 670289

A small 12th-century moated castle by the A495 on the outskirts of this north Shropshire village. Homemade scones, cakes and teabreads and freshly prepared sandwiches are served with a choice of tea blends in two separate rooms pleasantly furnished in cottage style.

Pot of tea and one cake average £1, set teas from £2.55
Open Tue–Sun 10am–5pm

WIGHT, ISLE OF   Gurnard   Map 04 SZ59

Bowspit Teashop
21 Princes Esplanade
Tel (0983) 291933

A small bungalow teashop facing the sea, serving farmers' lunches, snacks, homemade pies, quiches, freshly made sandwiches, cream teas and ice cream. Children and pets are particularly welcome. No smoking is requested.

Set tea £1.75
Open Easter–Nov, Tue–Sun and bank holidays, 10.30am–5pm

WILMINGTON   Devon   Map 03 SY29

Home Farm Hotel
Near Honiton
Tel (040483) 278

Warm homemade scones are served with generous helpings of clotted cream and strawberry jam in the comfortable lounge or pretty garden of this former farmhouse. The spacious well-kept lawns, floral borders and hanging baskets make this a particularly pleasant location for afternoon tea in the summer months.

Cream tea only
Open every day
1 2 3

WILMSLOW   Cheshire   Map 07 SJ88

Grape Vine Coffee Shop
Wilmslow Garden Centre
Manchester Road
Tel (0625) 525700

Though new greenhouses are being built at this garden centre, the coffee shop run by the mother and daughter of the family remains in the original complex. Here you can enjoy not only a good cup of tea – with toasted teacake, fruit pie, cheesecake or hot fudge cake, for example – but also meals and snacks throughout the day, with a 10% discount for senior citizens during the week.

Pot of tea and one cake average £1.50
Open every day 10am–4pm
Lunches and snacks

WILMSLOW   Cheshire   Map 07 SJ88

Menus 'The Coffee Shop on the Corner'
23 Water Lane
Tel (0625) 528013

A corner bistro-style café with additional outdoor seating in summer, located just off the centre of the main shopping area on the Altrincham road, is run by a husband and wife team who both prepare and serve a range of snacks and daily blackboard 'specials'. A choice of tea blends is available to accompany sandwiches, crumpets and a selection of pastries, fruit pies, sponges and gâteaux.

Pot of tea and one cake average £1.10
Open Mon–Sat 9.15am–6.30pm, Sun 12.15–5pm
Light meals and snacks

WIMBORNE MINSTER   Dorset   Map 04 SZ09

Kings Head
The Square
Tel (0202) 880101

A country-town hotel with good lounge facilities, modern and comfortable. Scones, cakes, sponges and sandwiches are served with a choice of Earl Grey or China tea.

Open all year, every day, tea served, 3–5.30pm
1 2 3

WIMBORNE MINSTER   Dorset   Map 04 SZ09

Quinney's
26 Westborough
Tel (0202) 883518

A small town-centre restaurant on two floors serving morning coffee, lunch and afternoon tea with a large selection of cakes and gâteaux provided by a bakery on the premises. A choice of tea blends is offered.

Cream tea £2.10
Open all year, (except one week Apr and Oct) Tue–Sat, 9.15am–5pm
Lunch

WINCHCOMBE   Gloucestershire   Map 03 SO92

Lady Jane's Tea Shop
7 Hailes Street
Tel (0242) 603578

A light, airy dining room with pretty tablecloths, china and fresh carnations. There are spindle-back chairs and attractive shell lightshades. A comprehensive menu is served, but teas are a speciality, with a good range of homemade cakes, meringue pies and cheesecakes. There are cream teas, a 'winter warmer' with hot crumpets, and a children's tea with honey sandwiches.

Teas £1.80–£2.30
Open all year, every day, 10am–6pm

WINCHELSEA   East Sussex   Map 05 TV92

Finches
12 High Street
Tel (0797) 226234

Conveniently situated next to the village post office, this period cottage restaurant features a varied choice of scones, crumpets, toasted teacakes and set cream tea; also a wide selection of homemade cakes, pastries and gâteaux. Freshly made loose leaf tea is served, and a choice of blends is available.

Set tea £2
Open Jan–Dec, Thur–Tue, 9.30am–6pm
1 2 3

WINCHELSEA   East Sussex   Map 05 TQ92

Winchelsea Tea Room
Hiham Green
Tel (0797) 226679

A shop dating back to Edwardian times, set beside one of this tranquil town's grass-verged, tree-lined roads, now serves three functions – being divided into bed and breakfast accommodation, an antique shop and a tearoom with good table cloths, attractive china, an array of pictures on the walls and pots and antique bric-à-brac on the Welsh dresser. Here, the main counter displays an excellent selection of such home-baked goodies as scones, caramel slices, rich fruit cake and carrot cake, to be enjoyed with Earl Grey, Darjeeling or standard blend tea.

Pot of tea and one cake average £1.40, set teas £1.70–£2.10
Open Wed–Sun 11am–5.30pm

WINCHESTER   Hampshire   Map 04 SU42

Lainston House Hotel
Sparsholt (outside Winchester off A272)
Tel (0962) 63588

Set in rolling parkland and well kept gardens, Lainston House dates back to the era of Willam and Mary and offers a most elegant, peaceful setting for a traditional afternoon tea, which may be served either in the beautifully furnished drawing room or in the gardens. Sandwiches, scones and gâteaux are all freshly made by the hotel kitchens, which have a high reputation for their cooking, and there is a good choice of blends of tea, all served by very friendly, cheerful staff.

Set teas £5.75–£8.75
Open all year, every day, 3–5.30pm
1 2 3 &

WINCHESTER   Hampshire   Map 04 SU42

Royal Hotel
St Peter Street
Tel (0962) 840840

This former convent is centrally situated. It has well tended gardens and a stylish garden lounge where Ceylon and China teas are served with sandwiches, biscuits, fruitcake or Danish pastry. Daily papers are available.

Pot of tea 90p
Open all year, every day, 10am–noon and 3–6pm
1 3

WINDERMERE   Cumbria   Map 07 SD49

Apple Cottage
21 Victoria Street
Tel (09662) 5234

A smart little teashop with a country Victorian feel to it is charmingly decorated to create a relaxed but civilised atmosphere. Light meals are served at lunch time, and a range of quality homebaked scones, biscuits and teabreads is displayed on a dresser. A choice of tea blends is available. Smoking is not permitted.

Pot of tea 50p–60p
Open all year, Mon–Sat, 10am–5pm
Lunches and dinners

WINDERMERE   Cumbria   Map 07 SD49

Aunty's Tea Shoppe
Church Street
Tel (09662) 88211

Beyond an attractive, green-panelled exterior, a typically English teashop, brightly decorated in yellow, with pretty floral table covers and fresh flowers, offers a particularly good range of tea blends – 26 in all – to accompany its sandwiches and homemade scones and cakes. A blackboard menu details a selection of snacks which are available all day. Smoking is not permitted.

Pot of tea and one cake average £1.75
Open Sat–Wed 10.30am–5pm

WINDERMERE   Cumbria   Map 07 SD49

Miller Howe Hotel
Rayrigg Road
Tel (09662) 4536

John Tovey has established an international reputation for this first-class Lakeland hotel. From the lounges where tea is served there are magnificent views across the lake to the Cumbrian fells beyond, a prospect to stimulate your appetite for the delectable cakes and pastries you are about to sample. The full afternoon tea comprises shortbread, scones with cream and fresh fruit, followed perhaps by very rich chocolate cake or a fresh fruit tart, with crème patissière. All this, and the good strong tea is beautifully served in Wedgwood bone china.

Set afternoon tea £4.50
Open all year, every day,
3–5pm

WINDERMERE   Cumbria   Map 07 SD49

Miller Howe Kaff at Lakeland Plastics
Station Precinct
Tel (09662) 6732

A small busy café which is part of the Lakeland Plastics Shop. Modern, light and bright but trying to be stylish. Exceptionally popular at lunch time as an eating place. Leaf tea is served in a silver pot with Wedgwood china. A small choice of homemade cakes and scones is available. Smoking is not permitted.

Pot of tea 60p
Open all year, Mon–Sat.
9.30am–4.30pm
Lunches

WINDERMERE   Cumbria   Map 07 SD49

Tea Shoppe
Field House
Bowness-on-
Windermere
Tel (09662) 2476

A pleasant basement tearoom overlooking a small garden close to the centre of town. Part of a guesthouse with self-catering units, the Tea Shoppe also sells a range of gifts. Freshly made sandwiches are served with homemade cakes and scones with generous portions of cream. A range of speciality teas is available. Smoking is not permitted.

Pot of tea 45p
Open all year, Fri–Wed,
10am–5.30pm

WINDSOR   Berkshire   Map 04 SU97

The Courtyard
8 King George V Place
Tel (0753) 858338

A small teashop located in a busy courtyard close to the river, the castle and the town centre. A choice of teas is offered with sandwiches, salads, pastries, croissants and gâteaux.

Pot of tea 65p–75p,
English cream tea £2.10
Open Jan–Dec (except
Christmas), every day,
11.30am–5pm (6pm
weekends)

WINDSOR   Berkshire   Map 04 SU97

The Hideaway
Sir Christopher Wren's
House Hotel
12 Thames Street
Tel (0753) 842186

A pleasant restaurant with exposed brick walls, modern prints and attractive drapes. A selection of speciality teas is served with scones, cakes, Danish pastries and gâteaux.

Cream tea £3.75
Open Jan–Dec, every day,
3–6pm for tea
☐1 ☐2 ☐3

WINGHAM   Kent   Map 05 TR25

**Little Crockshard
Farm**
Tel (0227) 720262

Tea garden open on sunny days from June to September serving homemade cream teas from the back door of the farmhouse. Kate Gibson makes lovely apple and walnut cake with lashings of cream. The farm shop sells some of its own fruit and vegetables.

Cream tea £2
Open Tue–Sun 2–6pm

WOBURN   Bedfordshire   Map 04 SP93

Annie's Place
2 Leighton Street
Tel (0525) 290300

A Georgian terraced building comfortably furnished throughout and with outdoor seating serving a bistro menu and afternoon tea. All dishes are made on the premises; a blackboard menu offers substantial meals, and cakes such as carrot and date and walnut are served along with pavlovas and gâteaux. A choice of tea blends is offered.

Pot of tea and one cake average £1.70, cream tea £2.30
Open every day & evenings Tue–Sat
Lunches and evening meals, licensed
☐1 ☐3

WOBURN   Bedfordshire   Map 04 SP93

**Woburn Country
Shop & Tea Room**
21 Market Place
Tel (0525) 290673

A tearoom with character, behind the country craft shop, heavily beamed with a large inglenook fireplace where a fire is lit in winter. A selection of good homemade cakes is displayed on a central table, and sandwiches, savouries, salads and pies are available with Twinings speciality teas.

Pot of tea and one cake average £1.25, cream tea £1.80
Open every day
☐1 ☐2 ☐3

WOKING   Surrey   Map 04 TQ05

BHS Country Table
British Home Stores
Commercial Road

Ideal for family parties – providing high chairs, and regarding children sympathetically – this conveniently placed ground-floor restaurant is surprisingly spacious, with ample room for movement between tables. Good use of wood and tiling echoes the 'country' theme suggested by its name, and the atmosphere is pleasant and relaxed. Hot and cold meals are available all day, together with a comprehensive range of sandwiches, filled rolls, buns, pastries and desserts, while the popular new 'set' afternoon meal provides sandwiches, crisps, a scone and a good mug of tea at a very economical price.

Pot of tea and one cake average 90p, set tea 99p
Open Mon–Thu 9am–5.30pm, Fri & Sat 9am–6pm
Hot and cold meals

WOKING   Surrey   Map 04 TQ05

Harvest Café
10–12 Wolsley Walk
Tel (0483) 771699

This small, unpretentious café stands beside the Harvest Bakery in one of the covered ways running parallel to the main street, the rustic theme indicated by its name echoed in corn dollies, arrangements of dried flowers and grasses, and the pleasant, flower-garlanded cream and brown crockery. Scones, teacakes, buns, Danish pastries and cakes from the range produced by the parent bakery can be enjoyed with a choice of tea blends. Sandwiches, salads and hot or cold snacks are also available.

Pot of tea and one cake average £1.05, cream tea £1.85
Open Mon–Sat 8am–5pm
Hot and cold snacks

WOLF'S CASTLE   Dyfed   Map 02 SM92

Nant-y-Coy Mill
Treffgarne
Tel (0437 87) 671

An old mill and farm beside the A40, near the Treffgarne Rocks, has been converted to create nature walks, an art gallery, craft shop, museum and – in the old milking parlour – a tea/coffee shop. Here, Dairyman's and Miller's lunches are served, as well as an array of teatime items which includes fruit and plain scones, fruitcake and chocolate cake (all baked without additives), served with a choice of tea blends.

Pot of tea and one cake average £1
Open summer Mon–Sat 10.30am–5.30pm, Sun 2.30–5pm, winter most days

---

WOODBRIDGE Suffolk Map 05 TM24

Mrs Pipers
65 The Thoroughfare
Tel (0394) 585633

A blue-painted teashop in the middle of the village, with exposed beams, Welsh dresser, white chairs and pretty tablecloths. There are pictures for sale and attractive displays of homemade cakes and sweets. Homemade lunches (special dishes displayed daily on blackboard) and light snacks are served. Afternoon tea comprises cucumber sandwiches, fruit scone, cream and jam. A choice of teas is offered.

Pot of tea 55p, cream tea £2.60, children's tea 1.65 Open Jan–Dec, Mon, Tue and Thur–Sat, 9.45am–5pm, Wed, 9.30am–2pm, Sun (Jun–Nov only) 11am–4pm

---

WOODBRIDGE Suffolk Map 05 TM24

Seckford Hall
Tel (0394) 385678

In the 34 acres of beautifully maintained grounds which surround this Elizabethan manor house, a recently converted Tudor tithe barn houses gymnasium, swimming pool, and the comfortable characterful Buttery serving set afternoon teas and a range of locally-made speciality ice creams as well as an all-day menu of freshly prepared meals and snacks. A choice of tea blends is available.

Pot of tea and one cake average £2.20, set teas £2.95–£5.75 Open Tue–Sat all day, Sun and Mon pm only

1 2 3

WOODFORD Greater Manchester Map 07 SJ88

Woodford Park Restaurant and Coffee Shop
Garden Store Garden Centre
Chester Road
Tel 061–439 2746

Recently completely refurbished, with a conservatory-style extension to accommodate the ever-growing number of guests, this restaurant displays a tempting range of homemade cakes, pastries and puddings – including such favourites as fudge cake, rum babas and lemon meringue pie as well as scones and gâteaux. A range of tea blends is available.

Pot of tea and one cake average £1.75 Open Tue–Sat (and Bank Holiday Mon), 9am–5pm Breakfasts, lunches (booking advisable), snacks

---

WOODSTOCK Oxfordshire Map 04 SP51

The Blenheim
17 Park Street
Tel (0993) 811467

Named after the Blenheim Orange apple tree, this neat country tearoom with its lacy cloths is conveniently situated near one of the entrances to Blenheim Palace. The menu offers an interesting range of salads (chicken, tarragon and Greek yoghourt, for example), with a choice of 23 tea blends to accompany a cream tea or slice of home-baked cake.

Pot of tea and one cake average £1.89, set tea £2.40 Open all year, every day in summer, Thu–Tue in winter (and for shorter hours)

1 2 3

WORCESTER Worcestershire Map 03 SO85

Shepherd's Purse
7 Severn Street
Tel (0905) 726770

This pretty cottage-style tearoom was once a fisherman's inn. It stands opposite the Royal Worcester Spode factory and is close to the cathedral and city centre. Good homemade scones, cakes and gâteaux are served by friendly staff and there is a choice of teas.

Pot of tea 55p Open all year, Mon–Sat, 10.30am–5.30pm Light lunches also served

WORKINGTON   Cumbria   Map 11 NX92   •

The Granary
6 Upper Jane Street
Tel (0900) 68188

Exposed stone walls decked with photographs and pictures provide an effective foil to the pine tables and chairs of this pleasant, fresh little coffee shop and restaurant in the centre of the town. A good cup of tea – with a choice of Earl Grey, Assam, Darjeeling, camomile, peppermint and lemon as well as the standard blend – complements a wide selection of hot meals, snacks such as jacket potatoes, sandwiches and sweets, and there is a separate children's menu.

Pot of tea and one cake average £1.50
Open Mon–Wed and Sat 9am–5pm, Thu 9am–6.30pm, Fri 9am–5.30pm

WORKINGTON   Cumbria   Map 11 NX92

Washington Central Hotel – Coffee Shop
Washington Street
Tel (0900) 65772

In the relaxing atmosphere of this very pleasant self-service coffee-shop with its stone-tiled floors, exposed brick walls and glass-topped tables, you can enjoy sandwiches or toasties (served with a demi salad), various snacks on toast and homemade scones, teacakes and cakes – notably deliciously sticky oatcakes. The assortment of tea blends available includes Earl Grey, lemon, rosehip, nettle and fennel.

Pot of tea and one cake average £1.30
Open Mon–Sat, 9.30am–4.30pm

WORTHING   West Sussex   Map 04 TQ10

Oojies Coffee Shop
Chatsworth Hotel
18A Marine Parade
Tel (0903) 203589

Fine teas and coffees are served in comfortable surroundings with Cornish cream teas or a selection from the pâtisseries. Daily 'homecooked specials' are available, also fresh fish and seafood dishes.

Open all year, Tue–Sun, 10am–5pm Tue–Sat, 11am–5pm Sun
Lunch

WORTH MATRAVERS   Dorset   Map 03 SY97

Worth Tea Shop
Tel (092 943) 368

An appealing teashop overlooking the village green and duck pond which has a pretty, partly-panelled, pink interior with a dresser displaying local produce for sale; seating is also provided in an attractive, flower-filled garden. In addition to the Dorset clotted cream tea, customers can enjoy a range of sandwiches – including those made with local crab – with homemade scones and cakes.

Set tea £1.80
Open Easter–Oct, every day, 10.30am–6.30pm (in winter Sun only).
Light meals

WROTHAM HEATH   Kent   Map 05 TQ65

**The Post House
Hotel**
London Road
Tel (0732) 883311

In an elegant and well-furnished foyer-lounge, which extends into a conservatory and small terraced patio garden, a formal tea is served between 3.30 and 5.30 each afternoon; Darjeeling, Earl Grey and China teas are offered as alternatives to Indian. An à la carte selection of light refreshments, open sandwiches and freshly squeezed fruit juices is also very popular.

Pot of tea and one cake average £1.70, set teas £1.95
Open Good Friday–end Oct, Mon–Fri, 10.30am – 5.30pm, Sat and Sun, 10.30am–6pm

WROXHAM   Norfolk   Map 09 TG31

Hotel Wroxham
Riverside Centre
Tel (0603) 782061

A popular meeting place in the town, the servery is an integral part of the hotel. Large windows overlook the river, or one can sit out in the large riverside patio area. There is a mouthwatering display of cakes and pastries from the hotel kitchen and hot food is also served.

Pot of tea 75p, cream tea £1.80
Open all year, every day, 10am–9.30pm
Hot meals
☐1 ☐2 ☐3 ☐&

WROXHAM   Norfolk   Map 09 TG31

**Ye Olde Mill Tea
Shoppe**
The Bridge
Tel (0603) 783744

A small friendly self-service café on the banks of the river offering a selection of light snacks and teas all day. Cakes and pastries are produced by a local baker. Seating is available indoors and out.

Teas £1.05
Open mid Feb–mid Jan, Mon–Sat 9am–4pm winter, every day Easter– Oct 8am–5.30pm
Light snacks

YARM   Cleveland   Map 08 N241

The Coffee Shop
44 High Street
Tel (0642) 790011

Situated over the Strickland and Holt department store in the main street of this attractive little town, stripped pine furniture gives a country feel to the Coffee Shop. All the food is homemade from natural ingredients. Breakfast and light lunches are served as well as scones, biscuits and a range of puddings and ice creams. A choice of five teas is offered.

Pot of tea 69p
Open all year, Mon–Sat, 9am–5pm
Breakfast, lunch

YEOVIL   Somerset   Map 03 ST51

Denners
High Street
Tel (0935) 74444

A modern coffee/teashop on the second floor of Denners department (fashion) store. The restaurant is glass-fronted with functional but comfortable furnishings. Food is displayed on a long service counter: cakes and scones are supplemented by biscuits and gâteaux. Hot dishes are also served with snacks such as toasted sandwiches for a light lunch.

Cup of tea 50p
Open all year, Mon–Sat, 9.30am–5pm
Lunch

Betty's Café Tea Rooms
6–8 St Helen's Square
Tel (0904) 659142

Just a short break from York Minister, Betty's is a branch of the renowned Harrogate tearooms founded in 1919 by a Swiss confectioner who settled there. The identity of 'Betty' herself is a House secret. The tearooms serve a huge array of delectable baking, made every day in the café's Harrogate bakery, combining traditional Yorkshire recipes with Continental pâtisseries to please every taste. The range of blends of tea is excellent and the service maintains the highest traditional standards. There are often queues of would-be customers. See also entries for Harrogate, Ilkley and Northallerton.

Pot of tea and one cake average £2.75, cream tea £3.48
Open every day (including most bank holidays), 9am–9pm
Other meals also served
1 3

The Conservatory at the Dean Court Hotel
Duncombe Place
Tel (0904) 625082

An hotel opposite the famous York Minster, built in 1850 as houses for the clergy, offers soups and salads as well as sandwiches and the scones, cakes and gâteaux baked in its own kitchens. A limited range of speciality teas is available.

Pot of tea 85p–£1.35, pot of tea and one cake average £1.85, cream tea £2.20
Open every day, tea served until 6pm
Supper menu from 6pm
1 2 3

Four Seasons Restaurant and Café
45 Goodramgate
Tel (0904) 633787

A pair of late 15th-century Tudor timber-framed houses in the centre of this historic city which have been a restaurant or tearooms ever since they were restored in 1929. In rooms retaining their original timbered ceilings and stone floors – or on an outdoor patio area – an extensive range of homemade cakes and biscuits, together with sandwiches, salads, hot dishes and puddings, gives a taste of typical Yorkshire fare. A choice of tea blends is served.

Pot of tea and one cake average £1.85, set teas £2.95–£3.25
Open every day 10am–10pm

Taylors In Stonegate
46 Stonegate
Tel (0904) 622865

Set in a 16th-century building at the heart of the city, above a busy shop which sells a wide range of Taylors Teas and Coffees, these quaint, cottage-style tearooms provide full waitress service with a section set aside for non-smokers. A delightfully old-fashioned menu offers hot snacks, salads and sandwiches as well as a wide range of cakes made at their own bakery, and a good choice of speciality teas.

Pot of tea and one cake average £3, set tea £3.48
Open every day 9am–5.30pm
Hot and cold snacks
1 3

Treasurer's House
Minster Yard
Tel (0904) 624247/646757

While situated inside the Treasurer's House, a National Trust property, admission to the tearoom is free. Located in the basement of the 17th-century building, spotlessly clean and furnished in pine, a range of homemade cakes is temptingly displayed. Choose from the like of pear and ginger cake, treacle tart and caraway seed bread. A blackboard menu offers daily 'specials', all homemade, and soups, salads, sandwiches and desserts. A choice of teas is available including fruit and herb varieties. Smoking is not permitted.

Pot of tea and one cake average £1.20
Open Apr–16 Dec every day
Light lunches

York Crest Hotel
Clifford Tower
Tower Street
Tel (0904) 648111

The ideal stopping place for visitors exploring the historic features of the city. Service is available in the cosy lounge or attractive cocktail area. Traditional afternoon tea with home-baked scones, cream and strawberry jam, sandwiches and a selection of cakes and pastries is served by courteous staff. A choice of tea blends is offered.

Afternoon tea £4.25
Open Jan–Dec, every day, 9.30am–5.30pm
1 2 3 &

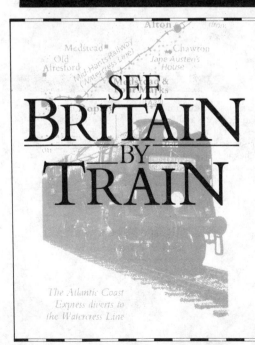

Readers' Recommendations

We realise that, as there are so many lovely places throughout the country to stop for tea, we may not have listed your own favourite, so we would be very grateful if you could let us know about any teashop, restaurant or hotel where you have enjoyed a particularly good afternoon tea.

We should also be interested to hear any comments you have on any of the places that we do list.

Please send your report forms, which will of course be treated in confidence, to:

The Automobile Association

Guidebook Publications Unit,

Fanum House,

Basingstoke,

Hants, RG21 2EA.

YOUR NAME _____

ADDRESS _____

_____

_____

AA MEMBERSHIP NUMBER (IF ANY) _____

IS THE ESTABLISHMENT LISTED IN LET'S STOP FOR TEA?   YES ☐   NO ☐

NAME OF ESTABLISHMENT _____

ADDRESS: _____

_____

_____

YOUR COMMENTS: _____

_____

_____

_____

_____

_____

_____

_____

IS THE ESTABLISHMENT LISTED IN LET'S STOP FOR TEA?   YES ☐   NO ☐

NAME OF ESTABLISHMENT _____

ADDRESS: _____

_____

_____

YOUR COMMENTS: _____

_____

_____

_____

_____

_____

_____

_____

IS THE ESTABLISHMENT LISTED IN LET'S STOP FOR TEA?   YES ☐   NO ☐

NAME OF ESTABLISHMENT _____

ADDRESS: _____

_____

_____

YOUR COMMENTS: _____

_____

_____

_____

_____

_____

_____

Readers' Recommendations

We realise that, as there are so many lovely places throughout the country to stop for tea, we may not have listed your own favourite, so we would be very grateful if you could let us know about any teashop, restaurant or hotel where you have enjoyed a particularly good afternoon tea.

We should also be interested to hear any comments you have on any of the places that we do list.

Please send your report forms, which will of course be treated in confidence, to:

The Automobile Association

Guidebook Publications Unit,

Fanum House,

Basingstoke,

Hants, RG21 2EA.

YOUR NAME _____

ADDRESS _____

_____

_____

AA MEMBERSHIP NUMBER (IF ANY) _____

IS THE ESTABLISHMENT LISTED IN LET'S STOP FOR TEA?   YES ☐   NO ☐

NAME OF ESTABLISHMENT _____

ADDRESS: _____

_____

_____

YOUR COMMENTS: _____

_____

_____

_____

_____

_____

_____

IS THE ESTABLISHMENT LISTED IN LET'S STOP FOR TEA?   YES ☐   NO ☐

NAME OF ESTABLISHMENT _____

ADDRESS: _____

_____

_____

YOUR COMMENTS: _____

_____

_____

_____

_____

_____

_____

IS THE ESTABLISHMENT LISTED IN LET'S STOP FOR TEA?   YES ☐   NO ☐

NAME OF ESTABLISHMENT _____

ADDRESS: _____

_____

_____

YOUR COMMENTS: _____

_____

_____

_____

_____

_____

_____

*Have you heard of a teashop or
hotel but are not sure where it
is? This index lists all the tea
places in the book in
alphabetical order*

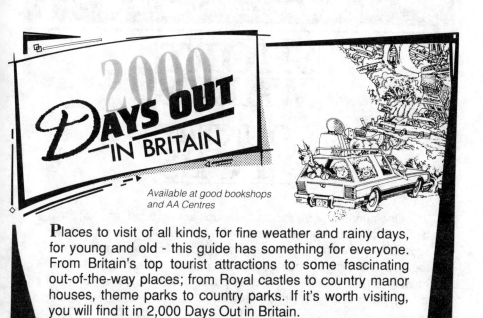

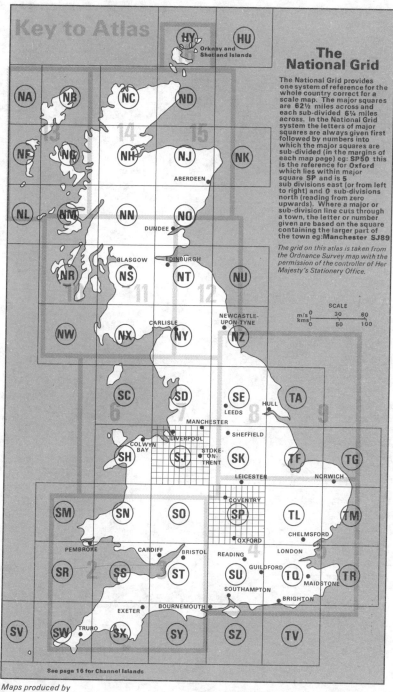

Key to Atlas

The National Grid

The National Grid provides one system of reference for the whole country correct for a scale map. The major squares are 62½ miles across and each sub-divided 6¼ miles across. In the National Grid system the letters of major squares are always given first followed by numbers into which the major squares are sub-divided (in the margins of each map page) eg: SP50 this is the reference for Oxford which lies within major square SP and is 5 sub divisions east (or from left to right) and 0 sub-divisions north (reading from zero upwards). Where a major or sub-division line cuts through a town, the letter or number given are based on the square containing the larger part of the town eg: **Manchester SJ89**

The grid on this atlas is taken from the Ordnance Survey map with the permission of the controller of Her Majesty's Stationery Office.

SCALE
m/s 0 — 30 — 60
kms 0 — 50 — 100

Orkney and Shetland Islands

HY HU
NA NB NC ND
NF NG NH NJ NK
ABERDEEN
NL NM NN NO NU
DUNDEE
GLASGOW EDINBURGH
NR NS NT NU
CARLISLE NEWCASTLE-UPON-TYNE
NW NX NY NZ
SC SD SE TA
LEEDS HULL
MANCHESTER
LIVERPOOL SHEFFIELD
COLWYN BAY
SH SJ SK TF TG
STOKE-ON-TRENT
LEICESTER NORWICH
COVENTRY
SM SN SO SP TL TM
OXFORD CHELMSFORD
PEMBROKE CARDIFF BRISTOL READING LONDON
SR SS ST SU TQ TR
GUILDFORD
SOUTHAMPTON MAIDSTONE
BRIGHTON
EXETER BOURNEMOUTH
SV SW SX SY SZ TV
TRURO

See page 16 for Channel Islands

Maps produced by

The Automobile Association from the Automaps database.
© The Automobile Association 1991.

This atlas is for location purposes only: see Members Handbook for current road and AA road services information.

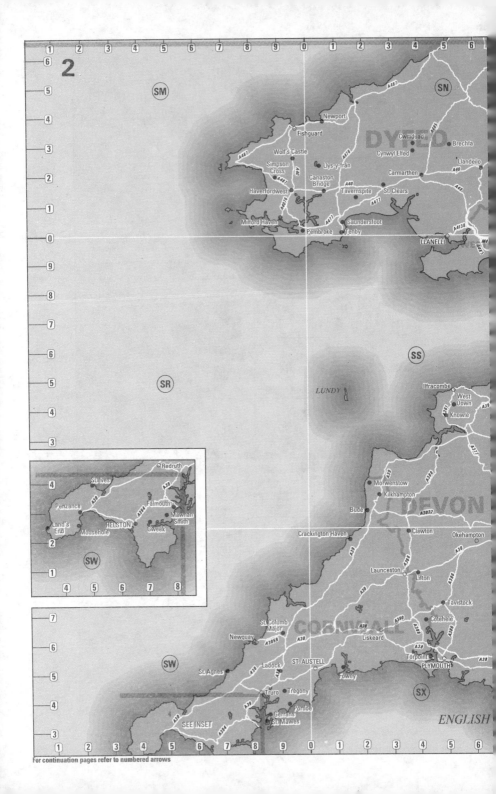

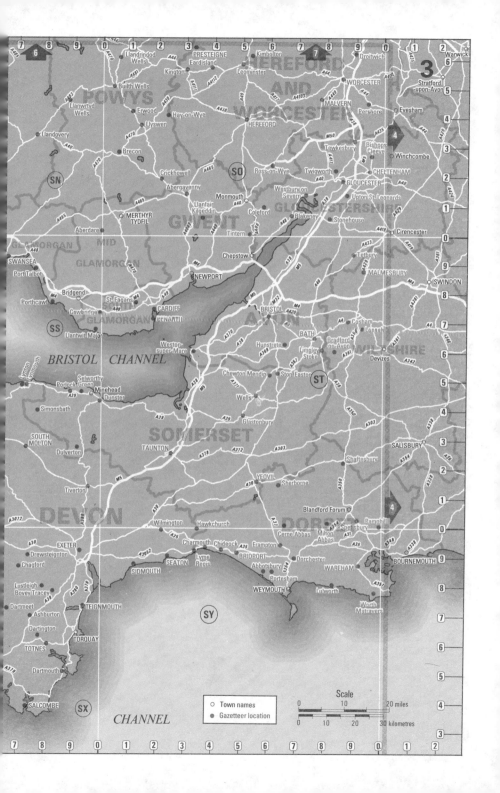

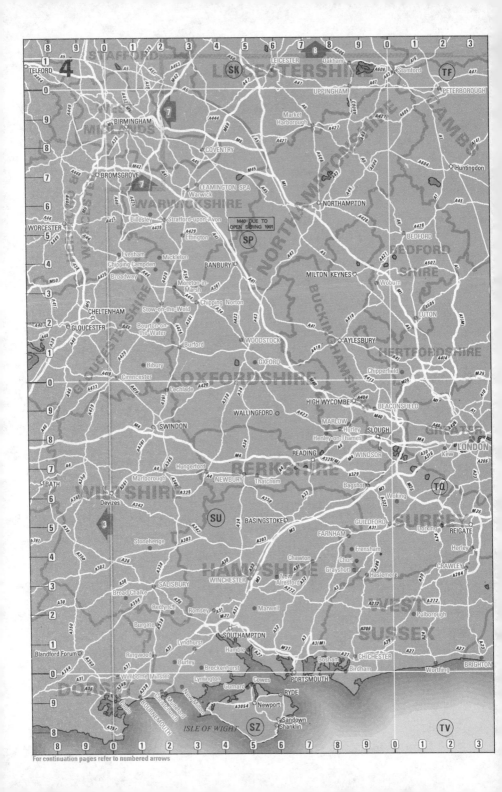

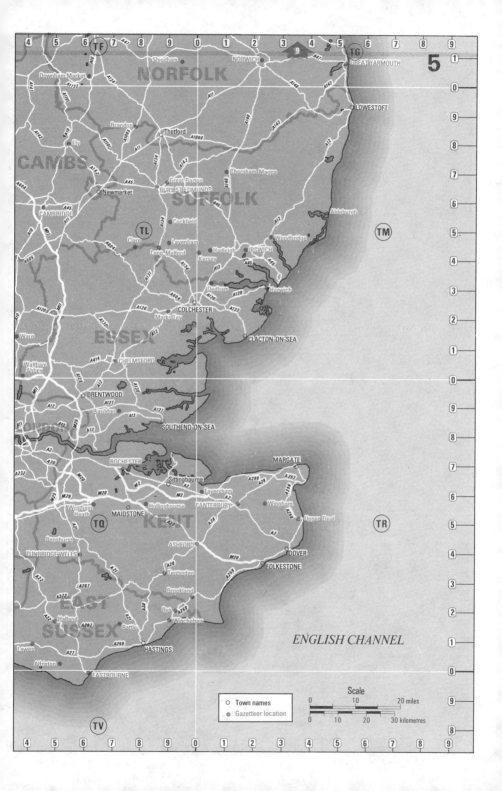

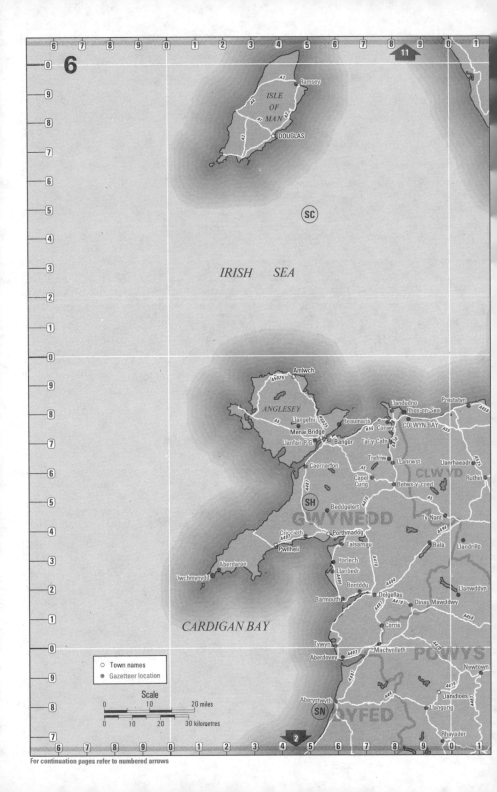

6

ISLE OF MAN

A3

Ramsey

A7

A3

DOUGLAS

SC

IRISH   SEA

ANGLESEY

Amlwch

A5025

A5

Llangefni

A5025

Menai Bridge

Llanfair P.G

Beaumaris

Llandudno

Rhos-on-Sea

Prestatyn

A548

A55

Conwy

COLWYN BAY

A55

Bangor

Tal-y-Cafn

A55

Caernarfon

Trefriw

LLanrwst

Llanrhaeadr

A525

A470

Capel Curig

Batws-y-coed

CLWYD

Ruthin

A5

A487

SH

Beddgelert

A470

Ty Nant

GWYNEDD

A490

Criccieth

A497

Porthmadog

Talsarnau

Pwllheli

Harlech

A496

Llanbedr

A470

Bala

Llandrillo

Aberdaron

A496

A494

Llanwddyn

Uwchmynydd

Bontddu

Barmouth

A493

Bontddu

A487

A470

Dolgellau

Dinas Mawddwy

A458

CARDIGAN BAY

Corris

A493

A487

Tywyn

A493

Machynlleth

POWYS

Aberdovey

Newtown

A470

A44

Llanidloes

Llangurig

A44

Aberystwyth

SN

DYFED

A470

A483

Rhayader

O Town names
● Gazetteer location

Scale

0   10   20 miles

0   10   20   30 kilometres

11

2

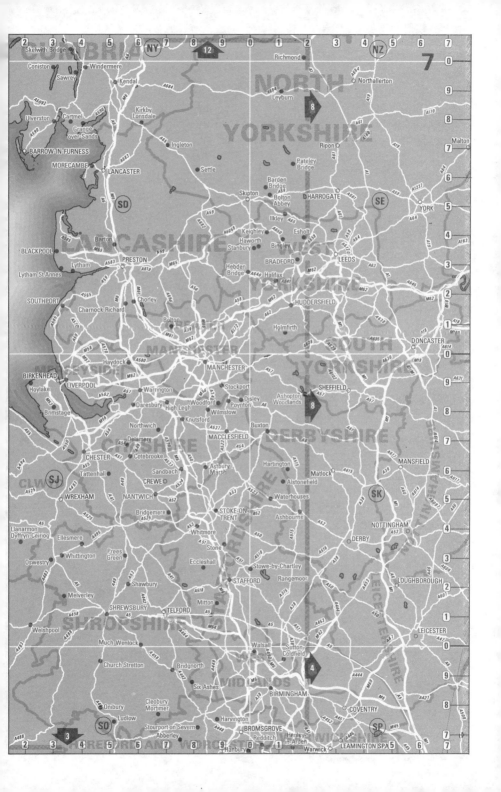

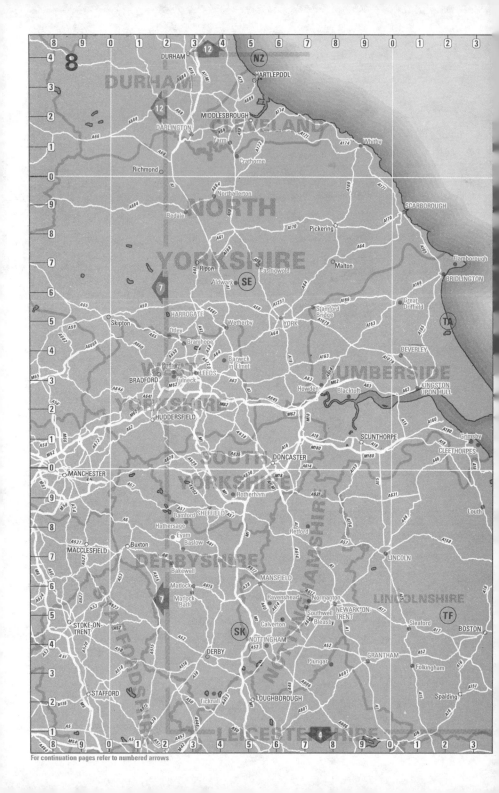

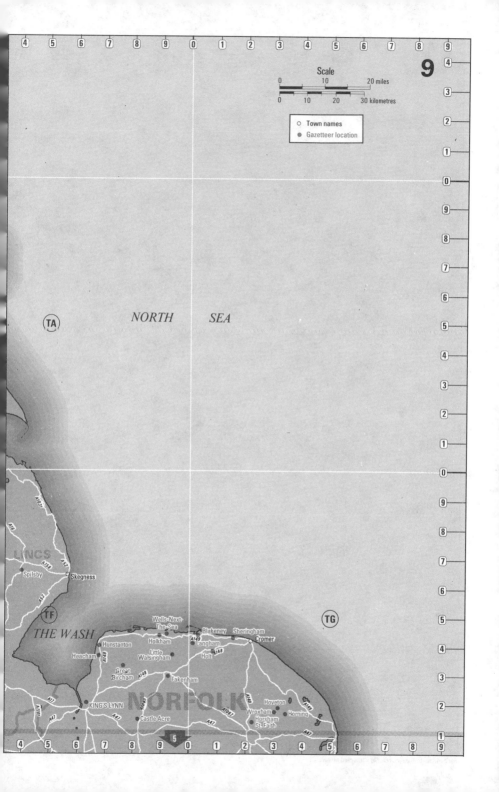

Scale

| 0 | 10 | 20 miles |
| 0 | 10 | 20 | 30 kilometres |

○ Town names
● Gazetteer location

NORTH   SEA

(TA)

(TF)

(TG)

THE WASH

LINCS

Spilsby

Skegness

Wells-Next-The-Sea

Blakeney   Sheringham

Holkham   Langham   Cromer

Hunstanton

Heacham   Little Walsingham   Holt

Great Bircham   Fakenham

NORFOLK

King's Lynn

Hoveton

Wroxham   Horning

Castle Acre   Horsham St Faith

5

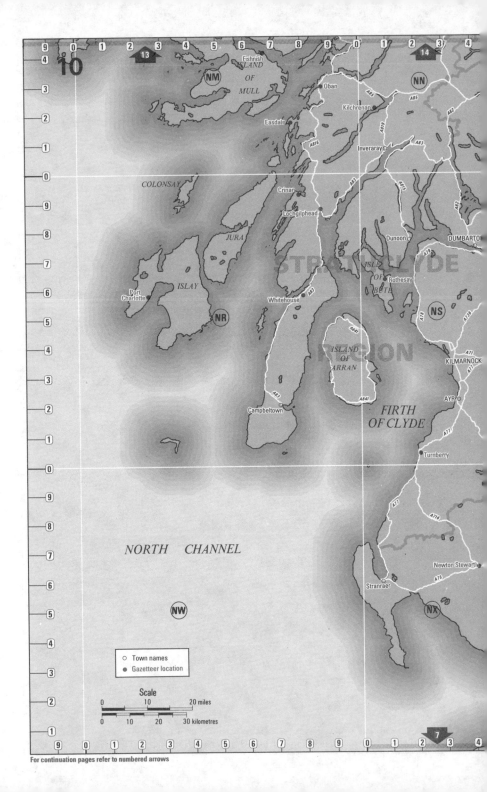

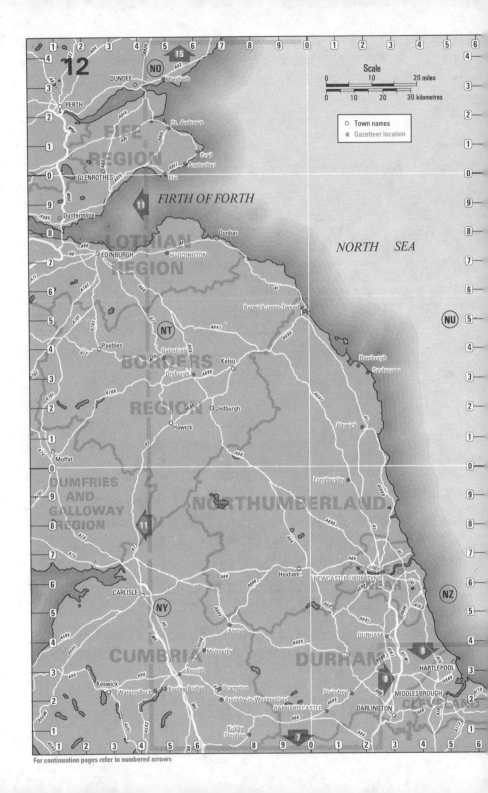

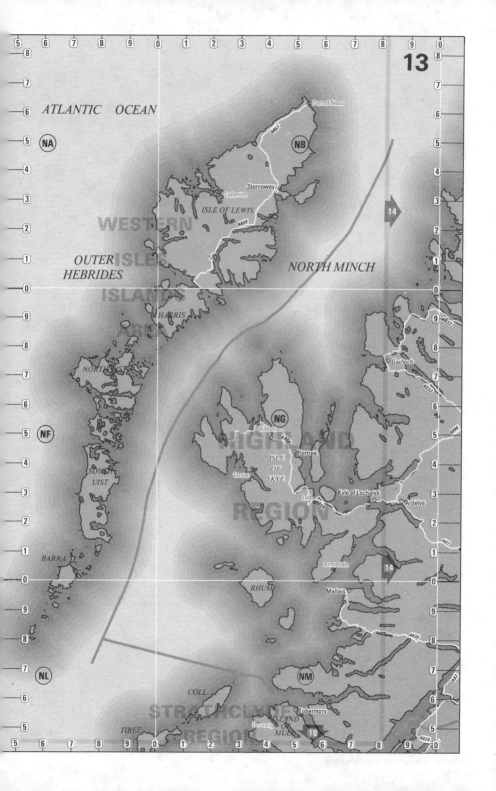

NORTH SEA

FIRTH

NORTH SEA

HIGHLAND

REGION

GRAMPIAN

REGION

REGION

Thurso

Wick

ND

NJ

NK

Elgin

Buckie

CULLEN

Fraserburgh

Fochabers

Banff

KEITH

Drummuir

ABERLOUR

Dufftown

Huntly

Oldmeldrum

ABERDEEN

Banchory

Ballater

Fettercairn

Montrose

ND

Forfar

Blairgowrie

12

Scale

| | | Town names |
| | | Gazetteer location |

Scale

0   10   20 miles

0   10   20   30 kilometres

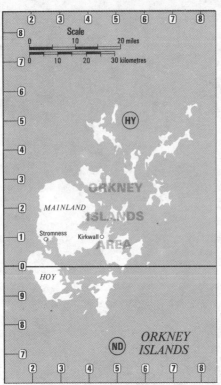

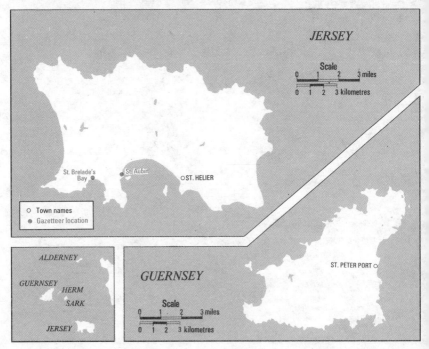